NAOMI B MCCORMICK, PHD
DEPT PSYCH, SUNY-PLATTSBURGH
PLATTSBURGH NY   12901
USA

p. 42 theoretical model
pp. 104- powerful path analysis in service of above.
110.

Ch 7 — study of clients; p 135—newer study
replicates this!

(pp 153— well concluded.
156

followed by policy recmm dtns.

PROSTITUTES WELL-BEING AND RISK

INE VANWESENBEECK

To my overseas friend
with the deepest affection,

Ine Vanwesenbeeck

VU Uitgeverij
Amsterdam 1994

VU University Press is an imprint of:
VU Boekhandel/Uitgeverij bv
De Boelelaan 1105
1081 HV Amsterdam
The Netherlands

tel. (020) - 644 43 55
fax (020) - 646 27 19

isbn 90-5383-301-3
nugi 711

cover design by Neroc Special Services, Amsterdam
printed by Wilco, Amersfoort

Acknowledgements

Many people have made indispensible contributions through the years of investigation and during the ultimate writing of this book. First, I wish to thank my co-researchers, Martine Groen and Sietske Altink, who worked with me in the early stages and Ron de Graaf in the latter stages, for their supportive and stimulating collegiality. It is because of their participation that throughout the book I speak of 'we' instead of 'I' when referring to the research. It almost goes without saying that the willingness of the respondents to share information, which was often sensitive, has been essential. I extend my enormous gratitude in recognition of them. I also want to express my appreciation to the intermediairies who helped us enter the world of prostitution and to the group of interviewers who assisted us in the fieldwork. In addition, my collegues at Tilburg University, the Mr. A. de Graaf Foundation in Amsterdam, the Netherlands Institute for Social Sexological Research (NISSO) in Utrecht and the Amsterdam School for Social Science Research have provided me with valuable and supportive comments on my work through the years. I am also grateful to the directors of these institutes for their nurturing of the projects and their financial support. My thanks as well to Meredith Pekerow who edited my English and to Francine van Remunt who helped me with the final lay-out of the book. And most of all, I wish to credit my supervisors, Aafke Komter and Nel Draijer for their inspiring tutoring.

CONTENTS

Chapter Three
FACTORS IN WELL-BEING AND RISK: THEORETICAL FRAMEWORK

Chapter Four
METHODS

Chapter Five
WELL-BEING OF PROSTITUTES

Chapter Six
PROTECTION STYLES OF PROSTITUTES

Chapter Seven
INTERACTION WITH CLIENTS

Chapter One
PROSTITUTION IN THE NETHERLANDS

Worldwide, millions and millions of women work as prostitutes. They work wherever clients are to be found: in streets, homes, bars and hotels in cities and villages, and near military bases, truckstops, borders and large conventions. The number of prostitutes is high, particularly in countries where sex tourism flourishes. For example, the number of women working as prostitutes in Thailand is estimated at 1 million from a population of 50 million (Roerink and Van der Vleuten, 1988). However, in the United States as well, it is estimated that 5 million American women between 16 and 64 years of age have ever engaged in various aspects of sex for pay (Janus and Janus, 1993).

In The Netherlands, the number of prostitution work places for female prostitutes is estimated at 20-25,000 (Visser, in press). It may be assumed that the number of women occupying them either full or part-time is higher[1]. Prostitutes in The Netherlands work predominantly in clubs and brothels and, to a lesser extent, in windows, as escorts, on the street and in their own private houses. It can be estimated that out of a population of 15 million, at least 250,000 women between 16 and 65 years of age have ever worked in prostitution.

Clearly their number is high, but there is relatively little systematic, empirical knowledge on how prostitutes fare and even less on the reasons they fare as they do. Neverthless, opinions on these matters run high. One extreme is the image of the prostitute as a pitiful drop-out, as the prototypical victim of society in general and ill-intended men in particular, who is all the more 'used up in a very rough way' (Winick and Kinsey, 1971:16) by working prostitution. The other is the image of 'The Happy Hooker' (Hollander, 1982), earning high amounts of 'easy' money in an exiting and enjoyable life style. Although these images are bound to reflect at least part of the truth for at least some of the women in prostitution, it is unclear to what extent, for exactly whom, and why they would apply. What are the conditions that make one woman have an enjoyable career in prostitution and another be 'destroyed' by it, if these extremes exist at all?

This is the subject matter of this book: how do prostitutes fare? Which differences present themselves in this respect? And how can these be explained? During the course of three different research projects on prostitution, we have had the opportunity to gather a substantial amount of information on the well-being of prostitutes in The Netherlands and on the conditions determining the differences

---

[1] Sterk-Elifson and Campbell (1993) estimate the number of prostitutes in The Netherlands to be approximately 40,000 (1993:198). They may have followed the line of reasoning mentioned above but, unfortunately, do not reveal their sources.

between them in this respect[2]. In this book, the findings of the two main studies will be reported. In the introductory chapter, the stage will be set by describing the legal status of prostitutes and attitudes towards prostitution in The Netherlands. We will compare the situation to those in other countries. The relevance of questions regarding the well-being of prostitutes will be discussed. We will consider some international developments which can be expected to affect both the position of prostitutes and the prostitution market in general.

1.1: Legal status of prostitutes and attitudes towards prostitution

Many consider The Netherlands a pioneer in liberal attitudes towards prostitution. They have seen or heard about the red light district in Amsterdam and assume that it is all perfectly permissible in The Netherlands. Some Dutch authors have also portrayed the country as a forerunner when it comes to attitudes towards prostitution (e.g. Belderbos and Visser, 1987; Boutellier, 1991). According to Boutellier, a 'post-modern morality' regarding prostitution has now come about in The Netherlands.

In this section we will reflect on the extent to which these judgements are right. The legal status of prostitutes in The Netherlands in comparison to other countries will be discussed. Then recent developments regarding long expected legal reforms will be considered. Next follows a discussion of general attitudes and an investigation of feminist views and the feminist lobby regarding prostitution. Conclusions will be drawn as to the question whether indeed The Netherlands is the liberal, pioneer country in relation to prostitution that it is often thought to be.

Legal status and law enforcement

Through the ages and throughout the world, prostitution has either been actively prohibited, tacitly condoned, formally regulated, or a combination of these. Prostitutes have seldom been left alone or received legal protection as workers.

Under a prohibitive policy, law enforcers and prostitutes continually play cat and mouse. Women working as prostitutes have to operate in such a way that the authorities are least likely to spot or trace them, which puts a heavy burden on their working conditions. A prohibitive policy thus gives way to all sorts of

---

[2] A first preliminary study addressed 'aspects of force and violence in prostitution' (see Vanwesenbeeck, 1986, 1987). Next, the two main empirical studies were conducted. One dealt predominantly with 'coping and well-being of prostitutes' (see Vanwesenbeeck, Altink and Groen, 1989; Vanwesenbeeck, 1990), while the second one focussed on 'protection behavior of prostitutes and clients in hetero-and homosexual prostitution' (see Vanwesenbeeck et al., 1992, 1993 and De Graaf et al., 1992, 1993). The first two studies were conducted at the Mr. A. de Graaf foundation in Amsterdam, by order of the Ministry of Social Affairs and Employment. The third study was conducted at the Netherlands Institute of Social Sexological Research (NISSO) and financed by the Counsel of Health Research (RGO).

exploitation. Authorities answer these iniquities by fighting prostitution and prostitutes themselves. This has proven to be a very expensive way of operating. In the United States where prostitution is illegal in all states except Nevada, the 16 largest cities spent an average of 7.5 million dollars on enforcing prostitution laws in 1985. Half of them spent more on prostitution control than on education or public welfare, and five spent more than on health services and hospitals (Weitzer, referring to Pearl (1987), 1991:25). Still today, the United States have the most repressive approach towards prostitution of all western industrial democracies (cf. Alexander, 1993).

On the contrary, in most European countries it is not illegal for individual women to engage in prostitution[3]. However, the organization and pursuit of prostitution are formal legal offences practically everywhere. This is the situation in The Netherlands as well. However, large differences exist between the European countries in the activities formulated under the denominator of 'prohibition of organization'. In The Netherlands, it bears on 'making a profession or habit of causing or encouraging indecent acts by others' (Art. 250bis, Dutch Penal Code) and 'living off the earnings of a prostitute' (Art. 432), while in countries such as Sweden, England, France and Belgium laws on organization also encompass renting a premises for the purpose of prostitution and public advertising for prostitution activity Regulations such as these can make it very difficult for prostitutes to organize their work and lives. This is the case to a much lesser extent in The Netherlands. Other measures such as the registration and medical examinations of prostitutes are also not mandated by law in The Netherlands, as they are in Austria, Greece and certain parts of Germany.

Furthermore, large differences exist between different European countries in the fierceness with which prostitution laws are enforced. The Netherlands is known as one of the least repressive countries for prostitution. Brothels, clubs and escort services are widely tacitly condoned and window and street prostitution is tolerated in specific districts. France or Britain on the other hand, are examples of more repressive regimes. Soliciting is illegal everywhere and prostitutes are routinely arrested and fined. Laws against procuring are enforced against prostitutes' families and against prostitutes who work together or share a flat. It is often taken for granted that one lives off the earnings of a prostitute when one lives with her. Still, varying forms of tacit condoning and toleration can be seen in all European countries. Since condoning is mostly limited to certain geographical areas, or to certain forms of prostitution, a policy of condoning is in fact often a policy of regulation, even if the activities being regulated are formally against the law.

---

[3] Belgium is one exception to this rule. Engaging in prostitution is formally illegal, although different forms of prostitution are widely tolerated. Spain is an exception of a different kind. There, no specific laws against prostitution exist, but women are prosecuted under laws against 'danger to society' (Alexander, 1993).

Considering the relatively mild legal restrictions put on prostitutes and the reticence of Dutch authorities to enforce the law against prostitution, it can be concluded that the Dutch policy is indeed a relatively liberal one. However, straightforward acceptance and decriminalization of prostitution also appears to be unfeasible in The Netherlands.

Law reform? No law reform!
One of the reasons The Netherlands has often been looked (down) upon as a 'mecca' for prostitution, is that for about a decade it seemed very likely that the prohibition statements would be deleted from the Criminal Code and that a policy was going to be adopted in which under certain conditions, the organization of prostitution could be legal business.

Political discussions about the topic started in 1983. At that time there appeared to be wide political support for a regulatory law on prostitution that would make it easier to on the one hand, regulate and control organized prostitution and fight exploitation and abuse with legal means and, on the other, improve the (legal) position of prostitutes. The opinion that the right of physical and psychic integrity and the right of sexual self-determination should make it principally possible for women to choose freely for prostitution was relatively widely shared in political circles in the eighties[4]. It was proposed that the laws prohibiting organization of prostitution would be struck out of the penal code and that municipalities would have the opportunity (and the duty) to regulate prostitution by means of local acts.

However, opposition to this law reform was too strong for the proposals to be accepted and the new rules to be introduced. A process started in which the original proposals came to be reformulated drastically because of the influence of persistent opposition to facilitating governmental interference with prostitution. In addition, a change of power in the government and the arrival of a new minister of justice in 1990, dealt a heavy blow to the 'post-modern morality' (cf. Boutellier, 1991), at least on the political level. Here was a minister who was absolutely unwilling to 'take charge of a legalization and by-law policy' or to 'make brothel keeping a commonly acceptable activity' (quotes from the Reports on Parliamentary Discussions 1990-1993). During the seminar on prostitution and the trafficking in women of the Council of Europe in Strasbourg in 1991, the official Dutch policy propagated is the government takes 'a pragmatic position as to prostitution (..), but believes the phenomenon of prostitution, even when voluntary, to be morally unacceptable' (Buijs, 1991).

The adaptation of the original proposals for law reform ended up in a final bill where the organization of prostitution was still in principle an illegal activity but

---

[4] It was in that political climate that research projects such as 'aspects of force and violence in prostitution' and the 'coping and well-being'-study were taken up by the ministries. The option for political change was clearly there and research was badly needed.

which granted local municipalities the option to license brothels and clubs with the caveat that brothel owners would be legally liable if they hired minors or non-EU residents. 'Decentralization' was proposed instead of 'legalization'. Prohibition law was again hauled in via a back-door. Improvement of the position of prostitutes as a political goal had by then disappeared from the discussions.

In november 1993 these adapted proposals ultimately came up for vote in parliament but did not receive enough political support. The arguments against the bill were that the local option and resulting local arbitrariness were in fact against the constitution (crimes should not be defined on the local level), that non-EU women were discriminated against, and that this reform would result in a large illegal circuit and even worse possibilities for control. The reform proposals were withdrawn. Apart from raising the sentence to six years for trafficking in women, the situation remained as it was. Experts in the field maintain that in the end moral considerations as well as the inability to properly distinguish prostitution-as-free-choice from prostitution-under-force, are the prime reasons for the legalization process to have taken this turn (e.g. Visser, in press). If the distinction was made at all, the limits of 'free choice' prostitution were all too easily and opportunistically put on immigrant women.

All in all, it is unclear what effect the excavated law reform would have had for the position of prostitutes. If one evaluates the political discussions, the regulation of prostitution has definitely been a more prominent goal than improvement of the position of prostitutes, particularly in the case of immigrant prostitutes. It has been shown that through the ages forms of regulation or legislation work more as a measure of control than as liberation for prostitutes (cf. Walkowitz, 1980; Otis, 1985). Even though regulation offers prostitutes some freedom like the possibility to organize, it still involves physical and geographical separation and punishment if they do not work by the book. Wage protection, sick leave or insurance have never been provided by regulation yet. As Van Mens (1992) has shown for The Netherlands, even under a (at that time still expected) regulatory policy, the Dutch government did not consider it their task to intervene in the area of labor laws or labor relations. Actual prescriptions for the organization of prostitution restrict themselves to the improvement of the physical work surroundings. The improvement of the position of prostitutes as workers must be considered only a declaration of intention (Van Mens, 1992:173). The law reform would probably have involved many duties for prostitutes, but hardly any rights.

Moreover, the social status of prostitutes does not change all of a sudden with a legal shift. Legalization or even decriminalization does not establish 'normalization'. Rejection by the public and social stigmatization can still remain intact, even if prostitution were formally considered a legal profession.

General attitudes towards prostitution

Most people agree that moral judgements on sexual activity have changed substantially the last few decades. The sexual revolution in the late 1960s has taken sex and lust out of the taboo sphere. Still, commercial sex is considered immoral by many. In the United States in 1983, 69% of the American population thought it very or fairly important 'that laws prohibiting prostitution be strictly enforced', a percentage that had risen since 1981 (when it was 65%) (Roper Poll, reported in Weitzer, 1991). In 1984, 60% still (strongly) disagreed with the statement 'it should be legal for a woman to receive pay for sex' and 53% with 'it should be legal for a man to visit a prostitute' (Illinois Survey Research Laboratory, reported in Weitzer, 1991).

Unfortunately, comparable data for The Netherlands are not available, but the moral climate around sexual matters seems to be less restrictive. Attitudes towards homosexuality appear to be more positive in The Netherlands than in the United States. In 1980, 78% of Americans found 'sexual relations between two adults of the same sex morally wrong' (National Opinion Research Center, cited in Weitzer, 1991). However, in The Netherlands in 1986, 93% agreed with the statement 'homosexuals should be left free to live their lives their own way' (Social and Cultural Planning Bureau (SCP), reported in Van Delft, 1991).

In reference to prostitution, moral judgement seems to be less harsh in The Netherlands as well. Prostitution is openly discussed as possibly 'another form of labor' by the public at large and in the media, and experts and authorities can hardly ever be caught uttering stigmatizing or denigrating remarks about prostitution. When prostitution is criticized or fought against by civilians, it is mainly because a concentration of prostitution in their neighborhood bothers them. Dutch attitudes seem to be more lenient and more 'matter-of-fact'. The Dutch typically take a condoning position toward prostitution, as toward other morally tainted matters (such as abortion and euthanasia). Emotions on moral issues do not seem to run as high as in the United States. No mass movement, comparable to the 'Moral Majority' in the US, exists in The Netherlands.

However, the open and liberal character of the public discourse contrasts with the widespread ambivalent or even negative private opinions and behavior. Having listened to many prostitutes describing their experiences with negative social reactions, one can not maintain that the Dutch population fully accepts them or their work, not to mention respects them for it. At best, prostitutes are met with a kind of compassionate awe for what they have to go through. Openly claiming a liberal attitude towards prostitution is one thing, but unequivocally and unproblematically approaching women who work in it with this attitude, is another. Negative public opinion apparently exists alongside 'Dutch leniency'. On close examination, in The Netherlands as well as in other countries, attitudes toward prostitution appear to be strongly ambivalent among many people. The stigmatization of prostitutes (see Chapter Three) seems to be intact here too, although perhaps more tactfully than elsewhere.

Feminist views; the feminist lobby

The second feminist wave even though it is historically connected to the sexual revolution, has only had a doubtful advantage for prostitutes. Feminist opinions on prostitution vary with the emphasis put on either the sexual objectification of women or on the restrictions of their being sexual subjects. Neither of these view points seem to tell the whole story about prostitutes.

Roughly, three feminist positions can be distinguished. In the first view, working in the sex industry is seen as by definition as violating women's human rights and repressing and subordinating women by sexualizing and objectifying them. Sex-work is viewed as 'bad', because it is considered to sustain, reproduce and reinforce patriarchal relations and its concomitant objectification of women. Prostitution is seen as a severe case of sex discrimination. 'Free prostitution' does not exist in this view: 'the distinction between forced and free prostitution only serves to make one form of exploitation more acceptable than the other' (UNES-CO/Coalition against trafficking in women, 1991:1). All prostitutes are assumed to enter prostitution out of economic necessity and/or because of a history of sexual violence. Prostitution is a priori detrimental to women: 'prostitution cannot exist as a right because it usurps and negates already established human rights of the prostitute women to human dignity, bodily integrity, physical and mental well-being' (UNESCO/CATW 1991:6). Dworkin (1990), Brownmiller (1975), Barry (1979) and Schrage (1989), for example, are strong advocates of this view. They reject sex-work and accuse prostitutes of degrading all women, and carry on a campaign to abolish prostitution.

A second view also starts from the premise that sex-work is part of systemic gender injustice, but judges it no more and no less reprehensible than other forms of female sexual behavior or 'women's labor'. Rosenblum (1975), MacMillan (1976), Dominelli (1986), Tabet (1987), Overall (1992) and Davis (1993) might be named as some representatives of this point of view. They stress the fact that all (hetero)sexuality implies an economical exchange, whether it is 'du don ou tarif' (Tabet, 1987) and that prostitution is wrongfully defined as 'deviant'. They do not reject sex-work as such, nor do they accuse prostitutes of reinforcing the existing patriarchal order. They consider the sexualization of women a subordinating mechanism, but also see it as a possibly advantageous choice for women to capitalize on their sexual objectification and earn money. Their position towards prostitution can be described as 'rather not'. They see prostitution only as an option which is sometimes logical and necessary because of the prevailing sexual and economic relations. As James puts it: 'As long as the definition of the 'normal' male sex role is broader than of the 'normal' female sex role, there must be 'deviant' women to take up the slack' (1976:195). Economic hardship and early victimization may play a role in women choosing prostitution, but are not a priori taken to be decisive factors for all prostitutes.

A third group of feminists does not so much stress the subordinating aspect of the sexual objectification of women, but highlights the fact that women have always been denied sexual autonomy and freedom. They would rather not talk about sexual victimization at all. The choice for prostitution, in this view, is seen by definition as a human right instead of as a violation of human rights. Many of these authors consider sex-work liberating, a manifestation of crossing the borders of strictly circumscribed femininity, and a possibility for women to use the (sexual) power that has been denied them by patriarchal traditions. Some representatives of this view are Alexander (1982), Vance (1984), Rubin (1984), Pheterson (1986, 1989, 1990) and Paglia (1990). Limitations of being 'a good woman' and the advantages of being a 'bad' one are put forward. Pheterson (1986) for instance argues: 'The pure madonna would probably have to do without a job, without sensuous desire, and without money' (1986:95). Pro-prostitution activists carry slogans such as 'good girls go to heaven; bad girls go everywhere'. They not only stress the individual gain of women who take advantage of a sexual ideology that is mainly used against women, but also view sexual freedom and the recognition of sex-work as an important and necessary step towards the (sexual) liberalization of all women. They acknowledge that the organization of prostitution at this very moment still reflects the societal power of men and the relative social and economical powerlessness of women, but consider the rights of prostitutes as workers as the main goal for which to strive. From the current apparent wrongs in prostitution, it does not automatically follow that commercial sex or sex as a professional service should be rejected, either morally or in principle. Criticism on 'sex negativity' is strong within this tradition. However, for those who stress the evils of the sexual objectification of women, the denouncement of sexuality as dangerous to women is more important.

Internationally, the feminist controversy over prostitution is still strong. Those (prostitute and non-prostitute) feminists who stress the liberating aspects of prostitution or those who consider prostitution as in line with other female activities have been a supportive force in the struggle for prostitutes' rights and the improvement of their social status. However, those stressing the violent character of prostitution and its reinforcement of the subordination of women have formed a substantial counter-force. In the United States particularly, where radical feminists have formed coalitions with the Moral Majority, they have built up a powerful anti-prostitution lobby. Radical feminists speaking out against prostitution would seem to be strongest in the US, but can be heard in other countries as well.

However, this is hardly the case in The Netherlands. The radical feminist view of prostitution as inherently opposing female human rights is considered too one-sided by most Dutch feminists. No longer are solely negative consequences attached to professional sex. The wishes of prostitutes to be recognized as professional workers are also widely acknowledged. Some feminists in The Netherlands subscribe to the 'rather not'-view, others the pro-prostitution view, and yet others endorse a bit of both. The first view is more strongly held in the case of migrant women who are considered to work because of economic necessity; the latter is particularly strong in relation to Dutch prostitutes who are considered mature and independent. The pro-prostitution view is also strongly advocated by some of the prostitutes themselves who have been organized in 'De Rode Draad' (the Read Thread) since 1985.

Dutch feminists and prostitutes are among the strongest advocates of decriminalization in Europe. In collaboration with some American advocates of the decriminalization of prostitution the First World Whores' Congress was organized in Amsterdam in 1985 and Dutch women were closely involved in the organization of the second one in Brussels in 1986[5]. One might say that as far as a feminist movement can exert influence on the position of prostitutes, Dutch feminists have been an important force in enhancing their social status in The Netherlands (see Boutellier, 1991).

Conclusion
The liberalization and decriminalization movement is stronger in The Netherlands than in other countries. The Dutch government adopts a less repressive policy than the governments of most other European countries or the United States. However, neither this substantial societal force nor the relatively liberal policies have so far succeeded in bringing about a radically different legal status for prostitutes. Moreover, the general moral climate toward prostitution does not seem to be substantially better than in other countries, perhaps only less openly and less negative. Ideological distinctions between 'good' and 'bad' women bother Dutch prostitutes as it does their colleagues all over the world. Even if the argument remains that working as a prostitute in a comparatively free, liberal, condoning and rich country is relatively comfortable, the Dutch prostitutes' situation differs only in gradation, not in principal from that of their colleagues in other countries.

Decriminalization would really make a difference for the status of prostitute women. However, this is still not an acceptable and too controversial an alternative for the Dutch government, just as it is not desired or viable in the United States or any other country. During the political squabble over this matter, improvement of the position of prostitutes seems to have gotten lost as a political goal. Historically speaking, the fact that this has recently been a topic during the political debate about prostitution in The Netherlands is exceptional. However, after ten years of fruitless debating, the baby seems to have been thrown out with the bath water.

1.2: The relevancy of the issue 'well-being of prostitutes'
Knowledge on the well-being of prostitutes is indispensable in order to develop the right policy. That is one reason why research on the topic is needed. Below, this first point will be stressed and followed by a short discussion of two examples of more or less recent societal developments which may affect the well-being of prostitutes and thus make insight into their well-being all the more relevant.

Lack of knowledge hinders correct policy
Through the ages, prostitution has been the subject of political debate with varying intensity, and will continue to be in the future. Incentives for debate and the resulting policy in whatever form have been either of a moral character and related to desired control over female sexuality and behavior in general, or related

---

[5] For a report on both congresses, see Pheterson (1989).

to public health (cf. e.g. Bullough, 1964; Alexander, 1982; Newburn, 1992 or Järvinen, 1993). The focus of debate or intervention has hardly been on the well-being of prostitutes. Traditionally, prostitution has often almost self-evidently been associated with sickness, pathology, unhealthiness and misery. The rise of AIDS has once more nourished the association with contagious diseases. In fact, moral arguments against prostitution are often strongly linked to the assumption that prostitution is detrimental to prostitutes and dangerous for society as a whole.

However, efficient and nuanced policy can not be based on assumptions. So far, appropriate political analyses are clearly hindered by a lack of knowledge of the actual well-being and risks of prostitutes and the factors which determine them. It has been noted that also feminist analyses often gets stuck in a lack of insight in whether prostitution is in fact beneficial or detrimental to the women involved (cf. Shameem, 1993). Not only should their well-being more explicitly be a topic of debate and a political goal in itself, but any intervention in prostitution should take the consequences for their well-being into account.

There is no doubt that the regulation of prostitution will at some time be back on the political agenda in The Netherlands. At the moment in Europe not only national interests are at issue, but international ones as well. Now that the European Union is starting to take shape national borders have been lifted for many forms of international traffic, and the EU is struggling with the coordination of social policies. The possibility for women from one EU-country to work in prostitution in another brings about a common political interest in regulating prostitution.

No matter how strong the need for national or international regulation is perceived in the near future, it would clearly be a positive development if the well-being of sex workers were taken into account in political considerations. This is already the case in other branches of professional activity deemed to carry certain physical or mental risks. Empirical knowledge on the subject is therefore indispensable.

Increasing migration and internationalization of prostitution
In the second half of the seventies, women from Southeast Asia were the first group of migrant women to come to work in prostitution in The Netherlands. In the beginning of the eighties, Latin American women (predominantly from Columbia and the Dominican Republic) joined them. Somewhat later, Ghanaians showed up and more recently, women arrived from Hungary, Poland, Rumania, former Yugoslavia, the Czech republic, Bulgaria, and Russia.

This development of increasing mobility and migration of women in prostitution is worldwide. Women and girls from Burma, Laos and China work in western sex-tourism in Thailand. Thai and Philippine prostitutes migrate to Japan and Australia. Great numbers of women from the former East bloc work in prostitution in Germany, and streams of Russian women travel to the Middle East and to China to earn money in prostitution. The business of prostitution seems not only to expand, but is also becoming more and more international. Important factors in this development are the collapse of the Soviet empire, the general increase in global mobility and the worldwide disparity of socio-economic conditions.

As more women worldwide find themselves in dead-end situations and migration because of economic necessity becomes more and more common for prostitutes all over the world, the exploitative and often abusive grip of traders on prostitutes becomes stronger. The trade in women flourishes the more women are dependent on and defenseless against intermediaries. Criminal organizations appear to control extended networks of prostitution, particularly in the former East bloc. We can not even begin to grasp the extent to which these practices involve deception, threats, extortion, or brutal force and violence. Every once in a while the media report horrifying stories on the victims of pimps and gangs. In June 1993, Time Magazine reported that 'a 1991 conference of Southeast Asian women's organizations estimated that 30 million women had been sold worldwide since the mid-1970s'. 'Such figures are at best guesses and at worst only the tip of the iceberg', the journalist concludes. We can only fear for the present and future well-being of these women. So far, knowledge about it is in large part fragmented and meagerly documented.

Furthermore, the fraction of migrant women who are not victims of force and violence by traffickers, but travel around the world independently in search of a better life, is largely still unknown. We have no knowledge at all of the consequences that these forms of migration have for their health and well-being. How do migrant women fare in the countries where they end up working in the sex business? The increasing migration of prostitutes and internationalization of prostitution calls for more insight into the factors which make prostitution, particularly for the migrant women involved, either an acceptable, enhancing way to earn a living or mainly a problem experience.

Changing sexual needs
The sexual revolution has brought women much more freedom and opportunities in the area of sexual pleasure. No longer are they restricted to the role of 'moral guardians of male sexual behavior' (Vance, 1984) and no longer is the sexually active woman the prototype of female evil. In the sixties and seventies, many expected the demand for commercial sex to diminish drastically now that women were increasingly permitted to realize themselves sexually and become more equal to men in other areas as well. However, the opposite seems to be the case; there is evidence that the demand for commercial sex is increasing.

The sex industry has currently developed thriving new forms of prostitution such as eros centers, sex holidays, sex telephone calls, sex therapy centers and dating services (cf. Davis, 1993). Economic growth, rising mobility, and the availability of cheap airplane tickets are probably important factors. There are also strong indications that a negative side-effect of the sexual revolution is that men have been strengthened in their feelings that they have a 'right' to have 'good sex', both in terms of quantity and quality. In The Netherlands, Komter (1985) has shown that women in private heterosexual relationships are confronted with different kinds of sexual requests from their partners more often. Men's sexual needs seem to have become even more taken for granted than they already were (cf. McIntosh, 1978). As the general preoccupation with sexuality increases, the appeal of commercial sex to many men seems to increase along with it.

Moreover, it has been suggested that men have become more insecure about their sexual identities because of changing gender relations. Some authors expect men to become more sexually compulsive as male sexuality in particularly may become problematical now that 'the context of separate and unequal social circumstances is waning' (Giddens, 1992). This compulsiveness is edged by potential violence. When there is a relatively high degree of freedom to design one's own sexuality, many people seem to loose track and have difficulties defining their limits (see also Van Zessen, 1993).

The increasing demand for (commercial) sex and the possibility of increasing addiction edged with violence may directly affect prostitutes' well-being. Prostitutes have always been relatively vulnerable to violent male sexual behavior. In the future, they might become even more the targets for male compulsion, frustration and aggression. In this context, the question of their well-being and risks, particularly in relation to their interaction with clients, becomes all the more acute.

1.3: A preview of the book

In the next chapter, an overview will be given of developments in social scientific theory and research on topics concerning health and well-being of prostitutes. In Chapter Three, a multi-causal theoretical model will be presented to analyze and explain differences in how prostitutes fare in managing well-being and the risks of Sexually Transmitted Diseases and HIV-infection. Relevant theory and research conducted among prostitute and non-prostitute samples will be described. Chapter Four describes sampling, subjects, instruments and operationalizations in the two empirical studies to be presented in this book. It also discusses the representativity and generalizability of the findings. In Chapter Five, the findings with regard to well-being and job satisfaction are presented. Where possible, comparisons are made with the general population. Relations with the factors put forward in our multi-causal framework are reported. The results of a path-analysis are presented and discussed. Qualitative material is quoted to illustrate and deepen the quantitative analyses. In Chapter Six, findings concerning the protection behavior of prostitutes are presented. Three different protection styles are described, as they have been identified in female prostitutes. In Chapter Seven, protection behavior is discussed again, but this time clients and prostitutes' interaction with them are addressed. In the final chapter, the findings will be summarized and discussed in the light of the theoretical framework and other research findings and the implications for policy and intervention and for theory and research will be considered.

Chapter Two
DEVELOPMENTS IN THEORY AND RESEARCH

Introduction
During the course of this century, an enormous amount of scientific literature on prostitution has been produced. Ever since medical scientists in the 19th century codified prostitution as a form of illicit sexual activity and 'deviant' behavior in their 'scientia sexualis' (Foucault, 1976), it has been the object of extensive scientific study as well as an important target of political, medical and therapeutic intervention. Scientists within a wide array of disciplines have felt compelled to tackle prostitution as either an individual or a societal phenomenon, to elaborate on its origins and existence, and to direct policies and treatment.

As a result, the body of literature is very diversified. In our review[1], we focus on social scientific empirical studies that address (aspects of) the health and well-being of prostitutes. This implies that the review will do less tracing of historical, anthropological, legal, or general descriptive studies, purely ideological and moralistic writings, or testimonial literature or philosophical essays. Moreover, we have limited ourselves predominantly to female prostitutes, although empirical studies on their clients will be reviewed briefly because of their relevance to health issues. For a review of studies on male prostitutes we refer to Earls and David (1989, 1990) and Coleman (1989). Furthermore, the review will focus mainly on studies of prostitutes in the western world. Psychological and sociological empirical research on women in the non-western countries is relatively scarce. However, some non-western studies will be discussed briefly as well.

Appraising the scientific literature on female prostitutes, it seems that feelings of abhorrence, astonishment, incomprehension and fascination have motivated many of the authors. Pressing questions seem to have been: Who are prostitutes?, and Why do they enter prostitution? The question How do they manage? has been asked less systematically and only relatively recently.

These three questions appear to form an appropriate, historical guideline for a review of the research to be discussed. First, this review will focus on (mainly psychological) studies, that address the question, who are they? Within this research tradition, implicitly or explicitly, prostitutes are taken to be the 'cause' of prostitution. Second, attention will be given to (psychological and sociological) research addressing contextual factors in 'the making of the prostitute': Why do they enter? Early abuse, the drift into prostitution and motives as reported by prostitutes will be discussed. In this section, research on (motives of) clients will

---

[1] Earlier, less extensive reviews for the social sciences have been published by for instance James (1976), Bullough and Bullough (1977), Newman et al. (1985), Earls and David (1989) and Van Mens (1992). Kantha (1991) wrote an extensive bibliography for the medical literature. Truong (1988) described the various images of 'prostitute' in social theory and politics.

also be reviewed since they constitute the leering market. Third, studies of 'prostitutes in their present and daily lives and work' will be discussed. This body of research encompasses social scientific as well as medical-epidemiological work: How do they manage? Finally, our own research problem and questions will be introduced.

introduce their hypothesest work

2.1: Who are prostitutes?

In connection with both the strong associations between prostitution and badness at the turn of the century and the biologistic-individualistic tendencies in early medical psychiatry, the first studies of 'the problem of prostitution' almost exclusively took the prostitute as the unit of analysis and focussed on the presumed 'evil characters' and 'sick personalities' of women in prostitution. This tradition still has its adherents today. We will discuss: biologistic explanations, psycho-analytical explanations, and clinical studies by personality researchers.

Biologistic explanations

Lombroso (1836-1909) and others believed to have detected an 'inborn moral insanity' in prostitutes as a result of degeneration and inheritance. By this they casted prostitutes as the ultimate female equivalent of the male criminal, genetically and biologically predestined to be who they were. The first physicians like Parent-Duchalet (1870) in France, Merrick (1890) in England, and Janovsky (1922) in The Netherlands, who described the women they met in the course of duty around the turn of the century, still grappled with this concept and were preoccupied with the presumed innate, stable and particularly 'evil' personality traits of prostitutes. They were described as lazy, idle, vane, mendacious, spurious, greedy, hypocritical, and insincere by nature, and by nature distinct from normal human beings. 'Social misery and bad working conditions' (Parent-Duchalet, 1870) or 'housing problems and youth getting acquainted with lasciviousness at too early an age' (Janovsky, 1922) were also mentioned as possible background factors in becoming a prostitute, but the emphasis quite clearly was with the innate, 'criminal' personality of the prostitute.

The idea that 'nature' made the criminal did not cease to exist in the 20th century. In the 1930s, the Danish sociologist Kemp (1936) who studied 530 prostitutes, also claimed that genetics prescribed the 'feeblemindedness' and 'socially destructive behavior' of the prostitute. Even more recently authors like Cowie et al. (1968) and Klein (1980) focus on biological characteristics and adhere to the notion of the 'inherent diseased nature of prostitutes'. Societal, economical, situational or psycho-developmental explanations for women choosing to work as prostitutes are sometimes considered, but nature overrides nurture within this tradition.

Disturbed psychosexual development

The focus on pathology in the individual prostitute has been thoroughly cultivated within the psycho-analytical tradition of the 20th century.

Psycho-analysts erected a theoretical model which 'conceptualized the whole institution of prostitution as psychopathology' (Bullough and Bullough, 1977: 154) and added to the idea of something being 'wrong' with prostitutes by suggesting a disturbed psycho-sexual development and resulting pathological psychodynamic make-up. Psycho-analytic authors often built their theories on the basis of a few patient contacts, although Choisy (1961) worked as a waitress in a brothel for a month and both Greenwald (1958) and Maerov (1965) interviewed 20 prostitutes extensively. These were either clinical or prison samples and control groups were not used.

As in relation to other objects of study, psycho-analytic theory concerning prostitutes focussed on parental rejection, fixation in Oedipal conflict, feelings of guilt or hostility, regression, and an interplay of various defense mechanisms. Some authors focussed predominantly on rejection by and consequent hostility towards the mother (Glover, 1943; Greenwald, 1958; Maerov, 1965). Others focussed on incestuous overtones in the relation with the father and consequent guilt and hostility (Choisy, 1961; Janus, 1967; Abernethy, 1975). Still others stressed both possibilities (Deutsch, 1947; Agoston, 1945). It was assumed that these pathogenic childhood relations result in regression, defense and/or counterphobic behavior on the part of the woman. Thus, she would eventually be unconsciously drawn to prostitution, either by self-destructive or by masochistic desires (Greenwald, 1958; Choisy, 1961; Mathis, 1974; Bess and Janus, 1975), by defense against (latent) homosexuality (Lampl de Groot, 1928); by incapacity for intimacy (Greenwald, 1958; Hollender, 1961); by the acting out of a pseudo-personality (Deutsch, 1947, Agoston, 1945); or by a castration (Abraham, 1922) or masculinity complex (Deutsch, 1947), taking revenge for the seduction, abuse and desertion expected from men. Deutsch (1947) argued that the rejection of paternal authority in the prostitute might have extended to the rejection of the institutions built by men, such as law and morality. Some (Agoston, 1945; Maerov, 1965) considered the prostitute to be driven by a combination of all these unconscious desires in her infantile polymorphous perversive orientation: 'Through her activities, the prostitute is able to indulge her sadistic, masochistic, and homosexual desires, and her scopophilic and exhibitionistic impulses, as well as the enjoyment of magical power over the sexual activity of the male', Maerov stated (1965: 693).

Some of these psycho-analytic notions might hold for the prostitute women who were analyzed (as they might for many others), but that does not mean that they should be the main reason for their working in the sex business. As Bullough and Bullough argued, 'used-car salesmen or surgeons may have certain childhood trauma's and personality traits in common with other members of their occupation, [but that does not mean that any] responsible authority is willing to argue that cars are bought and sold or that operations are performed merely to satisfy the emotional needs of these workers' (1977: 155).

However, despite the selectivity and limited size of their samples, psycho-analysts tended to generalize their views and made hardly any distinctions between individual prostitutes[2]. Even if background factors like broken homes, parental abuse and neglect, being forced into prostitution and other traumatic events were clearly present and ascribed to (some of) the prostitutes studied, these findings were not used to either differentiate between prostitutes or to consider the choice for prostitution a 'healthy' one. These experiences were invariably interpreted as a predisposition for the neurotic personality that all prostitutes are assumed to have: for most psycho-analysts, working in prostitution is a priori a sign of abnormality.

Prostitution was thus considered either a 'sexual aberration' (Glover, 1943) or a 'complex emotional aberration' (Maerov, 1965), at any rate a symptom of disease. Formed and blinded by Freudian images of 'normal' and 'healthy' femininity, psycho-analysts considered any deviation from this particular feminine personality as abnormal, at best neurotic and sometimes even psychotic (Mathis, 1974). The perspective of prostitutes themselves hardly ever appears in the writings of psycho-analysts. Moreover, reported rational motives like economic necessity have often been disqualified as a 'disguise for the oral-anal regression' (Glover, 1943) or the 'conscious over-valuation of money' (Maerov, 1965). Deutsch (1947), acknowledging the economic motive often to be the primary one, also stated that it is sometimes a rationalization of an underlying emotional motive.

The focus of early psycho-analysis in general has mainly been a very individualizing one, interpreting all human behavior as a result of the psycho-dynamics of early childhood and adolescence. However, in later years, psycho-analysts have broadened their views while 'thinking prostitution'. Some 15 years after he published his study on call-girls referred to above, Greenwald (1973) stated that 'the sociopathic attitudes of prostitutes must for a considerable part be due to society's attitude to their profession'. Glover (1943) pointed out that as a consequence of society's constraints on female sexuality, all women in one way or another might be construed as prostitutes. He referred to dowries and marriage contracts to support this view. Helene Deutsch also considered prostitution in the context of gender relations. She not only assumed the possibility of 'taking an anticipated revenge for the rape they expect' (1947) as a motivation for prostitutes, but she also shed critical light on the 'completely unmotherly portrayal of female prostitutes' by her colleagues as 'possibly a fantasy product in a certain type of men who have in their imaginations established a sharp division between sexuality (prostitutes) and motherliness (unsexual mothers)' (Deutsch, 1945:38). As well as by the image of the 'normal' woman, psycho-analysts must have been bothered by the whore-madonna split, just as many others in history before and after them.

---

[2]Some rough typologies were made though, for example by Glover (1943), who differentiated between the 'drab type', the 'gold digger', the 'enthusiastic amateur', the 'impulsive adolescent' and the 'flourishing professional'.

A search for pathology

Much of the psychological research done on prostitution outside the psycho-analytical tradition can be qualified as an ongoing search for pathology in prostitutes in order to explain 'who they are'. Many authors must have been heavily influenced by what Stein (1974) describes as: 'I kept looking for signs that the women were really miserable or neurotic, or self-destructive. I wanted them to be that way. I think I wanted call-girls to be 'sick', because I believed that anybody - at least any woman- who sold sexual access ought to be sick'.

However, many studies could not come up with unambiguous proof of pathology. Curran and Levine (1942), having administered a body image question-naire to 30 prostitutes and 30 female control subjects, found little difference between these groups on attitudes toward their own bodies, homosexuality or hete-rosexuality. Wei and Wong (1949), having studied 500 prostitutes in Shanghai, failed to find any outstanding psychological abnormalities among them. Jackman et al. (1963) emphasized that the lack of control of important dimensions of life created a psychological burden for prostitutes that could not be attributed to prior psychopathology though. Gebhardt (1969), having analyzed the data on 127 American prostitutes, denied presupposed nymphomania, homosexuality, frigidity and inability to form affectionate relations with men. Roebuck and McNamara (1973), after extensive fieldwork and interviews with 20 prostitutes in a Mexican border city, suggested that prostitution can be a relatively stable and even flourishing occupation with no apparent psychopathology among those selecting the profession. Spalt (1975) failed to find differences in prostitution involvement among people with different (affective and non-affective) psychiatric disorders. Miksik (1976) in a large Czechoslovakian study in which 238 prostitutes were compared with 238 women seeking advise about making contact with the opposite sex, found that prostitutes had dynamic interaction with the environment, a tendency towards risk-taking, social dis-inhibition and inertness to social pressu-res, while the other group had the opposite tendencies. Liss (1981) found no differences in social behavior between 32 full-time prostitutes and 32 controls working full-time in other occupations. Fields (1980), on the other hand, did find prostitutes to have a more 'detached interpersonal style' than a group of controls. Bour et al. (1984) comparing 25 prostitutes with 25 non-prostitute delinquents, found no evidence of psychotic or neurotic reaction and hardly any difference between the two groups in their scores on the Tennessee Self Concept Scale. And finally, Maiuro et al. (1983) administered the Bem Sex Role Inventory to 101 female juvenile prostitutes and 78 female juvenile delinquents and found a higher incidence of prostitution among those subjects with a higher masculine sex role orientation. However, by the time these findings were reported, they had lost their pathological ring, which was not yet the case with the psycho-analytic identificati-on of a 'masculinity complex' (Deutsch, 1947).

All in all, the findings presented here contrast strongly with psycho-analytical descriptions of prostitutes as 'psychological misfits, floundering in a pathological state of helplessness and confusion' (formulation by Exner et al., 1977: 474).

Some personality researchers have surely tried hard to find signs of pathology or abnormality in prostitutes and have compared them to the most remarkable groups in doing so. Foa and Krieger (1985) for instance, found prostitutes to have a 'greater need for status, love and services' than drug addicts, alcoholics and motor cycle racers! Despite such 'stunning' findings, there is strong evidence overall, particularly provided by those studies using control samples, that 'the stereotypical images of prostitutes are simplistic and that, as in other professions, a wide variety of personality types and traits must exist among prostitutes' (Surawitz, 1976).

However, signs of pathology were sometimes found when specific sub-groups of prostitutes were investigated. For example, Nolimal and Crowley (1989) found promiscuity and prostitution to be highly associated with an Antisocial Personality Disorder in 52 methadone maintenance inpatients, which is a sample that definitely can not be considered representative for all prostitutes. Research that differentiated between different groups of prostitutes did also come up with some evidence for pathology in some prostitutes. Exner et al. (1977), for instance, divided 95 prostitutes into call girls, in-house girls, street walkers, commuter housewives (also working the streets) and street walker addicts, matched them to controls and subjected them to a series of psychological tests. They found 'no evidence whatsoever to suggest pathology' among the call-girls and the in-house girls. However, the street walkers appeared to be 'more naive and self-centered, less well organized, somewhat more rebellious, and probably had less control over their emotions', although 'it would be inappropriate to identify [their scores] as pathological' (1977:483)[3]. The addicts 'appeared pathological' and the housewives' test configurations showed 'some of the classic signs of schizophrenia'. In addition, for these women, the data suggested 'the presence of considerable pain' and the streetwalkers indicated that their entry into prostitution did evolve directly from some 'interpersonal emotional trauma, usually a bad marriage'. Unfortunately no information on trauma or victimization was given for the housewives and the street walker addicts.

The findings of Exner et al. suggested a link between trauma and pathology, but the authors did not highlight this evidence. Had they, and other authors looking for evidence of pathology in prostitutes done so, trauma might have been found to be more closely related to pathology, than pathology to prostitution.

Trauma and pathology
Other studies have introduced trauma more explicitly and systematically as a factor into their research on pathology and prostitution. Fields (1980) found that

---

[3] In Belgium, where the Exner study was duplicated by DeSchampelaire (1990), it was found that the test configurations of 41 professional prostitutes (comparable with the in-house girls and streetwalkers in Exner's group) resembled those of the New York street-walkers.

the occurrence of rape, limited interpersonal involvement (that put the prostitutes at risk psychologically) and negative parent-child relationships, together, significantly differentiated a group of 42 prostitutes from 43 non-prostitutes. In another study, Ross et al. (1990) compared 20 patients with multiple personality disorder (MPD), 20 prostitutes and 20 exotic dancers on their histories of sexual abuse and measurements for dissociative disorders. Seven dancers met the diagnostic criteria for MPD and seven prostitutes met those for psychogenic amnesia. The percentage of sexually or physically abused women was very high in all three groups and did not differ significantly among them. However, the MPD-subjects, who were also found to be more dissociative than the others, reported a much longer duration of the abuse, more abusers and more forms of sexual abuse.

It can be concluded, that pathology has only been convincingly demonstrated in very specific groups of prostitutes, particularly when there was at least the suggestion of trauma. For the broader population, research in the past decades has revealed more and more associations between sexual trauma and psychological or psychiatric disorders (e.g. Draijer, 1988, 1990; Finkelhor & Browne, 1988; Nicolai, 1990; Hanson, 1990). For prostitutes however, the initial 'discovery' of sexual trauma and its psychological impact, surprisingly, shifted the attention away from their mental health. Sexual trauma in the context of prostitution came to be investigated in the first place as an explaining factor for entrance into prostitution per se.

2.2: Why do they enter?

As prostitution was less and less to be explained by the assumed pathological personality of prostitutes, attention shifted toward the question of why women would enter prostitution.

The (early) research on physical and sexual abuse of women revealed a relatively high percentage of prostitutes being among incest victims (e.g. Sloane and Karpinsky, 1942; Weiner, 1964; De Francis, 1969; Ferracuti, 1972; Lukianowitz, 1972). More recently in The Netherlands, Draijer (1988, 1990) found significantly more experiences with prostitution among women who were sexually abused as children (by family members) than among others. Many researchers have focussed on the prevalence of early victimization among prostitute (and control) samples and tried to find evidence for a link between (childhood) sexual trauma and prostitution on an individual, psychodynamic level.

Theoretically, the involvement in prostitution of victims of abuse can be interpreted as a form of counter-phobic behavior, in which the victim unconsciously repeats the traumatic experience in order to try and regain control and restore the disturbed images of self and the world. This mechanism could explain phenomena like the sexual acting-out of feelings of discomfort and/or prostitution. In modern trauma theory, prostitution is considered to be the repetition of early traumatic experiences and as such a possible part of the survival process (cf. Herman, 1981; Janoff-Bulman, 1985; Kleber et al., 1986; Draijer, 1988, 1990; Finkelhor and Browne, 1988). Others interpret the link between sexual trauma and

prostitution in terms of the development of a deviant self-image of 'prostitute' of
the victim, who may 'view herself as sexually debased or whose sexuality is more
than normally objectified' and thus 'may see prostitution as a natural or as the
only alternative' (James and Meijerding, 1977)[4].

At the same time as these psychological theories developed, 'new' sociological
approaches towards deviance, such as social control theory, labeling theory, social
interactionism, and stigma theory[5] became consolidated. The central feature of
these approaches is that deviance became interpreted as a result of social definition and control, labeling and reinforcement, more than as a static characteristic of
individual behavior as such. Research among prostitutes within this tradition also
often addressed violent, broken or non-loving families, but, instead of focussing
predominantly on the individual, psychological survival processes with the
victims, it highlighted the social interaction and 'feedback loops' between the
individual and her surroundings. In evaluating different theoretical approaches
toward prostitution, Newman et al. (1985) identified six features of this new
scientific approach to prostitution which in their opinion, began to emerge around
1970: 1. a focus on the individuals' interaction with society; 2. a view of society
as modifiable; 3. an assumption that the prostitute is neither simply victim nor
simply villain, but is instead an active participant in the construction of her life
and life style in so far as she is capable given her particular set of strengths and
weaknesses; 4. an assumption that much of the prostitutes' deviant behavior is
motivated by the same needs that everyone else in society has, namely the need
for love, a sense of self-worth, competence and power; 5. a focus on understanding how sex role and gender expectations contribute to female prostitution; 6.
a special emphasis on the complexity of the process by which the adolescent
female enters into prostitution (1985:84). The focus was on 'the processes of ego-
development, including ego's strengths, weaknesses, defenses and resources and
the nature of the ego-identity. The latter is crucial to an understanding of how a
girl comes to have a deviant self-concept' (Newman et al., 1985:85).

Below, the empirical evidence gathered in both the psychological and the
sociological approaches will be reviewed. In addition, the findings on motives as
reported by prostitutes themselves and the role of force by pimps and traders will
be discussed. Research on the possible association between drug use and prostitution will also be reviewed. Finally in this section, we will focus on clients. After
all, their sexual needs are at the basis of a worldwide institutionalized market for

---

[4] Theories on the psychological effects of childhood trauma and other forms of
victimization, will be discussed further in Chapter Three.
[5] Pioneering work in this field has for instance been done by Lemert (1951), Becker
(1963) and Goffman (1963). Lemert for instance views deviance as a 'progressive reciprocal relationship' (1951:76). Famous words by Becker are: 'Deviant behavior is behavior
that people so label' (1963:9). The companion notion of stigma, or 'spoiled identity' has
been thoroughly analyzed by Goffman.

commercial sex and thereby an important incentive for women to work in prostitution.

Early victimization as an explanatory factor

In the 1970s and 1980s, more and more empirical evidence became available from the study of prostitute samples which showed that prostitutes form a group of women with relatively many traumatic experiences with violence and abuse.

Rates of intrafamilial childhood sexual abuse among juvenile prostitutes reported in American studies vary between 31% and 66.7% (Weisberg, 1985). Jennifer James (1976, 1978) found that the prevalence of parental abuse-neglect among prostitutes was high among a sample of 136 prostitutes in New York: for 29% of the women studied, physical and emotional abuse appeared to be a significant factor in separating them from their families. The mean age at which they left their familial homes permanently was 16. 'Alienation from parents may result in a consequent inability on the part of the child to adequately socialize conventional mores of "respectable" society', James argues (1976:185). She suggests that sexual desirability may become a source of self-worth to compensate for parental neglect.

Silbert and Pines (1981, 1982, 1983) interviewed 200 (current and former) street prostitutes about their experiences with violence and found that 62% had been beaten as children, 45% on a regular basis. In more than three out of four cases the beater was male and in some relation of authority to the girl. 70% reported emotional abuse in the home environment. 60% were sexually exploited as juveniles with an average of two perpetrators each, 67% of those by father figures; and 70% claimed this had an influence on their choice for prostitution. A later analysis of their qualitative data (1984) showed that some prostitutes were also pornographically abused as children.

Bagley and Young (1987) in Canada, replicating the work of Silbert and Pines among ex-prostitutes, found 62% of 45 women to have been physically, and 73% to have been sexually abused as a child. More than half of these women judged their sexual abuse to have been a significant factor in becoming a prostitute. 'It appears that sexual abuse may have caused social and psychological isolation and/or maladaptive sexual behavior in at least two-thirds of those interviewed', Bagley and Young concluded (1987: 23)[6]. Still in Canada, Earls and David (1990) found 42% of 50 prostitutes having been physically abused at home and 26% having had a 'non-consenting sexual relation with (mostly an older) family member' at an average age of 10 and having left home at an average age of 13.7. 'The home situation of prostitutes may have been such that prostitutes were either

---

[6] It was also found by Bagley and Young that 42% of the women had been separated from a biological parent for more than 5 years before age 12, and in the multiple regression analysis with data from a control group this appeared to be an even somewhat stronger predictor for entering into prostitution than sexual and physical abuse before age 16.

obliged to fend for themselves at an earlier age or that they had more early sexual experiences', Earls and David conclude (1990:10).

Evidence for a link between sexual abuse and entering prostitution has also been found in the non-western world. For India, Singh and Singh (1980) showed that prostitutes suffered from lack of parental guidance, discovered that sex could be used as a means to get affection and other benefits, and experienced rape and incest, making them view themselves as sexually debased. In an Israeli study by Shoham et al. (1983), nine out of 67 prostitutes answered yes to the question of whether their fathers were interested in them 'not only as fathers' (1983:60). A Costa Rican study (Chacón et al., 1992) found that half of 32 prostitutes had been sexually abused before age 16.

Considering the fact that prevalence rates of child sexual abuse for the general population in the United States and The Netherlands are respectively 16% for incest (3-4% by father figures) and about a third (28-33%) for child sexual abuse in general (Russell, 1984; Draijer, 1988, 1990), it would seem that prostitutes have these experiences more often and more severe than other women. Several controlled studies empirically confirmed this supposition (see Table 2.1). When compared to the prevalence of sexual abuse and to family characteristics among the general population or among matched non-prostitute groups, childhood experiences of prostitutes were found to be significantly more negative. Prostitutes appear to come more often from families that were either broken, violent, or non-loving, to have left home earlier, to have had more experience with sexual and physical abuse in childhood, to have had sex at an earlier age and to have experienced more rape during adolescence.

However, in comparison to other non-prostitute 'delinquent' groups these differences did not show up. It would seem that trauma and negative childhood experiences can be a factor in the turning away from conventional, 'straight' life, but what form of 'deviance' will be 'chosen' also depends on other factors. Seng (1989), having analyzed data on 115 either sexually abused, or prostitution involved children (mean age 14), concluded, that 'the link between sexual abuse is not direct, but requires runaway behavior as an intervening variable. It is not so much that sexual abuse leads to prostitution, as it is that running away leads to prostitution' (1989:673). A very high percentage of runaways among prostitutes has been signalized by others as well. Lowman (1987), referring to the findings of the Juvenile Prostitution Survey in Canada, reported that only 5.5% of the female juvenile prostitutes interviewed said they had never run away from home.

On the other hand, Simons and Whitbeck (1991), comparing 40 adolescent runaways of whom 18% had been involved in prostitution, to 95 homeless adult women of whom 11% had done so, concluded that for both groups sexual abuse had a significant impact on the probability of becoming involved in prostitution. This was supported even after controlling for running away, substance abuse, and other forms of delinquent/criminal behavior (1991:375/6). The authors considered

Table 2.1: Overview of studies on childhood/adolescence experiences and family characteristics of prostitute and non-prostitute samples

Author (year)	country	N of samples	control group	prostitutes vs. controls
Nedoma & Sipova (1972)	Czechoslovakia	100/100	married women at prenatal clinic	more families without father more families torn by dissention more mean and domineering mothers earlier dating and intercourse no diff. educational guidance
James & Meyerding (1977)	western USA	92+136/idem	general population	less sex education from parents more sex. advances by elders more incestuous rel. w. fathers earlier age sexual initiation
Fields (1980)	L.A., USA	42/43	matched	more negative parent-child relat. no diff. childhood sexual abuse specific exp. more abusive more rape in adolescence
Liss (1981)	Illinois, USA	32/32	matched	sex at earlier age no diff. force in first sex exp.
James & Davis (1982)	western USA	136/133	engaged in other criminal activities	no diff. coming from broken homes no diff. age first intercourse no diff. number sex. relations
Shoham et al. (1983)	Israel	67/67	matched	more socially isolated as children more father-daughter incest run away from home more often
Bour et al. (1984)	New York, USA	25/25	age-matched delinquents	earlier first intercourse no diff. parental absence no diff. early abuse
Potterat et al. (1985)	Colorado, USA	14/15	patients at a VD-clinic/ matched	more often oldest child less often drop-out no diff. arrest records no diff. physical abuse no diff. sexual abuse no diff. age first intercourse
Bagley & Young (1987)	Canada	45/45	general population	more intrafamilial violence more physical and sexual abuse earlier leaving home
Earls & David (1990)	Canada	50/50	matched	more foster homes earlier leaving home more physical violence in youth gen. atmosphere home rated lower more sex interact. w. familymember earlier non-familial sex
Simons & Whitbeck (1991)	Iowa, USA	17/118	runaways and homeless women	more often sexually abused as child more often victimized during last year no diff. physical abuse as child no diff. criminal behavior no diff. substance abuse no diff. running away from home
Udegbe & Fajimolu (1992)	Ibadan, Nigeria	78/85	undergraduates	more polygamous fathers mothers higher number of marriages higher number siblings and cohabitants left home at younger age lower level of attachment to both parents no diff. need for affiliation or autonomy

their findings to support the 'direct effect model' of the impact of sexual abuse on prostitution which states that the 'specific experience of child sexual abuse fosters attitudes about oneself and the act of sex that facilitate the selling of sexual favors' (1991:363). They considered this to be at the expense of the 'indirect effect model' which supposes sexual abuse to be connected to prostitution by 'increasing the probability of participation in a deviant street culture and illegal activities' (1991:362). This indirect effect model has been investigated by several sociologists and will be further addressed in the next section.

In the interim, a critical remark must be made in regard to the evidence that prostitutes have been sexually victimized in childhood more often than other women. Many authors are inclined to conclude that 'separation, impaired quality of attachment and sexual experiences occurring in childhood and adolescence are antecedents in the development of women who become prostitutes' (Rubenstein, 1990). However, most research has been done among specific, select samples of prostitutes. They were, for example, exclusively street prostitutes (like the Silbert and Pines sample), or either working the street or recruited in jails (like the James and Meijerding sample) or exclusively ex-prostitutes recruited through social agencies (like the Bagley and Young sample). Since these samples are not representative of the whole population of prostitutes, they can not be generalized, neither with regard to the prevalence of abuse nor with regard to the conclusion that 'prostitutes' have been victimized in childhood more often than other women. In addition, the findings on the prevalence of abuse in groups of prostitutes are very divergent and even contradictory (see Table 2.1).

It should be kept in mind, that even if a large percentage of prostitutes had been sexually abused as children, another large percentage has not. The findings so far, call rather for differentiation between prostitutes than for generalizing statements with respect to early victimization.

The drift into prostitution

Scholars who study the process by which a woman enters prostitution from a more sociological, interactionist perspective, often consider explanations on a psychological level too one-sided. Psychological interpretations are deemed to focus too exclusively on the girl/woman without taking into account the surrounding structures, norms, relations, and reactions. Gail Pheterson (1986), for example, argued that it is not so much the psychological consequence of the abuse, but more the whore stigma that causes the relationship between abuse and prostitution: 'Because prostitution, unchastity, sexual abuse and badness are being brought under one stigmatizing denominator, the sexually abused girl has the choice to either repress her experiences or give away her reputation. (..) For women who have already been branded whores [as a consequence of the abuse], the step into prostitution is not as big as it is for those who cling to the status of being a decent woman. The tricky thing is, that in general not the whore stigma, but a damaged personality is seen as the link between an "unchaste" youth and prostitution' (1986:76).

Researchers within the interactionist, labeling and stigma tradition[7] emphasize the internalization of a deviant self-concept in response to informal labeling, public branding and subsequent stigmatization.

Davis (1971) studied a jail sample of 30 prostitutes and described the 'drifting process' as follows. First, in the interactional process with significant others, the girl achieves an identity as one who is 'different'. She is a person who is expected to behave in unconventional ways. Factors like low family cohesion lead the girl to seek street associates who will support the informally labeled degraded status. Motivational ambivalence is characteristic during the transitional phase and creates a zig-zag pattern of deviance for most prostitutes. They vacillate between conventionality and deviance. The development of adequate coping mechanisms is requisite if they are to continue. As the drift-process develops, the pick-up pattern has no longer an intrinsic appeal, while the sex-with-money act is viewed as a normal response to peer norms and an indication of emancipation, both social and financial. All this leads to the final stage of unequivocal perception of a deviant self and of sex as a vocation. Davis put a heavy emphasis on the implications of the criminalization of deviance: 'The social act of public branding as a crucial step in the individual's progress toward a criminal career', she wrote (1971:320). She saw deviance as shaped by the attitudes and actions of others. The stigmatization as immoral as a consequence of behaving unconventionally was seen as crucial to the development of a deviant identity and reducing the barriers to involvement in prostitution.

Rosenblum (1975), leaning heavily on Lemert's work and her own acquaintance with five call-girls, described the shift from 'primary deviance' to 'secondary deviance'. She explained the transformation of 'an incidental risk-taking action which is still socially excused and does not result in a change of status and psychic structure, into a situation where real or potential stigmatization, punishments, segregation, and social control become central facts of existence for those experiencing them, altering psychic structure, producing specialized organization of social roles and self-regarding attitudes' (1975:175).

There is empirical evidence for the 'drift-perspective': 60% of the women studied by James (1978) mentioned being labeled a prostitute before they actually entered prostitution. In the study by Silbert and Pines (1982), 90% of the women reported that their sexual activity caused them some sort of problem and in 93% of those cases, the problems involved 'bad reputations' (1982:483). Silbert et al. (1982) further illustrate 'the drift' and 'the narrowing of the funnel' by the diminishment of reporting feeling rejected as the girls grow older. In elementary

---

[7] Representatives of this tradition are Davis (1971), Rosenblum (1975), James (1978, 1980), Brown (1979), Schaffer and DeBlassie (1984), and for the Netherlands Van den Berg and Blom (1987).

school, 55% of the women felt rejected by peer groups to which they wanted to belong. In junior high school this was only 37%, while at the same time 65% of them already had close friends engaging in some form of deviant behavior. Finally in high school only 17% felt rejected. 'The picture which emerges', Silbert et al. write, 'is one of young girls of grammar school age who feel extremely isolated, lonely and rejected by a group of peers to which they want to belong, moving slowly out of isolation and finding friends among deviant groups where they do not experience rejection. By the time they have left school, the young women have turned their isolation and sense of rejection into a deviant identity (only 19% of the total sample at this point had friends who were straight). Clearly, at an age where peer involvement and acceptance and identity are critical, young women will choose to become involved with deviant behavior rather than to remain isolated' (1982:195). The same is argued by Schaffer and DeBlassie (1984): 'When children experience failure in the traditional setting, they find reinforcement on the streets and among peers' (1984:695).

On the other hand it has been stressed that 'the deviant label is not an automatic pass into the deviant career' (James and Davis, 1982:348). Conventional controls are loosened only by a series of unplanned and contingent events and factors that can function as stepping stones towards prostitution or as 'forks in the road' (James and Davis, 1982:348) towards alternative careers (see Table 2.2). As is shown, deprivation and/or abuse in the family is considered a crucial stepping stone by all the authors reviewed here, even though James and Davis (1982) did not find broken homes as a differentiating factor between prostitutes and non-prostitute female offenders. Those who consider the criminal justice system to be a negative influence in this context argue that teenage girls are overprosecuted and stigmatized by the criminal justice system, and that this instills further self-derogation. It is also noted that institutionalization results in 'contamination' with a deviant network and that acquaintance with other imprisoned prostitutes strengthens identification with hustler norms. Frustration at school is thought to possibly result in 'going for short-term gains' (Schaffer and DeBlassie, 1984). Other specific stepping stones mentioned, such as force by pimps and drug use, will be discussed more extensively further on.

More general aspects related to becoming a prostitute in this literature are of a general contextual nature, such as the need for money and the lack of employment possibilities. The congruity of sex-work with the female sex role and other female service professions is also mentioned by several authors. Furthermore, intrapsychic factors like feelings of guilt, anger, depression and hostility and a general feeling of disorientation and confusion are considered important. And, last but not least, rewarding aspects, such as the reinforcement of gained independence, 'quick' money, excitement and 'the fast life' are mentioned by practically everyone. However, Silbert and Pines (1981) concluded that for their research group, there was an absolute predominance of negative factors, and an almost total lack of attractive ones.

Table 2.2: Overview of factors facilitating a prostitution career, as brought forward by authors arguing for the 'drift' into prostitution

Factor	Authors
deprivation and/or abuse in the family	Gray (1973); James and Meyerding (1977); Brown (1979); Silbert and Pines (1981); Silbert et al. (1982); James and Davis (1982); Schaffer and DeBlassie (1984)
having run away from home	Brown (1979); Silbert and Pines (1981); Schaffer and DeBlassie (1984)
exposure to the prostitution life style, and a deviant social network	Davis (1971); Rosenblum (1975); James and Meyerding (1977); Brown (1979); Silbert and Pines (1981)
the juvenile justice system, criminal records, and institutionalization	Brown (1979); Silbert and Pines (1981); James and Davis (1982); Schaffer and DeBlassie (1984)
academic failure and frustration at school	Gray (1973); Brown (1979); James and Davis (1982)
getting involved with pimps	Gray (1973); Silbert and Pines (1981)
early drug use	Brown (1979); Silbert et al. (1982); James and Davis (1982); Schaffer and DeBlassie (1984)
(further) negative sexual experiences	James and Meyerding (1977); Silbert and Pines (1981)
incomplete pregnancies	James and Davis (1982)

Gray (1973) mentioned two elements that could 'break the cycle' of a girls' becoming increasingly involved in prostitution. The first is the formation of a close intimate attachment to a conventional person who strongly disapproves of her involvement; the second is the removal of the opportunity for her to engage in prostitution (1973:423). Gray admitted that the latter is unlikely because 'in the atmosphere of the prevailing sexual standards and attitudes in our society, the demand for prostitution as a market commodity is not likely to diminish rapidly' (1973:423). She has been proven right, because now, twenty years later, this situation has not changed.

The 'drift-perspective' in the study of prostitution has provided us with important supplements to the psychological evidence. In its emphasis on the interaction between the individual and society, the drift theory has a broader scope than theories that limit themselves to the intrapsychic level. Factors in adolescence have also been studied in addition to those in childhood. This gives insight into a multi-layered process and more explicitly takes the perspective of the prostitute into consideration. Less than in the other studies reviewed so far, it is (either implicitly or explicitly) argued that prostitutes are the reason for the existence of prostitution. The societal reality of a leering consumer demand, the worldwide institutionalization of the sex industry, and the 'logic' of choosing prostitution considering economic and sexual gender relations are given credence. The same is true for the enormous survivorship capacities of many street women (cf. Davis, 1993:4). Because of all this, the drift perspective is less reductionistic than the other perspectives discussed earlier.

However, as a consequence of the attention to the process of becoming a prostitute, many studies focus solely on the younger girl. Some authors interpret this as a sign of putting the limit of the 'acceptable' with juvenile prostitution (e.g. Rio, 1991). The perceived unacceptability of young women working in prostitution is also demonstrated by the recurring recommendations to protect young girls from the drift. We tend to see this focus on the younger girl as a limitation in the study of prostitution.

There is still reason, here as well as in the evidence reviewed in the previous section, to question the extent to which the girls studied represent the entire population of prostitutes. It is clear that the samples being studied are still small and quite specific. The over-representation of women working the street and women recruited in jails and through agencies applies to these studies as well. In addition, these findings are apparently built for the most part on studies of women with negative experiences and negative motivations. This leaves a presumably large group of prostitutes out of the picture. In spite of this, generalizations are made easily by authors within this tradition and by the public at large. Particularly where stigmatized individuals are concerned, people tend to quickly think that they are 'all alike'. The drift perspective has not come up with a clear differentiation between prostitutes either. On the contrary, a bow-net has been described, of which we do not know to how many prostitutes it applies.

Finally, it is clear that also within this tradition, western women have been studied by western researchers almost exclusively. A look at the more conscious motives for entry attributed by prostitutes themselves, suggests that there might be differences with prostitute women in non-western countries.

Motives as reported by prostitutes themselves

As prostitutes' own perspectives were considered more important, researchers increasingly focussed on conscious motives as reported by the women themselves. Motives often include independence, adventure and an exiting life style, but the strongest motive showing up in every study is money.

Gebhard (1969) analyzed the data on 127 prostitutes and concluded that for nine out of ten women, money is the prime motivation. James (1976) stated that 'economics is the pervasive theme of prostitution, and this reality is indicated by the fact that money is mentioned as a motivating factor in virtually all of the literature' (1976:178). In the western world, it is definitely not always extreme economic deprivation 'forcing wretched creatures into prostitution'. The majority of prostitutes choose prostitution as the occupational alternative that affords them the highest attainable standard of living. Boggs (1991) studied 100 Scandinavian prostitutes and found that they predominantly entered prostitution on a part-time basis to supplement their income, have fun, or satisfy their curiosity. In James' study of 136 prostitutes, only 8.4% claimed to have started because of economic necessity, while 56.5% were motivated by a desire for money and material goods (1976:179). For North American women, she concluded that 'a combination of a higher income and an independent, exiting life style is the major motivating factor for most prostitutes' (1976:194). For the women in her study, answering the question 'What are the advantages of being a prostitute?', the economic motivation overwhelmed all other categories, and in the second response, independence had first place.

More than in the western world, severe economic necessity in a situation characterized by very few societal opportunities seems to be the prime motivation for women in the non-western world to enter prostitution. Wei and Wong (1949), studying the motivations of 500 prostitutes in Shanghai, said that the majority gave 'poverty' as the major reason and that 82% of their subjects were 'illiterate'. Some similarities as well as possible cultural differences also become clear in a study by Pillai (1982). Among 50 prostitutes in Delhi the following motivations of working as a prostitute were found: poverty, ignorance, search for a glamorous life, marriage against subject's wish, negligence or desertion by the husband, ill-treatment by the in-laws, lack of education at school and home, bad associations and imitation of 'western life'.

Despite differences between western and non-western women, it must be acknowledged that women all over the world still have limited money-making options. There are virtually no other occupations available to unskilled or low-skilled women offering an income which compares to prostitution. It is indeed, as Davis (1937:750) already mentioned 'not the hard question why so many women become prostitutes, but why so few of them do'.

Force by pimps and traders

The role of physical and emotional coercion by third parties to force women into the trade has been the subject of research all through the century and, it appears, has very often been overstated. 19th century feminists are an example, as DuBois and Gordon (1984) have shown: 'First they exaggerated the magnitude of the 'white slavery', including virtually all women engaged in casual sex. Then, they consistently exaggerated the coerciveness of prostitution. They denied the prostitute any role other than that of passive victim. They assumed that prostitution was so degrading, that no woman could freely choose it, not even with the relative

freedom with which she could choose to be a wife or a wage earner. Thus, the
"fallen woman" was always viewed as a direct victim' (1984: 33).

This conviction, even though held by many throughout the century, has not
been unequivocally confirmed by empirical data. In Gray's study of 17 young
prostitutes, the pressure applied by pimps in recruiting women appeared to be
'generally minimal' (Gray, 1973: 412). James (1976) found only about one in five
women having been 'recruited by pimp, pimp's woman or madam' (the level of
force is unclear). Only 4% of the 127 prostitutes in Gebhards (1969) study had
been 'forced'. In Canada, Bagley and Young (1987) come up with a somewhat
higher percentage of 13.3% of 45 former prostitutes having been forced by pimps.
Eighty percent of the women in this study said they 'did not have any alternative',
but 'did it to survive'.

Even though the actual force used by pimps to lure women in the job might
be considered lower than expected, this does not mean that most prostitute-pimp
relations are without violence. Silbert and Pines (1982) in their study of 200 street
prostitutes, found that 66% of these women had been physically abused by pimps.
However, it must be said that particularly street-women, who comprise this entire
sample, depend on pimps for survival on the job.

Until now, no reliable figures exist on the number of women who were the
victims of international women traders. In Chapter One, an estimate of 30 million
women having been sold world-wide since the mid-1970s was mentioned.
However, the level of actual force is not clear. In The Netherlands, Buijs and
Verbraken (1985) estimated the number of women trafficked to be 'probably
thousands'. Altink (1993) mentioned 'about a thousand'.

One of the difficulties with the figures on trafficking and force by traders is
the differences in the definitions used. While some define any mediated migration
that leads to prostitution as trafficking, others refer only to those cases where
actual force and/or deception were used. A proper mapping of the size of the
group of women who were victims, particularly of force and deception, is one of
the areas that definitely needs more research in the near future.

Drug use

Drug use is one area that has been researched as a factor in becoming a prostitute,
as well as being a characteristic of the working life of prostitutes. Many studies
have been conducted to investigate whether prostitutes are more drug dependent
than others and whether entrance into prostitution can be related to drug use. Drug
use had already been identified as a 'stepping stone' towards a career in prostitution by several researchers in the 'drift' tradition. This evidence will be elucidated
here and supplemented by a review of other studies on the topic.

James and Davis (1982) found early drug use (before age 15) to be
significantly higher among prostitutes than among non-prostitute delinquent
women. Silbert et al. (1982) concluded that their study of 200 street prostitutes
'documented a high prevalence of alcohol and drug abuse in their family of
origin, during the drift into prostitution, and as a part of prostitution' (1982:197).

Fifty five percent of their subjects reported being addicted prior to their involvement in prostitution, 30% became addicted after it, and 15% concurrently with
their prostitution involvement.

Partly because Silbert et al. did not differentiate between types of drugs, other
studies contradicted these findings. Gebhard (1969) found only 4% of 127
prostitutes to have ever been addicted to hard drugs, while another 5% experimented. Bour et al. (1984) found 25 non-prostitute delinquents to be more prone to
drug use than 25 prostitutes. And Marshall and Hendtlass (1986) compared 115
prostitutes on the use of drugs and alcohol with the general community in
Melbourne and concluded that the frequency of drug use and abuse among
prostitutes is generally overstated. Prostitutes seemed to have experimented
somewhat more though, and street prostitutes used more drugs than other prostitutes. This is a recurring theme in many studies on drugs and prostitution: that
mainly women working the street use drugs. In The Netherlands, this has also
been found (De Graaf et al., 1993). The high incidence of drug use in the studies
by James and Silbert et al. must be looked at bearing this in mind.

Goldstein (1979) did a very thorough study on drug use and prostitution. He
studied 60 users, among whom 45 were prostitutes and concluded, that the addicts
tended to become prostitutes almost twice as quickly as prostitutes became addicts
(1979:145). His differentiation between different drugs and their different
functionality in relation to prostitution is interesting. Heroin appeared to be
economically related to prostitution (working to support the drug habit), barbitura-
tes psycho-actively related (using to keep up the energy), and alcohol was found
to be functionally related (drinking in the course of 'turning tricks'). Drug use by
prostitutes was shown to vary historically, geographically, and with the level of
professionalism. The more a prostitute had a professional attitude, the more
functional the use of drugs, resulting in eventually less drug use. With a non-
professional attitude, drugs (in this case predominantly heroin) were used to blot
out the realities of being a prostitute.

Philpot et al. (1989), in a comparison of 277 prostitutes and 95 non-prostitutes
in an STD-center in Sydney, found no difference between the groups on
intravenous drug use (both groups 12%). However, they concluded that 'substan-
ces such as alcohol, tobacco, sleeping pills and amphetamines were at least partly
used to counteract some of the adverse effects of working in prostitution, and
their pattern of use tended to be dictated by the demands of the job. (..) Where
differences existed between prostitutes and non-prostitutes, they are mainly work
related' (1989:504-505).

The picture that emerges is that hard drug use is related to entrance in
prostitution for only a specific group of prostitutes, particularly street prostitutes.
Furthermore, for women who do use drugs of whatever kind, where drugs were
not a factor in their entrance into prostitution, an interaction between the work
and drug use seems to occur.

The market: needs of clients

Research on the demand and need for commercial sex is a last area we would like to review under the heading 'why do they enter'. We consider this to be one of the prime factors for prostitution to exist at all.

The scientific study of prostitutes' clients, although not as extensive and varied as the study of prostitutes themselves, chronologically shows more or less the same development as the prostitutes'. Until after the first half of this century, a search for pathology characterized the studies, that revealed alcoholism, non-integrated personality structures, inability of emotional attachment and masochism (Ellis, 1959; Gibbens and Silverman, 1960). Next, a bulk of writings appeared in which the absence of pathology in the men being studied was claimed (Winick, 1962; Pomeroy, 1965; Stein, 1974; Simpson and Schill, 1977; Armstrong, 1978; Holzman and Pines, 1982; Velten and Kleiber, 1992). Stein studied hundreds of clients with the help of in-house prostitutes and concluded: 'most clients were agreeable, reasonably attractive, upper-middle class men, business men or professionals. My lawyer, my accountant, my father's business associates, indeed my father, would not have been out of place among them' (1974:10).

However, some form of pathology was still brought up by other authors, such as 'compulsive need for variety' (Basel, 1970), 'the idea that sex is dirty and can only be enjoyed with a woman who is degraded in the patron's opinion' (Bullough, 1970; Basel, 1970), 'regression to an "Id" state of complete freedom from all restraints of civilization and acculturation' (Winick and Kinsie, 1971) and 'the excitement of sexual relations in an illegal or "I'm OK, you're deviant" situation' (James, 1978:182). Differences with other men that could not immediately be called pathological were found as well. Wilson et al. (1992), for instance, found 77 clients in Zimbabwe to have lower achievement orientation, lower desire for detailed, unambiguous knowledge, and higher impulsivity, pleasure seeking, exhibitionism and ego-defensiveness than 67 controls.

Research on motives as reported by the clients is relatively more prominent than in the case of prostitutes. One group of motives that has been stressed in almost all studies (sample sizes vary from very often thirty or so to hundreds in some cases), is the desire for sex and sexual variety or certain specific acts. Ellis (1959), Bullough (1970), Cave (1970) and Van Herk (1985) noted the fact that often a deprivation felt in marriage, or an unwillingness or inability to perform certain acts within the marriage is at the basis of this need. The same authors found evidence that the lack of emotional involvement in contacts with prostitutes is particularly attractive for many men. Others found that less shame and anxiety, less fear of pregnancy and less risk of refusal than is the case in non-commercial sexual contact were characteristic motives (Ellis, 1959; James, 1977; Holzman and Pines, 1982). Practical motives, like being away on business trips or army service (Bullough, 1970; Cave, 1970) or unavailability of the wife due to pregnancy (Cave, 1970; James, 1977) have also been mentioned. Mystery and excitement (Holzman and Pines, 1982) and visiting prostitutes being an 'ego-boosting activity' (Bullough, 1970; Van Herk, 1985) were given as a motivation as well.

Others brought up more social motives, like the search for companionship (Holzman and Pines, 1982; Van Herk, 1985), the desire for intimacy (Bouchier and De Jong, 1987), and the therapy-like quality of visiting prostitutes (James, 1977).

Velten and Kleiber (1992) on the other hand, interviewed 218 clients in written correspondence and 380 on the phone and concluded that sexual motives by far outweighed the social motives. Differentiating between their subjects, they identified 'the playboy', 'the loser' and 'the family father'. Responses to three scales of a standardized personality test revealed that the men were, on average, neither especially inhibited, insecure or shy of contact, nor especially self-confident, casual or open to contact. As in the general male population, some indicated a particularly high tendency toward aggressive behavior. Overall, the men tended to have an above-average level of inhibition in spontaneous or reactive terms. It was a striking result in this study that many men were decidedly dissatisfied with their present life circumstances and expressed a negative view of life.

In scanning the literature, we noticed that in comparison to prostitutes, clients appear much more as subjects, as individuals with conscious and rational motives, and as trustworthy respondents whose answers need no doubt. Researchers seem to identify more easily with clients than with prostitutes and to have less difficulty with their perspective. It seems to be true when Pheterson (1986) states: 'Whores are being reduced to one image, that neither encompasses mother nor wife, while clients are supposed to represent "the secret side" of every man. While prostitutes are being reduced to "whores", the "john" is being seen as an individual with a certain identity, who also visits prostitutes' (1986:38).

2.3: How do they manage?

As a result of the major interest in being (2.1) and becoming (2.2) a prostitute, the reality and consequences of working as a prostitute have been studied much less. Psycho-analysts and psychologists studying prostitutes' possible mental health problems, have mostly done so in relation to the choice for prostitution, not in relation to their actual and present situation. Many researchers seem to loose interest for the women once they are in the job. The exceptions to this rule will be discussed in this section. The studies pertain to work, well-being, and the risk of Sexually Transmitted Diseases (STD's).

Prostitutes at work

Studies focussing on prostitutes at work are comprised of a very diverse collection of topics. The areas which have had the most systematic attention are: working routines, job satisfaction, occupational ideology, and sexual response.

Working routines

Hirschi (1962) was probably the first to study working routines. He contested the judgement of Davis (1937), that prostitutes were getting 'something for nothing' by pointing out the skills necessary to find customers, 'sell' them, provide a suitable place in which to transact business, please the customer, collect her money, protect herself from disease, pregnancy and physical injury, and avoid the police. Gebhard (1969) described methods of client-selection on the basis of age, cleanliness, race and health. Heyl (1974, 1977) studied occupational mobility and the training of in-house prostitutes by madams. Brecher (1975) described the routine-like guarding against venereal disease, such as the 'pre-coital short-arm inspection'. Girtler (1984), studying the way prostitutes deal with the job, mentioned that they use various methods to distance themselves personally and internally from their clients to counteract degradation by being treated as merchandise. In The Netherlands, Van Gelder and Van Roekel (1989) concentrated on temporal and spatial features of the sexual interaction between street prostitutes and their clients. Potterat et al. (1990) studied career-longevity and found that the majority of women remain in prostitution for only a short time. Only 35% of a thousand prostitutes could be classified as long term residents; those who stayed in the business for about four or five years.

Most of these studies are descriptive and for the most part based on small samples. When it comes to working routines, the autobiographical literature (Adler, 1955; Hollander, 1982; Barrows, 1985) and the literature where prostitutes themselves have the floor (McLeod, 1982; Groen, 1987; Bell, 1987; Delacoste and Alexander, 1988) is more informative. Reports 'from within' until now have given a clearer picture of the daily practice of prostitution than scientific studies of it.

Job satisfaction
In 1949, Wei and Wong were very surprised to find that 56% of the 500 Shanghai prostitutes studied were enjoying their type of life, that 50% had no desire to get out of the profession, and that 'only 26% were hoping to meet rich husbands and have a home' (1949:237). Considerable job satisfaction has been reported by other authors as well. Pomeroy (1965) stated that 60% of 175 white prostitutes do not regret being a prostitute and Liss (1981) found no differences in job satisfaction between 32 full-time prostitutes and 32 women working full-time in other professions. Prostitutes did report a greater tendency to withhold the nature of their work from relatives though.

On the other hand, Silbert and Pines, who studied 200 street prostitutes, pictured women 'trapped in a life style they do not want' (1982:132). Bagley and Young (1984) concluded for their group of 45 ex-prostitutes: 'All hated doing it, and left as soon as they could' (1984:23). Lowman (1987) also reported 'negative appraisals' and 'thoroughly ambivalent' feelings about prostitution among street prostitutes. Apparently job satisfaction varies a lot between different groups of prostitutes, not the least between prostitutes and ex-prostitutes or street prostitutes and others. Findings may also vary according to different perspectives of researchers. There have been no differentiating studies yet which have provided insight into determinants of job satisfaction.

Occupational ideology

Hirschi (1962) described prostitutes' occupational ideology as containing justifications based upon functional premises ('prostitution is needed') and impugning the squares' integrity ('they are prostitutes themselves'). Bryan (1966) signaled a discrepancy between prostitutes' occupational ideology (in which negative attitudes toward customers and positive attitudes toward colleagues prevail) and their individual attitudes (in which women refuse to stereotype clients, and in fact, have positive attitudes toward them, while relationships with other call-girls are marked by interpersonal conflict, disloyalties, and mutual exploitation) (1966:444). Day (1990) described the construction and elaboration of a 'counter-ideology' among London prostitutes. The counter-ideology contradicts stereotypes concerning prostitutes and affirms that 'they are simply working and doing business'. A division is asserted between work and home and their private selves: 'certain types of sex can legitimately be relocated in the sphere of "work" and separated from reproduction, which is kept at home' (1990:30). As regarding job satisfaction, there have not yet been any differentiating studies on occupational ideology.

Sexual response

A specific area that has drawn the attention of some researchers is the sexual responsiveness of prostitutes. The general tendency here is to contradict prostitutes' presumed indifference to sex. Pomeroy (1965) concluded that prostitutes were 'more sexually responsive in their personal lives than women who were not prostitutes and that even in their contact with paid partners they were more responsive sexually than one might have anticipated' (1965:183). The data obtained from 46 street prostitutes by Savitz and Rosen (1988) produced 'a consistent picture of prostitutes who usually derive pleasure from both lovers and customers' (1988:206). They found that for over 60% sex with customers was at least sometimes (or more frequently) orgasmic, and that 'the higher the sexual enjoyment in the prostitutes' private sex life, the greater the erotic pleasure reported in their professional realm' (1988:205). In the differentiating study by Exner et al. (1977), only the street-walker addicts were found to have significantly fewer orgasms during intercourse in their private lives than their controls.

On the other hand, Nedoma and Sipova (1972) found that prostitutes report more negative and painful reactions and more 'orgasmus deficiens' than their controls, although they found no differences in sexual need. Tollison et al. (1977) found 20 prostitutes to have more conservative attitudes towards sexual intimacy than 20 college coeds and 20 secretary clerks. Again, much seems to depend on the sample studied.

Managing well-being and risk
Problems

In the study by James (1976), prostitutes reported police-jail-legal expense, danger from customers, emotional stress, and physical stress and venereal disease as the four major disadvantages of being a prostitute. A study by Paterson-Brown and Finnerty (1986) investigating problems among 40 London prostitutes, revealed them as 'an unhappy group of people, with little social life outside of work and few satisfactory relationships with boyfriends' (1986:260). Thirty-five percent of all the girls interviewed had attempted suicide at least once (1987:261). Some studies revealed a greater likelihood of gynecological problems among prostitutes (e.g. Nedoma and Sipova, 1983). Dutch research revealed bad working conditions such as long working hours, bad hygiene and feudalistic working relations with employers (Altink, 1989). It also reported difficult and disappointing interaction with helping agencies (Groen, 1989). The work situation especially for migrant women was found to be problematic (Brussa, 1989; Van Mens, 1992). Although Brussa (1992) also found that compared to previous work and living conditions prostitution was not found to be so stressful by Latin American migrant women in The Netherlands. Migrant prostitutes who work in an organized setting are often forced to stick to rules that Dutch women do not accept and often get an even smaller percentage of what the client pays for their services (Van Mens, 1992).

An overwhelming problem for prostitutes signalled by many, not in the least by prostitutes themselves, is the stigmatization of their work and their personalities. Pheterson (1986) revealed the consequences stigma has for prostitutes at the legal, social and psychological level. Since this research, as well as other literature on the topic, is mainly descriptive, it will be discussed further in the next chapter. Some empirical studies of victimization on the job which was identified as one of the consequences of stigmatization by Pheterson and others, will be discussed below.

Victimization and emotional well-being
In addition to the findings on the high prevalence on violence and abuse in childhood, several studies have shown that prostitutes have a high risk of experiencing violence in their adult life, both on and off the job. In the study by Silbert and Pines (1981, 1982) it was found that 70% of the women studied experienced customer rape, with an average of 31 times; 65% had been abused or beaten by a customer, with an average of 4.3 times; and 73% had experienced rape unrelated to the job. Bagley and Young (1987) found, that in addition to the reported child sexual abuse, 31% of the women studied had been raped before entering prostitution; 62% had been raped after entering by someone other than a client; and 93% of the women had been severely beaten at least once by either a 'trick', a pimp, the police or another person.

Silbert and Pines (1982) explicitly linked these forms of victimization to their earlier experiences of abuse. 'A history of victimization at home (..), coupled with a series of abuses on the street after leaving home, resulted not only in learned helplessness, but often in an even more extreme reaction, which we have termed "psychological paralysis"', they wrote. 'For the street prostitute who was trapped in a cycle of victimization, "psychological paralysis" is characterized by immobility, acceptance of victimization, feeling helpless and hopeless, and an inability to take the opportunity to change' (1982:131).

Bagley and Young (1987) also found sexual victimization to have grave consequences for prostitutes' emotional well-being. They found the mental health of the ex-prostitutes they studied to be 'dramatically poorer than that of their controls. They were three times as likely to have attempted suicide, and more than four times as likely to have Poor Mental Health (on the Middlesex Hospital Questionnaire), and Devastated Self-esteem (as measured by the Coopersmith)' (1987:14). Relating these mental health data to those on early sexual abuse and the practice of prostitution, they found that 'severity of sexual abuse before the age of 16' was a more important predictor of Poor Mental Health than 'practice of prostitution' was, even though the latter did also relate to Poor Mental Health. Leaving the controls out of the analysis, they found that 'time spent in prostitution' and 'separation from a parent before age 12' were the most significant predictors of Poor Mental Health of prostitutes.

To a large extent, experiences with violence and abuse thus seem to explain the emotional problems reported by ex-prostitutes and street prostitutes. The findings by Bagley and Young further suggest that the emotional well-being of ex-street prostitutes is threatened more the longer they work in prostitution. We have not come across research such as this among other, more representative groups of prostitutes, nor have we found studies that relate the emotional well-being of prostitutes to factors other than childhood trauma and adult victimization.

Managing risk of Sexually Transmitted Diseases (STD's)
The amount of research on prostitution, STD's, and condom use is enormous and has grown to astonishing proportions since the rise of AIDS. Prostitutes in non-western countries are now also the object of extensive investigation since these countries have become 'Pattern II countries', i.e. countries where heterosexual contacts are an important factor in the spread of AIDS.

Since many studies are medical-epidemiological and are therefore for our purposes not particularly interesting, and others are social scientific and will be discussed in more detail in the next chapter, we confine ourselves here to a short, general reflection on this body of work.

The association between prostitution and contagious disease is as old as the profession itself. There is a high level of unanimity in historical studies over what Alan Brandt (1985) has called three dominant themes in the history of STD's: 1. they are considered a disease of behavior and a punishment for sexual adventurers; 2. STD's are always employed in pleas for a more restrictive moral code; and

3. they are viewed as a symptom of another disease: a fundamental moral and sexual derailment[8].

As a consequence, the epidemic rise of a certain STD often brings about a 'moral panic' (Rubin, 1984; Weeks, 1985). In a moral panic, guilt and fear about the epidemic are projected on a scapegoat, notably those who do not adhere to the conventional norms of sexual conduct: 'During a moral panic, such fears attach to some unfortunate sexual activity or population. The media become ablaze with indignation, the public behaves like a rabid mob, the police are activated, and the state enacts new laws and regulations' (Rubin, 1984:297). This is exactly what, according to many authors (e.g. Pheterson, 1990; King, 1990; Carovano, 1991), has happened to homosexual men and female sex workers with the rise of AIDS, although, for example, Mooij (1993) argues that, for The Netherlands, the appearance of AIDS did not lead to a revival of the traditional forms of moralism.

As far as AIDS intervention programs have been directed at women, they focussed almost exclusively on women in the sex industry (and to a lesser extent on pregnant women): 'In essence, only bad girls are perceived as being at risk for AIDS' (Carovano, 1991:132). Pheterson (1990) noted that scientific inquiry on the AIDS-epidemic, all too easily takes prostitutes as a category and that 'even the category prostitute is based more upon symbolic and legal representations of the bad woman than upon an actual set of characteristics within a population of persons' (1990:398). This moralizing, categorizing, unifying and stigmatizing approach to prostitutes in AIDS research has since been criticized by many and, what is more, proven wrong in empirical research (see for overviews Padian, 1988; Campbell, 1991; McKeganey, 1992; Estébanez et al., 1993).

From the empirical evidence it appears that fear of the entire prostitution circuit as the focus of infection is not justified. In The Netherlands as well as in the rest of Europe and the United States, HIV-positive prostitutes are found mainly among intravenous drug users (Hooykaas et al., 1989; Campbell, 1991). Intravenous drug-use was found to be the single most important risk factor for HIV in female sex workers, both in Europe (European Working Group, 1993), and in the US (Rosenberg and Weiner, 1988; Miller et al., 1990). The Special Committee on Pornography and Prostitution in Canada (1985) stated that 'any notion that prostitutes play a decisive role in the spread of this disease is unsubstantiated' (1985: 395).

---

[8] Walkowitz (1980) has documented these mechanisms in clinical research focussing on prostitution at the turn of the century. Syphilis and gonorrhea were considered the consequence of not just any sexual conduct at that time, but the consequence of 'impure' sexual intercourse, a result of sin as well as bodily imbalance and excess or the consequence of a 'way of life'. Venereal disease was seen as the symptom and the punishment of 'impure' and unchaste behavior. The spread of syphilis was not thought to be caused by promiscuous sexual contact in general, but only by 'promiscuous sexual contact with diseased prostitutes' (Walkowitz, 1980:48).

The role of prostitution in the spread of HIV appears to be more important in non-western countries, such as Africa (Piot et al., 1987; Van de Perre et al., 1985; Quinn et al., 1984; Kreiss et al., 1986; Hunt, 1989) or India (Sikka, 1984; Correspondent, 1990). The incidence of HIV among prostitutes varies and can only be interpreted in relation to the broader features of the epidemic in a particular area, to the wider organization of sexual activity in that area, and to the organization of prostitution (cf. Day, 1988).

These considerations call for research on determinants of condom use in paid sex contacts, more than for a focus on prostitutes as a category or risk group. Moreover, research on determinants of condom use in prostitution should also take the contextual and situational characteristics into account that have been discussed in this chapter, such as the level of victimization, well-being and job satisfaction, and, for the clients, their motivation for visits to prostitutes. So far an integration between different scientific traditions, more specifically clinical epidemiology and the social sciences, has only begun to be established and in the context of prostitution this has hardly been done yet.

2.4: Conclusion; research problem and questions of this study

In the introductory chapter of this book, we stated that relatively little is known about the well-being of prostitutes. The abundance of research reviewed in this chapter may seem to belie this appraisal. However, the literature is widely diverse, scattered, fragmented, unsystematic and sometimes sketchy and anecdotal. Most researchers make a single, specialized contribution to the field and few attempt to integrate findings or to follow up on previous studies. The concept mental health is, apart from in a few studies, seldom related to trauma and victimization, and neither of those have yet been related to protection behavior and risk management.

The main part of the reviewed research either focusses on prostitutes' presumed personality characteristics or tries to explain why women enter prostitution. Much of the scientific theory and research sees prostitution a priori as a form of deviant behavior and searches for associations with unhealthiness, sickness, pathology, and the distortion of 'normal' human existence. Another part of the research, in reaction, tries to prove these associations wrong. Researchers often use select, very specific samples of prostitutes. As a result, we have no coherent, representative picture on the well-being of prostitutes yet. With our research, we have tried to make a contribution to the development of a more coherent picture on the well-being and risk management of prostitutes, on the differences between them, and on the factors determining these differences.

Our research problem is the following:

'To what extent, and in what way are (differences in) prostitutes' well-being and risk management (particularly condom use) related to their experiences with abuse and violence (both in childhood and adult life), to context-related factors (such as demographics, work place and working conditions), to person-related factors (such

Hypotheses

as Health Locus of Control and other cognitions), and to their interaction with clients?'

We seek to answer the following research questions:

1. How well are prostitutes in The Netherlands generally doing, both physically and emotionally?
2. What is the prevalence of experience with abuse and violence among them?
3. How do they deal with possible complaints and problems, and with abuse and violence?
4. How do prostitutes manage to protect themselves against STD's and HIV-infection?
5. What differences exist between them on these four aspects?
6. To what extent are these differences interrelated?
7. To what extent are these differences associated with other context- and person-related aspects?
8. And, in terms of protection against STD's and HIV-infection, how and to what extent does the interaction with clients play a role?
9. How do clients manage to protect themselves against STD's and what factors are related to the differences in this respect?

In the next chapter, carrying the aspects brought forward in these research questions further, we will introduce a multi-causal theoretical model to study and explain the differences in well-being and protection behavior among prostitutes.

Chapter Three
FACTORS IN WELL-BEING AND RISK:
THEORETICAL FRAMEWORK

Introduction

In the previous chapter it was concluded that generally speaking, the health and well-being of prostitutes were in the first place mainly addressed in terms of individual pathology as an explanation for their involvement in prostitution. Then, the focus was on unfortunate developments and conditions, particularly on trauma and victimization, both as explanatory factors and as the result of working as a prostitute. In recent years, research has been predominantly epidemiological, and the health of prostitutes has mainly been addressed in terms of the risk of HIV as a property of sex work. We consider these approaches to health and well-being rather limited. Moreover, they concentrate on prostitutes as a homogeneous group instead of on the differences between them.

We want to take a broader approach. It is our aim to gain insight into the levels of the general well-being and into the protective behavior of women who work as prostitutes and into the factors and processes that differentiate them.

In this chapter, we introduce a multi-causal[1] theoretical model which explains well-being and protection behavior of prostitutes. We draw on theory and research among prostitute as well as non-prostitute samples. The central question in this chapter is: what should one consider in studying the well-being and protection behavior of prostitutes? Well-being and protection behavior will be addressed in paragraphs 3.1 and 3.2. Expectations regarding the factors in both dependent variables are summarized in the concluding paragraph.

3.1: Well-being

Well-being is not a static, isolated phenomenon. It is the result of an ongoing interaction between person and environment. Freely following De Ridder's (1990: 14 e.s.) transactional model of mental health, several notions regarding well-being are considered crucial. First, well-being is seen as the result of a process of adaptation to (ever changing) environmental demands and the management of stressful life events. Second, the factors determining this adaptation and management are considered context-related as well as person-related. These factors can be either stressful in themselves, or on the other hand, a source of protection. They exert their influence via the coping process which mediates between stressful events or conditions, protective resources, and individual well-being. Third, the dimensions 'experience' and 'subjective meaning' are considered important. The

---

[1] We acknowledge that the matter of causality is a difficult one in a study with cross-sectional data. In this chapter causal relations are theoretically presupposed. In the Chapters Five, Six and Seven while discussing the findings, we check to what extent the evidence supports these suppositions and elaborate on the question of causality.

very impt
then . model

A cognitive
envir
model
like
George Kelly

adaptation process is influenced by previous experiences. However, the significance of circumstances and events is not the same for all individuals. Well-being is thus seen as a result of reciprocal and dynamic interaction between person and environment. The environment not only either stresses or protects the individual, but the individual through the coping process also helps to shape her own reality.

In this study, the well-being of prostitutes is seen as reciprocally related to the context and the person, (previous and actual) stressful life events and coping behavior. Childhood trauma and adult victimization particularly, are studied as stressful life-events, although it is acknowledged that many other life-events might also be worth studying. The context-related factors which are considered important in relation to prostitutes' well-being are: stigmatization, financial need, migration, working conditions and demographic aspects (age, educational level). Although stigmatization is not empirically investigated, it is thought to be a background factor of prime importance for all prostitutes and will be discussed as such. Health Locus of Control will be studied as a person-related factor. The relation of these factors to well-being is considered to be mediated by the coping process. Well-being is presumed to be dynamically related to situation, person and events[2]. In figure 3.1 this theoretical framework is schematized.

Figure 3.1: Factors in well-being of prostitutes

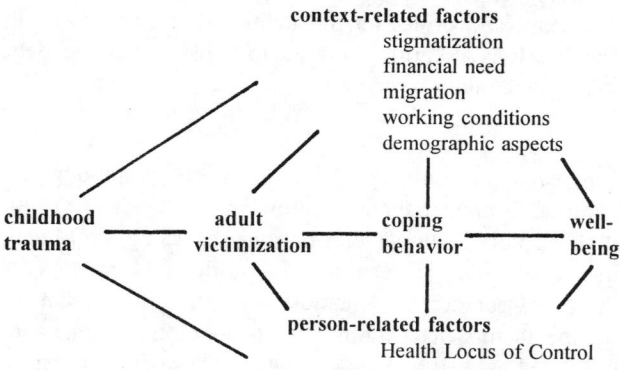

<hr>

[2] The use of concepts such as context- and person-related factors is somewhat problematical in a model in which all factors are presumed to interact. The context-related factors are considered to influence the person-related factors and vice versa. Coping behavior as well as the dependent variable well-being are person- and context-related as well. Despite these difficulties, we will use those terms as 'organizing' constructs. Context-related factors refer in the first instance to the situation a person is in, while person-related factors refer in the first instance to internal processes.

Well-being itself is broadly conceptualized as 'how someone fares'. We focus on emotional and psycho-social well-being and on the physical aspects of well-being. Body and mind go together in constituting well-being. Physical matters can be psychologically stressful and psychological problems can express themselves somatically. Mind and body cannot be meaningfully separated in matters of health and illness. Physical health is inextricably interwoven with the psychological and social environment (Taylor, 1986:6) and vice versa. Therefore, in investigating the general level of well-being of prostitutes, we study both the psychological and somatic aspects. A state of positive well-being refers to the absence of somatic complaints and to the absence of emotional or psycho-social problems. Moreover, it is assumed that physical health and emotional well-being influence each other; the better the one, the better the other.

In the context of prostitution, job satisfaction (the extent to which a woman feels at ease on the job, likes the atmosphere among her colleagues, feels positive about clients and about contact proceedings, and does not experience negative stress because of the work), is also presumed to be an important aspect of general well-being. Less job satisfaction is assumed as somatic complaints and emotional and psycho-social problems increase.

Coping behavior as a mediating variable

It is generally acknowledged that individuals react differently toward stressful situations and events, and that this has different consequences for their health and well-being. There is ample empirical evidence that coping responses (according to Silver and Wortman, 1980, broadly defined as 'everything a person does, feels or thinks in reaction to a negative, stressful or victimizing condition or event'), function as a mediator in stressor-illness relationships (Lazarus et al., 1974; Folkman and Lazarus, 1988; Vingerhoets and Van Heck, 1990).

Many classifications of coping responses have been developed and employed in research, but the most current distinction is the one between 'problem- and emotion-focussed reactions' (Lazarus, 1966; Lazarus et al., 1974; Snyder and Ford, 1987). While problem-focussed reactions refer to a manipulation of the stressful situation and/or attempts to change external problematic conditions, emotion-focussed responses indicate an internal manipulation of one's own fee-lings or cognition in order to be able to bear the emotional distress which is the result of the stressful situation or event. Examples of problem-directed responses in the face of a stressful condition are: direct intervention, purposeful action, getting information on how to solve a problem, asking for help or resisting abuse and violence. On the other hand, seeking diversion, wishful thinking, self-blame, tension reduction, identification with the aggressor, dissociation, denial and re-de-fining the problem could be taken as examples of emotion-directed responses. 'Doing nothing', depression, distancing and avoidance can also be brought forward as emotion-directed because they are often accompanied by a certain degree of emotion manipulation and do not necessarily imply a change in proble-matical conditions.

The frequency and likelihood of the employment of one of the responses is considered a function of (the nature and severity of) the event or problem itself, the situation in which it is experienced and the personality of the person dealing with it. There is ample empirical evidence that internal, emotion-directed coping responses are more likely as anxiety and tension increase (e.g. Girelli et al., 1986) and/or the problem or problem situation lasts longer or is more severe (Peterson and Seligman, 1983; Walker, 1984; Draijer, 1988). Situational and external factors that may influence the 'choice' of coping responses, are for example: available social support and socio-demographic variables (e.g. Pearlin and Schooler, 1978; Dunkel-Shetter et al., 1987; Holahan and Moos, 1987; Rim, 1986; Eckenrode, 1991; Kleber and Brom, 1992).

Subjective appraisal of both the problem and situation is considered crucial. The central supposition within coping theory is that if the coping resources in the situation are not appraised as sufficient (called 'secondary appraisal' by Lazarus and Folkman, 1974) *in relation to* the perceived seriousness of the problem ('primary appraisal'), it is more likely that emotion-directed instead of problem-directed responses will be employed. Intra-psychic coping mechanisms will be used more readily when circumstances do not allow for direct action. Comparable results have been found by Dweck and Goetz (1978), who state that helpless reactions are more likely than 'mastery-oriented' reactions when the situation is considered unsurmountable. Taylor and Brown (1988) presume more use of positive illusions as the situation is perceived as increasingly hopeless. In general, it seems that the more coping resources such as status and control are available to people, the better they fare (Eckenrode, 1991). We would like to add that the fewer the protective resources, such as social support, the greater the likelihood that people turn to emotion manipulation and distancing.

The crucial question about coping responses in relation to health is how effective, how 'healthy' they are. Generally it is assumed that internal responses like denial and repression are adaptive in the short run (e.g. Lazarus, 1985), but they may be associated with psychosomatic and psychosocial problems in the long run (Suls and Fletcher, 1985; Draijer, 1988). The beneficial aspect of emotion-directed responses may be the protection they offer against having to deal with the implications of the problem all at once. However, they are found to be unhealthy in the long run, especially when emotion-directed reactions interfere with and undermine problem-directed action (Wortman, 1983; Wethington and Kessler, 1991). There is the possibility that this negative interference does not necessarily last for ever, as shown in some of the women who were sexually abused by their male partners and at first became more helpless, but gradually experienced an 'internal change' and managed to get away from their abusers (Van Rappard, 1988; Römkens, 1989).

One other reason why reactions like denial and avoidance may be harmful is the fact that they may give rise to unhealthy behavior like smoking and drug abuse (Friedman, 1992). Drug abuse is often considered a palliative or avoidant coping measure in itself, a means for not feeling overwhelmed by negative emotions. We therefore study drug abuse under the heading of coping and expect it to be associated with emotion-directed responses.

In regard to the effectiveness of problem-directed responses many authors have presumed that problem-directed reactions are especially harmful and frustrating when change is altogether impossible (e.g. Baum and Gatchel, 1981; Wethington and Kessler, 1991). The seeking of social support which is a strategy often associated with problem solving, also does not necessarily reduce stress and might even bring about higher psychological costs (Eckenrode, 1991). Spontaneously offered support need not have this effect.

We expect prostitutes to use more emotion-directed coping strategies than non-prostitutes because we expect them to deal with relatively more negative stress while having relatively fewer coping resources. However, we expect to find differences among prostitutes as well. We expect many of the factors which have not yet been discussed to relate to coping behavior. One relation can be made clear right now: we expect an increase in complaints and problems when more emotion-directed coping is used and vice versa.

Context-related factors
Stigmatization

All prostitutes have to deal with the stigmatization of prostitution and of everyone associated with it (cf. Pheterson, 1986). Sex for money is considered immoral by many people and is definitely a form of sexual conduct that is low in the 'hierarchical valuation of sex acts' (Rubin, 1984). We can expect grave consequences for well-being: 'As sexual behaviors or occupations fall lower on the hierarchical scale, the individuals who practice them are subjected to a presumption of mental illness, disreputability, criminality, restricted social and physical mobility, loss of institutional support, and economic sanctions' (Rubin, 1984:279). She continues: 'They have less protection from unscrupulous or criminal behavior, less access to police protection, and less recourse to the courts. Dealings with institutions and bureaucracies -hospitals, police, coroners, banks, public officials- are more difficult' (1984:293). Women working (or having worked) in prostitution get stigmatized as 'whores' and are imputed a 'spoiled identity' (Goffman, 1963). As a consequence, they run a higher risk of being undervalued, socially excluded, and discriminated against. Opportunities on a broader societal level become worse as the result of stigmatization, or, as Edwin Shur states, 'the practical consequences of being stigmatized can include the reduction of his or her social acceptability, a blocking of important social and economic opportunities, a diminishing of overall life chances' (1984:38). Being stigmatized may be seen as making one's external conditions more stressful and less protective.

The burden of stigma and the pervasiveness of its consequences on social encounters of all kinds has been excellently described by authors such as Goffman (1963), Katz (1981) and Schur (1984). The following subtle processes have been identified as the consequence of stigmatization: people are more likely to isolate the stigmatized, to stereotype them and think that they are 'all alike', to be aggressive and punish them, to differentiate strongly between 'them' and 'us', to feel uncomfortable in their presence, to be extremely curious, to interpret all behavior in terms of the deviant characteristic and to generalize and attribute negative characteristics to them. An example of the latter is the observation by Carter (1979), that the shrewdness of the businessman is interpreted as greed when encountered in a prostitute. Overall, limits are set on the behavior of the stigmatized; 'they shouldn't press their luck' (Goffman, 1963:121). As a consequence of all these interactional mechanisms, prostitutes who are stigmatized women may end up with relatively little 'social capital' (Bourdieu, 1989). Seen on the level of day-to-day social interaction, stigma is also stressful and detrimental to protective resources.

On the other hand prostitutes, influenced by the effects of stigmatization, are - as stigmatized people- often troubled by feelings of shame and guilt and likely to draw back from many forms of social interaction. The influence of stigmatization on a person's behavior can be so pervasive that it may be considered more important than the influence of personality characteristics. Stigmatization is a stressful process, and as has been shown above, there is ample reason to assume the emotional and social well-being of prostitutes as a group are negatively influenced by it. Coping behavior is presumably also influenced by stigmatization. Emotion manipulation and dissociation of problematic feelings are more likely when one is socially isolated and there are fewer protective resources.

As a consequence of the process of stigmatization, prostitutes may be identified as a risk group for sexual and physical violence. The whore stigma is not only an accusation of unchastity in women, but also acts as an invitation to and legitimizes the presumptuous and aggressive behavior of men towards them (cf. Pheterson, 1986). Once one is considered a 'bad' girl as opposed to a 'good' one, men are more likely to claim all sorts of sexual rights. According to Katz (1981), the feelings of ambivalence toward the stigmatized can be taken as an explanation for extreme behavior directed at them. In the case of prostitutes this ambivalence may be enhanced by the ambiguity of her being both the idol and the scape-goat of sex, worshipped as well as despised. This ambivalence can be seen in attitudes towards women in general as a consequence of the sexualization of their bodies. It is also a core factor in violence against women in general, but prostitutes are subject to it in the extreme. Secondary victimization is also more likely when one is stigmatized, because institutions involved with victim-care consider violence against the stigmatized more legitimate. In one Dutch study (Ter Mors, 1978), it was found that people working with the police vice squad judge the rape of a prostitute walking the streets alone at night as the least serious of all rapes. This is another example of how stigma diminishes protective resources. In this case, there is less automatic acknowledgement of harm being done to a woman.

Women who are prostitutes do not differ basically from non-prostitute women. However, stigmatization and its consequences are considered an extra and a heavy burden on prostitutes' lives.

Demographic aspects

'Low-status'- groups seem to be more vulnerable to illness and people from lower social classes have more psychological problems (De Ridder, 1990; Vereijken and Bauduin, 1992). The conditions of their lives may be considered more stressful and their possibilities for dealing with their conditions may be less favorable. Important reasons are that low status groups often have fewer health-protecting resources and less access to health care systems. People of higher social status, as reflected in educational and occupational attainment, have consistently been shown to have higher levels of coping resources (such as access to social support), and to engage in more effective coping behavior (Eckenrode, 1991:6).

The relationship between class and psychological disturbances has often been explained by (either actual or perceived) lack of control over one's own existence, or by connected internal factors like learned helplessness and lack of flexibility. Relying on ample empirical findings, Eckenrode states, that 'fatalistic beliefs about the world, often associated with people living in poverty, may seriously compromise coping efforts in that the motivation for active, problem-focused responses is undermined. The poor, not having access to the range of social support from their informal networks that more privileged people have, must often rely on institutional structures that too often are unresponsive and fail to bolster the individual's own ability to cope with stressors they are experiencing' (1991:6). People from the lower classes have less opportunity to acquire important internal skills for coping with stress (Kleber and Brom, 1992:164).

Obviously, prostitutes differ in their socio-economic background. Although, as a result of stigma, social status and coping resources may be relatively low for all of them. As shown in the previous section, stigma does not only complicate contacts with institutional structures, but also diminishes overall social status and coping resources. Still, educational level may be expected to differentiate the levels of well-being in prostitutes.

Financial need

The same is true for financial need. Many women in prostitution face problems like poverty and unemployment. Often prostitution is the only way out of the poverty trap and the only key to social mobility and economically more favorable conditions. Conditions of poverty are stressful in themselves, can frustrate one's further aspirations and are a possible threat to one's health and well-being. However, prostitutes obviously differ in their levels of financial need. Different responsibilities for household-incomes, differences because of having or not having other incomes, and differences in expenses for drug-dependencies, may also be expected to differentiate the levels of well-being in prostitutes. Besides, greater financial need may weaken a woman's position in interaction with clients and may bring about more violence by customers.

Migration

Women who have migrated to get out of the poverty trap may find themselves in an even more unfortunate situation. They have often experienced extremely problematical situations in their countries of origin and come to a country where they do not speak the language. They may have to deal with xenophobic attitudes and racism and acquire an even lower status as members of an ethnic minority. Their interaction with indigenous clients may be more difficult. They may also suffer a lack of information on supportive and social services. As a consequence, migrant women often end up in extremely isolated positions, particularly when they stay in a country illegally. Their financial need is often great, particularly when they have only a short time to earn their money and/or they have incurred debts to intermediaries or traders. The worse the situation in their country of origin, the more vulnerable they are to this kind of exploitative 'intervention'. The conditions just described are considered stressful and not very protective and offer few coping resources. They can be expected to be a threat to the well-being of migrant prostitute women and to increase the likelihood of violence by customers. It is assumed that migrant women have more complaints and problems, and less job satisfaction. Having been born in the country where one lives, and where one is not a stranger, is thought to be an advantage in terms of general well-being.

Working conditions

Besides stigma and the other factors which have already been mentioned, there are other, more specific sources of work stress. In a report on prostitution, the Municipality of The Hague (1988) for instance states: 'Prostitutes are often in stuffy and smoky rooms for large periods of time. Working hours are often long and irregular. Physical strain is particularly high in window prostitution. One is often obliged to stay in tiny rooms for a very long time. Psychological strain is caused by, among other things the extreme demands and threats and humiliation of customers, force by the partner or boss, and also by societal disapproval and the necessity to keep the work a secret' (1988:8).

Hochschild (1979, 1988) points to another form of work stress which applies to what she calls 'emotion work'. Emotion work refers to these forms of labour where 'rules about how to feel and how to express feeling are set by management, where workers have fewer rights to courtesy than customers do, where deep acting (acting that begins as an act and transforms one's own feelings) and surface acting (behavior that one feels to be false) are forms of labour to be sold, and where private capacities for empathy and warmth are put to corporate use' (1988:456). 'One general source of stress', says Hochschild, 'a thread woven through the whole work experience, is the task of managing an estrangement between self and feeling and between self and display' (1988:466). This description of emotion work definitely applies to prostitution. Prostitutes engage in deep and surface acting towards clients and, especially in male organized and male controlled forms of prostitution, their capacity for warmth is put to corporate use. The management of estrangement between self and display may therefore be assumed to be a specific source of work stress for prostitutes.

Prostitution is not yet an area of research within the now firmly established social-scientific tradition on 'health at work' (see Barnett et al., 1991; Weiss, 1991; Frankenhaeuser et al., 1991; Winnubst and Schabracq, 1992; Muchinsky, 1993). A view of the existing research however, leads to some unfavorable hypotheses concerning the well-being of prostitutes. Winnubst and Schabracq (1992) have identified 'compatibility with other situations' as one of the major criteria by which the functionality of working situations may be judged. Other criteria are the 'ability to treat working situations more automatically and self-evidently' (and thus with less stress), and 'inspiration of confidence and safety'. Very often the prostitution situation, because of its illegality generally organized by the laws of the jungle and strictly hidden from other activities and situations, is hardly characterized by any of these. The protective qualities of the prostitution work setting can be considered very low.

Other authors within the health-at-work-tradition, Barnett et al. (1991) (whose research is particularly applicable here because they studied female subjects, whereas many other samples are predominantly male), identify as general 'job concerns' in licensed practical nursing and social work: overload, dead-end job (monotony and little chance for advancement), hazard exposure, poor supervision and discrimination (1991:101). All of these seem to apply to a large extent to many prostitutes' situations. 'Job rewards', as formulated by Barnett et al. seem to be less applicable: helping others at work, decision authority, challenge, supervisor support, recognition, and satisfaction with salary. Barnett et al. found that job rewards related to low reports of physical symptoms and job concerns related to high levels. Applying these findings to prostitution work gives reason for concern about the likelihood of physical symptoms associated with it.

At the same time it seems that different sorts of prostitution (for example window and street work in comparison to club and brothel work) are characterized by different levels of job concerns and job rewards. The organized context may offer more safety and protection and more social support than the worker in the 'unorganized'[3] setting is provided with. There may be less client violence in the organized context. On the other hand, working relations in clubs and brothels are often extremely exploitative and one may have to answer to various forms of house-regulation and control. Other possibly stressful factors, like more or less comfortable interaction with bosses and colleagues, the number of clients, the speed of the working routine, and the earnings, may also differ from situation to situation. Even if work stress is considered generally high for all prostitutes, more specific working conditions as regards work settings, relations, and routines may be seen as differentiating to an important extent the amount of work stress

---

[3] Since a certain level of organization is of course present no matter what working site is concerned, we put the term unorganized between quotation marks.

individual prostitutes have to deal with. It is expected that work stress is highest when one serves a large number of clients, in a rapid work routine, with relatively low earnings. Working in an 'unorganized' versus an organized setting may be judged differently by individual prostitutes, but we expect independence of (control by) bosses to be highly appreciated by prostitutes and thus causing less irritation and stress.

Person-related factors: Health Locus of Control

A person-related factor thought to be relevant to health and health behavior is the (Health) Locus of Control. The Locus of Control theory maintains that behavior occurs as a function of chronic expectation of reinforcement in a given situation (Taylor, 1986:73). Individuals with an internal Locus of Control expect to be reinforced by the consequences of their own behavior, while 'externals' expect reinforcement to be controlled by external agents, such as their surroundings, experts, fate or luck. Stronger internal Health Locus of Control (and other personality characteristics like high self-esteem or high 'mastery beliefs') are associated with trying harder to solve problems, because of a greater desire for control over a situation (e.g. Kleber and Brom, 1992) and thus reciprocally with higher levels of well-being. On the other hand, manipulation of thoughts and emotion can also bring about perceived or psychological control, which is also found to be beneficial to well-being (e.g. Fiske and Taylor, 1984).

Experiences of control may be not so much stable personality properties but are dependent to a large extent on past personal experiences and situational conditions. The experience of childhood trauma may, aside from having a direct relation to health as is shown below, have dramatic effects on an individual's intrapsychic make-up, with regard to Locus of Control among other things. Still, Health Locus of Control in itself may also be considered a factor in well-being. It is thought that higher levels of well-being relate to a stronger internal Health Locus of Control.

Childhood trauma and victimizing life-events in adolescence and adulthood

The life-events which are considered crucially important to the level of well-being are traumatic experiences such as physical or sexual violence and abuse, whether it is in childhood, in private adult life, or on the job. Long term detrimental effects of childhood (sexual) trauma have been demonstrated in many studies (Herman et al., 1986; Wyatt and Powel, 1988; Draijer, 1988; Schoemaker, 1991). The central issue in all relevant theories[4] is the fact that the overwhelming emotions associated with the abuse cannot be handled, are warded off and cause

---

[4] Draijer (1988) discusses cognitive coping theory, emotion theory, psychoanalysis, dissociation theory, script theory, object relation theory and modern trauma theory. Here the focus is predominantly on the latter, in which many aspects of the other theories are taken into account.

psychological damage in the long run (Draijer, 1988:251). The symptoms associated with this process are now generally described as Post Traumatic Stress Disorder.

In modern trauma theory, the response to trauma is characterized by denial, repression and avoidance of the (memory of) the painful experience on the one hand, and the involuntary re-living of them in intrusive images, nightmares, or involuntary 'repetition' of the shocking events in thoughts, phantasies, bodily sensations and behavior on the other hand (Draijer, 1988:252 a.f.). Complaints related to denial may be: disturbances in concentration, depression, emotional numbing or aloofness. Avoidance may manifest itself in running away from home, difficulties with intimate relationships, vaginismus or a general aversion to men and/or sexuality. The need to suppress painful feelings may give rise to psychosomatic symptoms, or the abuse of alcohol, sedatives and drugs. Internal coping strategies, once learned in childhood may generalize themselves into an ongoing inclination or readiness of the adult individual to use them.

Re-experiencing the childhood trauma may express itself in nightmares, sleeping problems, anxieties, panic, inexplicable pain and bouts of anger. Unconscious repetition of the traumatizing events may manifest themselves in counter-phobic behavior in an attempt to regain control and restore the disturbed images of self and the world. Revictimization, sexually 'acting out' or prostitution itself may be seen as the effect of unconscious repetition. Finally, dissociation (the disconnection of associated levels of awareness) as a strategy to ward off the overwhelming emotions is often seen in cases of multiple and long lasting abuse. This warding off can result in various dissociative symptoms such as depersonalization, feelings of estrangement from self and others, loss of contact with reality, loss of memory, concentration problems, psychosomatic problems, and the disconnection of emotion and cognition in stressful situations. Different forms of non-feeling may manifest themselves in self-destructive behavior like eating disorders and selfmutilation. In the worst case, dissociative symptoms may take the form of a multiple personality disorder (MPD) (cf. Boon and Draijer, 1993).

The overwhelming nature of the sexual abuse of children, in combination with the pressure to keep it secret, hampers the process of coming to grips with traumatic events and strengthens the need for internal coping strategies. As long as integration of the shocking events has not taken place, traumatized people may suffer from a variety of complaints and problems. It has been noted by Schoemaker (1991) and others, that even when victims seem to function relatively well for periods of time and seemingly manage to 'keep the burden under', minor or major life-events can uncover the old overwhelming anxiety again. Kleber et al. (1986)

state that 17 to 27 percent of traumatized people never reach complete integration[5].

Victimization in adult life causing another form of violent trauma is shown to be more likely when one has been abused in childhood. Sexual abuse in childhood particularly is found to be a risk factor in regard to revictimization by private partners (Römkens, 1989:152). Further, victimization by private partners also has an independent negative effect on health and well-being (Römkens, 1989). There is ample evidence that rape, either by strangers or acquaintances, may cause grave emotional distress like anxiety, fear and depression, and may have long term effects upon social adjustment in marriage and the family, as well as in professional and leisure functioning. Gynecological complaints and sexual dysfunction are among the most long lasting consequences of rape (Koss and Harvey, 1991).

However, people may perceive victimizing experiences differently. One explanation for the effects of trauma is that people's assumptions about a just and meaningful world, and a worthwhile self have been shattered (Janoff-Bulman, 1985; Wortman, 1983). When one has been traumatized earlier, these assumptions may have been already profoundly harmed, and later victimizations may be perceived and appraised differently. In fact, after childhood abuse, positive basic assumptions may have hardly been developed and revictimization may be appraised as 'back to normal' (cf. Schoemaker, 1991:118). However, this does not mean that the effects of victimization on well-being are necessarily less serious.

The extent to which women in prostitution suffer from childhood trauma, or have experienced violent and/or sexual victimization in adult life has been the topic of much social scientific research on prostitution, as was shown in Chapter Two. The prevalence of trauma among prostitutes in The Netherlands has yet to be established. Even though not all prostitutes are certain to be victims of violence, it is assumed that because of the possibility of prostitution being a reaction to early sexual abuse and the workings of stigma, a relatively large percentage of them are. Violence on the job particularly may be considered to exert a negative influence on job satisfaction which is seen here as an aspect of

---

[5] All in all, the long term effects of childhood sexual trauma on health and well-being of the victims can be explained in different ways. Draijer (1990:37-53) includes the following ones: first, a direct connection has been postulated: later complaints directly result from the warding off of traumatic memories. Second, defense mechanisms might enhance vulnerability in an indirect way. Third, context and background factors associated with the abuse, like emotional neglect, have also been presented as the cause of later complaints. A fourth explanation is that symptoms are largely due to later stressful experiences as a consequence of the urge to re-live the early trauma. Fifth, negative social reactions might be the cause of the problems experienced in adult life. Self-blame (feelings of being bad, guilt and shame) is stressed in a sixth explanation and finally, the specific effects of forced secrecy might be the cause for the detrimental effects of childhood sexual abuse on health and well-being.

well-being. The same applies to the possibility of being forced into prostitution. Working under force is probably associated with negative job satisfaction. Having overcome the forceful relations and presently working 'for one's self' may, on the other hand, bring about more job satisfaction. Thus the relation between being forced into prostitution and well-being may not be a rectilinear one. However, for those prostitutes who have been victimized, research on the long term effects of childhood trauma and later victimization suggests a great burden and a negative influence on their general well-being.

3.2: Professional protection behavior

Compared to other professional hazards (such as being burdened by stigma or violence from customers), protection against infection by Sexually Transmitted Diseases (STD's) and the Human Immunodeficiency Virus (HIV) seems relatively easy if one uses condoms consistently. Condoms are frequently used in commercial heterosexual contacts. In a recent Dutch study it was found that only 7.6% of all the female prostitutes' vaginal contacts were unprotected (De Graaf et al., 1992). In the United States, a study by the Center for Disease Control (CDC, 1987) found that 78% of the prostitutes reported using condoms with paying partners. Thomas (1989) found that about three quarters of Edinburgh prostitutes use condoms either usually or always in commercial sex. Spina et al. (1992) even found that 52 out of the 53 prostitutes in seven Italian towns always use a condom with clients[6]. At the same time it should be noted that there are specific groups of prostitutes and clients who engage in unprotected sex relatively often and run a substantial risk of infection. In the Dutch study mentioned above, 19% of the prostitutes and 25% of their clients do not take precautions consistently when engaging in commercial sexual activity (De Graaf et al, 1992).

Still relatively little is known about prostitutes' and clients' reasons to either use condoms or engage in unprotected sex. Many epidemiological studies have been conducted to investigate HIV-prevalence and its risk factors among prostitutes (see for overviews Day, 1988; Campbell, 1991; McKeganey, 1992; Estébanez et al., 1993). The use of condoms is often presented as an explanatory variable of infection rates. Relatively few prostitution studies focus on the determinants of condom use. Furthermore, little differentiation has been made between different categories of prostitutes.

Protection behavior among non-prostitute samples has often been studied as a process of personal weighing and deciding, in which cognitive, rational factors prevail. Although we acknowledge the possible relevance of these factors, we

---

[6] Prostitutes in the non-western world seem to use condoms less often. For example, in Kinshasa less than 15% were found to use condoms regularly with customers and in Nairobi only two out of 418 sex workers reported using barrier methods of contraception (Estébanez et al., 1993). These are very low figures. Wilson et al. (1989) found that 54% of the prostitutes studied in Harare had used a condom in their last paid sexual act.

think that they alone give too little insight into the complexity of the matter. Generally speaking, in sexological and social-psychological studies of risk behavior, sexual behavior is too often seen as straightforward activity and is stripped of its socio-cultural context and complexity of meaning and significance to the individuals studied (see also Tiefer, 1991). However, the context and significance of sexual behavior may be crucial in the development of sexual risk behavior. An important distinction should be made between sexual risk behaviors that are voluntary, and those which are not under control of the individual[7].

Instead of focussing on condom use as a property of individual behavior, we consider protection behavior to be the outcome of an ongoing dynamic interaction between person and environment and thereby a 'health-outcome' in much the same way as general well-being is. Interaction between sex partners is also considered crucially important. Again, we study the dependent variable 'protection behavior' from a multi-causal theoretical framework. It is our aim to identify the conditions influencing the professional protective behavior of prostitutes and to differentiate between them in that respect.

There is evidence that for many prostitutes unprotected sex with private partners carries greater risk for infection with STD's and HIV than their work does, since the rate of condom use with private partners is much lower (Darrow et al., 1988; Day et al., 1988; Hooijkaas et al., 1989; Spina et al., 1992; Dorfman et al., 1992). Still, in this study, protection behavior is addressed primarily in the context of prostitution work. Protection behavior is conceptualized as the degree of condom use by prostitutes in sexual contacts with their clients. In regard to the fact that variations are expected in prostitutes' personal conditions, the context of prostitution does not have the same significance for all prostitutes (see De Zalzuondo 1991). Therefore, we talk about different *protection styles* which are conceptualized as types of protection behavior in relation to the subjective definition of prostitution work. These protection styles, then, are thought to have developed in relation to context, person, life-events, coping and interactional processes.

In general, our theoretical model of protection styles is very much like the one presented earlier in the context of well-being. We consider financial need, migration, and working conditions to be important context-related factors in relation to the protection style of prostitutes. 'Social norms' regarding condom use are considered as an additional context-related factor, although only qualitative data have been gathered on that variable. Health Locus of Control is studied as a person-related variable. In addition, AIDS-related cognition and attitudes presented in social psychological models on health behavior (such as risk perception), as

---

[7] At the VIII International Conference on AIDS/III STD World Congress in Amsterdam, both John Gagnon and Gail Wyatt called for a contextualizing of data on sexual behavior and condom use in order to better understand why people behave as they do and why they take the risks they do.

well as somatic and emotional well-being and job satisfaction are studied as person-related factors. Childhood trauma and adult victimizing life-events, both in private life and on the job, and their relation to protection behavior are also investigated.

Figure 3.2: Factors in professional protection behavior of prostitutes

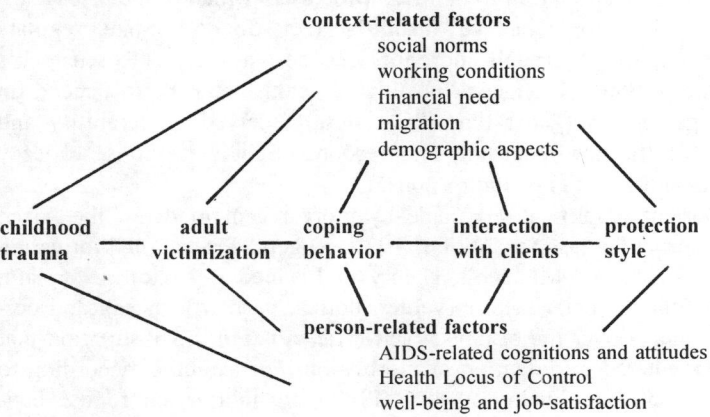

The most crucial amplification of the previous model concerning well-being is the introduction of interaction with clients as a factor. We consider interactional processes, as well as individual properties and contextual factors, to be crucial in sexual behavior in general and protective behavior more specifically (cf. Ingham and Van Zessen, 1994). It is, in fact, remarkable that interactional aspects have been studied relatively little in relation to sexual protection behavior, since sexual risk-taking is so clearly a matter of more than one individual. The focus on interactional aspects is by no means meant to put the role of either cognitive or contextual aspects aside, nor to ignore the role of the personal significance of the prostitution context or the sexual encounters themselves. In fact, interactional processes between prostitute and client are the moment where cognition, context and import for both participants ultimately take shape. As much as the other factors, interaction is thought to be a significant component in the dynamic process in which condom use or condom abstinence by prostitutes comes about.

In the following section, theory and research on the role of person-related factors is discussed. We choose to start with those because social-psychological models addressing them have been dominant in research on protection behavior among the population at large. Next, an argument is presented to point out the limited value of these models and coping behavior will be considered, since it is conceptually connected to the role of internal factors. Finally, context-related factors, childhood trauma and adult victimization, and interaction with clients are discussed.

Person-related factors
AIDS-related cognition and attitudes
    Traditionally, social psychological models addressing health behavior in general, lean heavily on rational and cognitive processes. Modern social psychological theories on why people behave 'healthily' (e.g. do not smoke, regulate eating habits, use condoms) are all more or less derivatives of Rosenstock's Health Belief Model (1966). Rosenstock postulated health behavior to depend on two factors: risk perception (general health values, perceived vulnerability and perceived severity of the health hazard) and response beliefs (response efficacy and perceived costs and benefits of the response).
    The most important amplifications made by more recent models (like Ajzen and Fishbein's Theory of Reasoned Action, 1977; Rogers' Protection Motivation Theory, 1983; and Ajzen and Madden's Theory of Planned Behavior, 1986) are: the taking into account of social factors (values, norms, peer influences), and perceived behavioral control over the response (self-efficacy), and the postulation that actual behavior is mediated by intention or motivation. For example, according to Rogers' (1983) protection-motivation theory (PMT) the motivation to use condoms is high if 1) one believes in the effectiveness of condoms (response efficacy), 2) has complete confidence in one's competence to use them (self efficacy), 3) the costs associated with condom use are low, 4) the intrinsic and 5) extrinsic (social) benefits are high, 6) the threat of AIDS is taken seriously and 7) one considers one's own risk of being infected as high. A high protection motivation is thought to be able to predict actual health behavior.
    In a meta-analysis on the results of 150 independent samples studied from the perspective of the Theory of Reasoned Action (TRA), it was shown that 38% of the variance in actual behavior is indeed explained by intention (Van den Putte, 1993). Van der Velde and Van der Pligt (1991) found the protection motivation theory (PMT) in the case of AIDS protective behavior even to have an explaining power of 49% for heterosexuals, but less (22%) for homosexuals. AIDS-related cognition and attitudes, as conceptualized in these psychological models, seem to be related not only to intention, but also to protective behavior itself. For prostitutes, as well as for their clients, we expect the extent to which they consider AIDS a serious disease, their personal risk perception and their fear of AIDS to be related to their protection style. AIDS-related knowledge will be investigated qualitatively, but we do not expect many differences between prostitutes in this respect. There is evidence that knowledge of AIDS may be quite high among prostitutes. Kuhns and Heide (1992) found 53 prostitute arrestees to be more knowledgeable about AIDS than 47 female non-prostitute arrestees, even after controlling for demographic characteristics. Mak and Plum (1991) on the other hand, concluded for prostitutes in Gent, Belgium that they too often incorrectly

assessed the risk of different sexual techniques. We will also consider clients' attitudes towards condoms and towards their prostitution visits.

Health Locus of Control

Since an internal Health Locus of Control is generally related to problem-focussed behavior (Strickland, 1978), consistent condom use might be considered more likely with 'internals'. Less consistent condom use may be more likely if one experiences less control over one's own health.

Well-being and job satisfaction

In connection to this, it is expected that levels of well-being are also related to protection behavior. In general it has been found that good health behavior is more likely when self-esteem is higher, and when there is a sense of psychological well-being and a belief that one's health is generally good (Taylor, 1986:66). Stiffman et al. (1992) found a higher number of risk behaviors associated with mental health complaints in 602 young adults. For the subjects in our study, we expect consistent condom use to relate to higher levels of well-being. The same applies to job satisfaction: higher job satisfaction is expected to relate to more consistent condom use with clients.

Coping behavior

In the studies of health behavior done according to the models presented in the previous paragraph, the cognitive aspects of attitudes and intention are usually correlated. This not only poses problems regarding causality (do attitudes predict intention or vice versa?), but of validity as well since cognition may be strongly manipulated by the individual in the coping process. Self-report surveys of attitudes and intention may be strongly influenced by fears, the wish to be consistent, and by actual behavior. People tend to construct their own reality to a certain extent, especially including their cognition and attitudes corresponding to their actual practices, emotions, and opportunities.

A telling example in this context has been provided by the study of personal risk perception. Here, the coping process influencing reported cognitive aspects is particularly clear. Personal risk perception is sometimes found to be related to risk behavior in a completely different way than was predicted by the protection motivation theory: higher risk appraisal may in fact be related to high risk behavior (Otten and Van der Pligt, 1991), or, particularly in high-risk groups, it may only be a modest factor in explaining risk behavior (Van der Pligt et al., 1992). The reasons for this are sought in increased defensiveness and 'unrealistic optimism' (-i.e. the tendency to think that risks mainly apply to other people and not to oneself). Unrealistic optimism has an indirect effect on protection motivation because it decreases worry (Weinstein, 1982) and can be seen as a form of emotion-directed coping behavior. People with high risk behavior in particular, may be more strongly inclined to unrealistic optimism because they have a stronger wish to reduce fear and maintain self-esteem[8].

Connections between risk behavior and emotion-directed coping behavior have been shown in other studies as well. De Wit et al. (1991) found that continuing risky sexual behavior among homosexual men was related to having more reassuring thoughts and seeking less social support. Drug abuse (considered here as a form of coping) has not only been identified as a major risk factor in HIV-infection rates in both prostitutes and others (e.g. Van der Hoek, 1988; Miller et al., 1990), but has also been related to risky sexual behavior (Sterk, 1989; Leigh, 1990), although not explicitly in connection to emotion-directed coping.

On the other hand, consistent protection against HIV-infection has been associated with problem-directed coping responses. Hooijkaas et al. (1989) studied the coping responses regarding the threat of AIDS of 52 women (of whom 36 were sex workers) and 28 men (of whom 18 were sex customers) and found that a rational-analytical pattern of coping behavior (considered to be more effective by the authors than the contrasting denying, panic response) was most likely with the female prostitutes who had high knowledge on AIDS and a high risk-perception. Recently, active coping has even been related to the (more favorable) workings of the immune system in homosexual men (Goodkin et al., 1992), thereby connecting the psycho-social to the physiological.

Limiting ourselves here to the psycho-social level, we assume that prostitutes' emotion-directed strategies may be effective in the short run in regard to emotional well-being in the context of HIV-risk since they reduce worry. They may be especially 'welcome' when consistent condom use is impossible to realize. Defensive coping may be more present in those whose behavior is more risky. However, problem-directed coping responses are expected to be related to consistent protection behavior by the use of condoms.

Context-related factors

The assumption mentioned in the PMT, that intention cq. motivation predicts behavior appears to be at least partly faulted. One can have all the positive intentions in the world and still end up not using a condom (see Becker and Joseph, 1988; Rademakers, 1991). In general, apart from cognitive factors, demographic, social, and emotional factors, personal goals and perceived symptoms, as well as access to health care systems, are considered important to health behavior (see for instance Taylor, 1986).

---

[8] Furthermore, unrealistic optimism will be stronger when there is higher perceived controllability, an egocentric bias, lack of experience with the negative event, and a stereotypical belief about AIDS-victims (Weinstein, 1982; Van der Pligt, 1991). Other factors found to reduce risk perception and worry, but which enhance risky behavior related to AIDS, are for instance sensation seeking tendencies (Fisher and Misovich, 1990) or multiple testing of sero-status (Lagergren et al., 1990).

In addition to this, the PMT and related theories imply a relatively stable individual protection-motivation for different situations. However, it is more probable that protection behavior varies with the specific context in which protection strategies are employed. Without any doubt, the perceived (dis)advantages of condoms (and other factors which have been mentioned) play an important role in whether or not they are used. However, the perception of these costs and benefits will probably vary with the context in which the sexual contact takes place and the subjective definition it has for the sexual partners. Within the context of prostitution, the following context-related factors are considered important in relation to condom use.

Social norms
Whereas the social-psychological models generally address social norms as a factor in protection behavior in terms of peer influences, prostitution has a much broader and structural norm and tradition of condom use. That the prostitution context alone is of some importance regarding protective measures, can be seen from the fact that the prevalence of unsafe sexual behavior is significantly higher in unpaid contacts than is the case in paid contacts. For example, among Dutch heterosexual subjects without a permanent sexual partner, only 15% consistently used condoms (Van Zessen and Sandfort, 1991). In The Netherlands, as well as in the United States, differences in the rate of condom use with paying or non-paying partners were also found among prostitutes (Hooijkaas et al., 1989; Darrow et al., 1988). Commercial sex apparently calls for condom use more strongly than non-commercial sex does. These differences notwithstanding, positive social and peer norms regarding condom use have been found to relate to their use among the general population (Van de Velde and Van der Pligt, 1991). Habits and previous behavior regarding condom use have also been found to be of importance. The more experience one has using them, the more likely it is that one will use them again (Richard et al., 1991; Van de Velde and Van der Pligt, 1991). These factors are thought to play as strong a role in commercial sex. However, habits and the social norm of consistently using condoms will probably not be equally strong in all cases.

Working conditions
There is evidence that the rate of condom use varies in different working surroundings. Both Jackson et al. (1992) studying prostitutes in Toronto, and Woolley et al. (1988) in Sheffield found substantial differences in risk taking in different types of prostitution. Women working on the streets were found to use fewer condoms than women in saunas or call-girls. Pickering et al. (1993) conclude for the Gambia, that condom use is determined more by the type of establishment and the clients' characteristics than by any fixed tendency among the prostitutes. It has been found in several countries that condom use is more likely when a prostitute serves fewer clients and the earnings per client are higher

(Sittitrai et al., 1990; Wilson et al., 1990; Siraprapasiri et al., 1991; Pickering et al., 1993).

In The Netherlands, the most supportive and thereby safest extreme of a continuum may be represented by working in an organized setting where condoms are available, there are house rules for consistent condom use, the working routine is rather relaxed, earnings are relatively high and the safety of the workers is controlled to a certain extent. (Let us be clear that not all clubs and brothels conform to these characteristics). The most risky extreme may be represented in working the streets where there is little protection from aggressive behavior from clients, little social support, relatively low earnings and a relatively high quantity of clients, and no ready availability of condoms. In this context, Jackson et al. (1992) proposed that 'in areas that are especially dangerous, prostitutes may be more interested in responding to immediate street dangers than in discussing HIV and the long-term consequences of unsafe practices' (1992:285). Besides, some areas of street (or window) prostitution or brothels and clubs may be known by customers as affording the possibility of unprotected sex with at least some of the workers. This may result in more pressure to abstain from the use of condoms and less social and norm-support to consistently use them. In addition, working relations where third parties, whether a pimp or boss, exert force on a woman to earn as much money as possible, are seen as having higher risks for inconsistent condom use. Unsafe sex still earns more.

Demographic aspects
Condom use may also be related to demographic aspects. Among the population at large, in the United States as well as in Europe, low status groups are found to be more at risk for AIDS (e.g. Miller et al., 1990; Schneider, 1992). In The Netherlands, consistent condom use was found to be more likely among the higher educated (Sandfort et al., 1989). It was also by the same authors found to be more likely the younger one is. For health behavior in general, Taylor (1986) states that good health behavior is generally practiced by younger, more affluent, better educated people under low levels of stress with social support available. Higher levels of stress and/or fewer resources which are more common in people of low socio-economic status are associated with more health compromising behavior (1986:66).

Financial need
Moreover, we suspect inconsistent condom use to be more likely when a woman works because of severe financial need. Evidence supporting this supposition has been found in several studies. In Surinam, Terborg (1990) found prostitutes' objective external conditions, more specifically their financial situation, to be related to condom use. In Toronto, Jackson et al. (1992) found 'economic incentives for risk taking to be quite common' among prostitutes (1992:282). We expect that the more a woman is solely responsible for her (or others') household income and the less she can fall back on other sources of income, the more she wants to

earn as much money as possible in as short a time possible, or the more she depends on prostitution to finance a drug habit, the more likely it is that she does not use condoms consistently.

Migration

Some of the problematical aspects mentioned above often seem particularly present in migrant womens' situation. As sketched earlier, their situation often offers extremely low protection or support and their economic position is weak. We expect these conditions to be related to inconsistent condom use.

Van Haastrecht et al. (1992) found that among other factors, low socio-economic status, being Latin American, and having been in The Netherlands less than three years, were important predictors of inconsistent condom use by prostitutes in Amsterdam. Generally, ethnic minorities are found to be more at risk for AIDS (e.g. Miller et al., 1990; Schneider, 1992). In line with these findings, we assume inconsistent protective behavior to be associated with migration.

Childhood trauma and victimizing life events in adolescence and adulthood

Childhood trauma and victimization in adult life are considered to relate to protection behavior as they do to well-being. Not only may they indirectly relate to protection behavior by influencing personal perception of risk, level of well-being, and the coping process, but, in their long-lasting consequences, they are also thought to constitute the personal context in which (commercial) sexual behavior takes place. Sexually traumatized or victimized women may attach a different significance to prostitution than non-victimized women. From a symbolic interactionist point of view, it is assumed that people do not as much react to the objective characteristics of a situation, but to the significance the situation has for them and to the way they subjectively define the situation. A history of victimization may relate to Locus of Control and the coping process, as well as to general levels of well-being, job satisfaction, and to the meaning prostitution work has for an individual prostitute, and thus (indirectly) to protection behavior.

Childhood trauma has recently been empirically connected to HIV-risk (Allers and Benjack, 1991; Fullilove et al., 1992). In their study of 52 HIV-infected (predominantly male) adults, Allers and Benjack (1991) found that 65% of them were victims of physical or sexual abuse in their childhood. One third had experienced physical abuse only; the rest had also been sexually abused. To explain the higher risk among adult survivors of childhood abuse, the authors suggest several explanations. There is the possibility of a lack of assertiveness and the ego-strength necessary to set appropriate, safe limits with sexual partners. Another explanation is the possibility of sexual compulsion and subsequently more frequent sexual activity with a greater number of partners. The authors also suggest exposure to HIV as a possible form of self-destructive or passive suicidal behavior resulting from low self-esteem, chronic depression and feelings of hopelessness and helplessness. For the same reasons, victims may fail to internalize safer-sex guidelines or lack the motivation to follow precautionary recommendations, or both. And finally, there is the possibility of increased use and abuse of alcohol and drugs which may result in more risky sexual behavior.

The relationship between childhood abuse and protection behavior is, in this view, largely mediated by the negative effects of the abuse on well-being which may cause victims to cope with risk and interact in sexual encounters differently. These psychological and interactional factors might play a role in the protective behavior of survivors of childhood abuse who are prostitutes. The abuse not only decreases the general level of well-being, but (partly as a result) also reduces the likelihood of consistent condom use.

The relation between adult victimization and protection behavior has not yet been the subject of research studies. Nevertheless, it is obvious that forms of victimization such as working under force from third parties and sexual violence by customers (or others) may have a direct effect on the use of condoms and HIV-risk. We expect victimization in adult life to be related to more risky behavior.

Interaction with clients

There is evidence from non-prostitute samples that interaction between sexual partners plays a role in risky sexual behavior. Some interactional aspects found to be important are: anticipated negative affective reactions with the partner (Holland et al., 1990); communication skills regarding condom use (Ross, 1988; Catania et al., 1989; Worth, 1989; Holland et al., 1990; Rademakers, 1991); and actual control over the behavioral goal (Worth, 1989). Several authors have stressed the relative powerlessness of women in general in implicit or explicit negotiations about sex and condom use (Worth, 1989; Kane, 1990; Holland et al., 1990; Carballo, 1990), but what exactly comprises powerlessness (either the prostitutes' or the clients') in the context of prostitution is much less clear. Several studies have shown that refusal by clients to use a condom is the prime reason for prostitutes to engage in risky sex (Estébanez et al., 1993). Bloor et al. (1992), in a study of male prostitutes found that unsafe sex is associated with control by clients, while safer sex is associated with countervailing strategies of influence by the prostitute, such as opening hidden agendas. These authors insist that protection behavior in prostitution must be explained as a dyadic act, not as an individual response.

We assume that both actors bring their personal backgrounds and goals into the interaction and that the course of these interactions depends on which two actors meet, the subjective definition the sexual encounter has for them and what kind of contact they want to establish, how they perceive each other, and what actions and influence strategies they undertake. From a symbolic interactionist point of view, self-perception and perception of the other are considered important to interaction processes. Self-perception and personal goals determine the way one presents one-self. Self-presentation often contains a message; one communicates what one hopes to achieve with the other. We will study, for both prostitute and client how the variations in context and in the significance of prostitution translate themselves into interaction and result in different self-presentations, mutual perceptions, lines of action, and 'working agreements', particularly with regard to condom use.

We will study which implicit and explicit influence strategies are being employed by both prostitutes and clients. In line with Bloor et al., (1992) explicit influence strategies are presumed to be more effective with regard to condom use. Explicit strategies are expected to be more likely when context-related conditions and person-related factors are more favorable. In addition, we will investigate where prostitutes localize control over contact proceedings. It is expected that the less control experienced by the prostitute, the less likely consistent condom use is.

3.3: Main research expectations *Summary of hypotheses in Ch. 3*
On the basis of the theoretical model and the research presented in this chapter, we have the following main expectations regarding our research findings on the well-being of prostitutes in comparison to other women:

- Considering the possibility of prostitution work as a response to childhood sexual trauma in addition to the workings of stigma and the nature of prostitution work, it is presumed that prostitutes as a group are traumatically victimized more often than non-prostitute women, both in childhood and in adult life. Furthermore, victimization in adult private life is presumed to relate to childhood trauma, and victimization on the job is expected to relate to victimization in the private sphere, as well as to childhood trauma.
- Considering the high level of stress and relatively low levels of protection related to the workings of stigma, as well as the amount of stress and the lack of protection inherent in sex work, and considering the expected higher levels of victimization among prostitutes, it might be predicted that prostitutes as a group have more somatic complaints and psychosocial problems than non-prostitutes. Somatic complaints are also expected to be related to psycho-social problems. Job satisfaction is probably inversely related to complaints and problems.
- Considering the workings of stigma, the amount of stress and the lack of protection inherent in sex work, and considering the expected higher levels of victimization, it is expected that prostitutes as a group employ more emotion-directed and less problem-directed coping behavior, and seek less social support than non-prostitutes. Further, drug abuse is expected to relate to emotion-directed coping behavior, and drug abuse and emotion-directed coping are expected to be inversely related to problem-directed coping behavior.

We expect levels of prostitutes' well-being and job satisfaction to be higher as:
- victimization, be it in childhood, adult life, or on the job, is less severe;
- emotion-directed coping responses, particularly dissociation and denial, are used less and as the use of drugs decreases;
- problem-directed responses are used more;

- financial need is lower, educational level is higher, and one has not migrated;

- working conditions are more favorable, more specifically when one works in an 'unorganized' as opposed to an organized setting, has fewer clients, earns more per client, and client contacts last longer.
- one has a stronger internal, rather than external Health Locus of Control.

Why not examine
risks taken with
non commercial
partners

We expect risky protection behavior by prostitutes in commercial sex to be more likely as:
- levels of victimization, in childhood, adult life, as well as on the job, are higher;
- well-being and job satisfaction are lower and the subjective significance of prostitution work is less positive;
- one employs more emotion-directed coping behavior, uses more drugs and employs less problem-directed coping behavior;
- financial need is higher, educational level is lower, and one has migrated;
- working conditions are less favorable, more specifically when one works in an 'unorganized' as opposed to an organized setting, has more clients, earns less per client, and client-contacts are of shorter duration;
- norm-support regarding condom use is lower;
- AIDS-related knowledge, perception of AIDS as being a serious disease, personal risk perception and fear of AIDS are less strong;
- external Health Locus of Control is stronger than internal Health Locus of Control;
- one uses fewer explicit influence strategies in interaction with clients and experiences less control over contact proceedings.

Those who wish to replicate can view Appendices

Chapter Four
METHODS

Introduction

The evidence relevant to the investigation of the expectations formulated in the previous chapter has been gathered in two empirical studies. In the first one which we will refer to as the 'coping and well-being'-study, the problems prostitutes and ex-prostitutes deal with were investigated. The study also aimed to discover why these problems remain relatively indiscernible in social work and therapeutic assistance and to make recommendations in this area. The study has been carried out by order of the Dutch Ministry of Social Affairs and Employment at the Mr. A. de Graaf Foundation in Amsterdam. Initial results have been published in a ministerial report (Vanwesenbeeck, Altink & Groen, 1989).

The second study is referred to as the 'protective behavior'-study. Funds were granted by the Counsel for Health Research (RGO) and the study was carried out at the Netherlands Institute of Social Sexological Research (NISSO). The focus of the study was on determinants of condom use in hetero- and homosexual prostitution and its initial results have been reported in a series of publications by Vanwesenbeeck et al. (1992, 1993) and by De Graaf et al. (1992, 1993).

Both studies clearly had their own rationale and own focus and were not set up originally to come up with comparable findings. Nevertheless, in both studies, valuable information was gathered which could be further analyzed and adapted to answer the questions posed here. This chapter will outline the sampling procedures, subjects, and instruments and operationalizations in both studies which are relevant to the subject matter of this book.

4.1: Sampling

In the 'coping and well-being'-study, the target population were prostitutes in different work settings and in different parts of the country. Ex-prostitutes also took part in the study since we had an equal interest in their well-being. The recruitment of respondents took place in the summer of 1988. Prostitutes and ex-prostitutes were invited to engage in a face-to-face anonymous interview about all the possible sorts of problems they experienced which were related to their work as well as to their day-to-day lives, and the way they dealt with them. It was stressed that we would also be interested in talking to them even if they did not experience any problems. A fee of 100 guilders was offered.

The recruitment of subjects for the 'protective behavior'-study took place two years later. The target population was female prostitutes who had been working in prostitution for at least one year at the time of the interview, as well as the male clients of prostitutes who had at least two commercial contacts in the previous year[1]. Again the aim was to recruit prostitutes from different work settings and from different parts of the country. Recruitment took place under the denominator of 'sex and health'. Prostitutes were given 75 guilders; clients did not receive any money.

Several tracks were followed to contact the target populations. Table 4.1 gives an overview of the procedures. In the 'coping and well-being'-study, (ex-)prostitutes were recruited predominantly via intermediaries and snowballing, while in the 'protective behavior'-study, most of the prostitutes were reached at their work places through outreach fieldwork. Clients were contacted through advertisements in national and local newspapers.

It is difficult to give a non-response rate for the sampling in the 'coping and well-being'-study. The intermediaries were successful in their recruitment, but invited only those women to participate whom they suspected to be willing to cooperate. Of the women who reacted to the advertisements, it is estimated that about one third of the serious reactions eventually resulted in an interview. In the outreach fieldwork it is estimated that about one in five women who were contacted agreed. The snowball method proved to be quite successful as well, but without any doubt had the same (dis)advantage as recruitment by intermediaries; namely that only subjects who were expected to be willing to participate were contacted. In the 'protective behavior'-study approximately one out of three women contacted at their work places consented to an interview.

In both studies, women in the target group who were contacted personally, but would not agree to an interview mostly said they did not want to participate because of fear of loosing anonymity. Another reason frequently mentioned, particularly in the 'coping and well-being'-study was, that they did not want to talk about problems and difficulties, and certainly not with an outsider. The denominator of 'problems' may be one reason for the somewhat higher non-response in the fieldwork in the 'coping and well-being'-study. It is also possible that prostitutes had become somewhat more willing to talk about their lives and work in those two years. In two instances during the recruitment phase in the 'coping and well-being'-study, it became clear that women had been forbidden by their partners to participate. In some other instances, women seemed to be dissuaded by their bosses to engage in an interview. We did not come across such overt dissuasion in the 'protective behavior'-study.

Of the clients reacting to the advertisements, eventually one third consented to an interview. The main reason for the men to not consent to an interview was 'unwillingness to enter the face-to-face situation'.

---

[1] Male prostitutes and their clients were also targeted and recruited as subjects in the 'protective behavior'-study (although to a lesser extent than the heterosexual population), but will not be described in this book. For findings on the partners in homosexual prostitution, see De Graaf et al. (1992, 1993).

4.2: Subjects

Demographic and other characteristics of the study samples are put together in Table 4.1. Here, the two groups will be compared and their representativity considered.

A crucial difference between the two samples is the presence of ex-prostitutes in the first one, as opposed to their absence in the second. In the 'coping and well-being'-study, about one third of the women still working report doing so 'only sometimes' at the time of the interview and describe themselves as 'retired'. Women still working and those no longer working can therefore be said to be somewhat equally represented. In the 'protective behavior'-study, all the women still work in prostitution and have on average worked about the same period as the women in the first study. Their mean age is somewhat lower. Clients are, on average, significantly older than prostitutes and have a longer history of involvement in prostitution.

Most of the respondents were born in The Netherlands, but due to our extra effort in the second study to reach migrant women, the percentage of prostitutes who were born outside The Netherlands is higher there. Those born in another Western European country are predominantly German, and those born outside Western Europe are predominantly Latin American (n=20). The others are from Morocco, Surinam, the Antilles, and Eastern Europe. On average, these women have been in The Netherlands for a period of ten months.

In both studies, the majority of the women work(ed) in one of the four big cities. The division of women working in other regions is comparable in the two studies, although the percentage of women who moved frequently is somewhat higher in the first sample.

Differences in educational level between the two samples (there is a smaller group of more highly educated women in the second sample) are probably due to our own formulations. In the first study we asked for the most advanced education ever started, while in the second we asked for completed studies. Therefore, proper comparison between the two groups of prostitutes regarding educational level is difficult. Compared to about the same age group of the female population in The Netherlands, the percentage of prostitutes at the lowest educational level in the 'protective behavior'-study seems to be higher (44% as compared to 34% of the female population between 25 and 44 years of age). Furthermore, the percentage of prostitutes at the highest level of education seems to be considerably lower (5% as compared to 18% of the female population between 25 and 44) (Central Bureau of Statistics -CBS-, 1991). The middle groups are about the same (51% and 48%). On average prostitutes seem to have a somewhat lower educational level than women in their age group. Clients, on average, are more educated than prostitutes.

Relatively many prostitutes are either single or divorced/widowed. Comparing the marital status of prostitutes to that of the same age group of women in The Netherlands, considerably more are single (56% versus 21%), more are divorced

Table 4.1: Overview sampling and subjects in the two studies

	The 'coping and well-being' study	The 'protective behavior' study	
		Female prostitutes	Male clients
target population	prostitutes and ex-prostitutes	prostitutes working >1 year	clients with two or more contacts last year
recruitment	in the summer of 1988, under the denominator 'dealing with problems in work and private life'	July 1990-March 1991 'sex and health'	July 1990-March 1991 'sex and health'
	N (%)	*N (%)*	*N (%)*
outreach fieldwork	6 (10)	85 (67)	-
intermediaries	25 (42)	24 (19)	-
snowball technique	15 (25)	13 (10)	-
advertisements	14 (23)	5 (4)	-
			91 (100)
non-response	unknown	approximately 60%	approximately 60% of those who called in
N	60, of which 23 (38%) are ex-prostitutes	127	91
mean age	32.2 (SD=8.5)	29.8 (SD=8.1)	45 (SD=13.5)
av. period prostitution experience	6.7 years (SD=6.5)	6.8 years (SD=6.7)	17.3 years (SD=11.7), 27.2 (SD=30) last year
place of birth	*N (%)*	*N (%)*	*N (%)*
the Netherlands	54 (90)	83 (64)	89 (98)
other Western European country	4 (7)	16 (12)	0 (0)
non-Western European countries	2 (3)	28 (24)	2 (2)
region of work			
the four big cities	35 (58)	75 (59)	30 (33)(main region prostitution visits)
medium-sized city	12 (20)	29 (23)	31 (34)
village/rural area	6 (10)	19 (15)	30 (33)
varying	7 (12)	4 (3)	-
educational level			
primary school	21 (35)	56 (44)	23 (25)
secondary education	21 (35)	65 (51)	41 (45)
advanced study	18 (30)(started)	6 (5)(completed)	27 (30)(completed)

	N (%)	mean age	N (%)	mean age	N (%)
civil status					
single	unknown		71 (56)		32 (35)
married	unknown		27 (21)		40 (44)
divorced/widow	unknown		29 (23)		19 (21)
steady partner last year					
male	unknown		86 (68)		0
female	unknown		6 (5)		49 (54)
children					
no	30 (50)		63 (50)		unknown
yes	30 (50)(mean: 1.5)		64 (50)(mean: 1.3)		unknown
financial responsibility household					
mainly with respondent	50 (83)		84 (66)		unknown
shared	9 (15)		39 (31)		unknown
mainly with partner	1 (2)		4 (3)		unknown
work place		mean age		mean age	
club	14 (23)	32	32 (25)	31	26 (29)(sorts visited by:)
brothel	14 (23)	33	27 (21)	30	33 (36)
window	16 (27)	33	27 (21)	30	47 (52)
street	4 (7)	30	29 (23)	28	16 (18)
escort	3 (5)	25	5 (4)	34	20 (22)
own house	3 (5)	33	7 (6)	38	28 (31)
combination	6 (10)	35	-		51 (56)(visited more than one sort:
					16 (18) visited three sorts or more)
period worked					
< 1 year	4 (7)	22	10 (8)	27	
1-2 years	5 (8)	25	18 (14)	24	
2-5 years	21 (35)	31	35 (28)	27	
5-10 years	13 (22)	31	28 (22)	30	
> 10 years	17 (28)	39	36 (28)	36	
working position					
madam/manager	13 (22)		5 (4)		
employee	21 (35)		54 (43)		
independent	26 (43)		68 (54)		

(23% versus 8%) and many fewer are married (21% versus 71%) (CBS, 1992). However, the percentage of prostitutes with a steady male partner (68%) resembles the general percentage of married women. In both samples half of the women (50%) have one or more child(ren). Prostitutes, then, seem to have slightly more children than women under 38 in general, of whom 43% have one or more child(ren) (CBS, 1988).

Regarding financial responsibility for households, the low percentages of women in both samples being financially supported by a partner is noteworthy. Comparing the 66% of women who have the main responsibility for household finances in our second sample to the 4% of (un)married women with a male partner in the general population contributing more financially to the household than their partners (Hooghiemstra et al., 1993), it must be concluded that prostitutes carry a high financial responsibility. This responsibility of prostitutes in many cases exceeds their own households and partners. In the 'coping and well-being'-study, six women (10%) have at times been financially responsible for other family members as well. In the 'protective behavior'-study, 40 women (32%) have financial responsibility for other family members and/or friends.

Comparing both samples of prostitutes with respect to their working situation the remarkable differences are: in the 'protective behavior'-study, a larger percentage of women work the street, a larger percentage has worked less than two years, and a smaller percentage of women have a position as madam or manager.

4.3: Representativity of research samples

To what extent are our samples a good reflection of the whole population of prostitutes in The Netherlands? The out-reach procedure followed in the second study (as opposed to the recruitment through intermediaries and snowballing in the first) may be considered more appropriate with regard to representativity (cf. Markos et al., 1992:94). However, in both studies, motives for not wanting to participate, such as not wanting to drag up the past or wanting to hide difficulties, combined with the explicit dissuasion by third parties in some cases, gave rise to the supposition that with the exception of those who were recruited by intermediaries, the non-responders suffered relatively worse conditions than those who consented to an interview. The more neutral recruitment-approach in the second study may have resulted in a more diverse and representative sample with regard to problems and attitudes towards the work, but as in the first sample, women working under duress or living in abusive relationships at the time of the interview were not present in this group either. As has been noted by others (e.g. Lowman, 1987), women who have relationships with pimps are extremely reluctant to participate in interviews. As a result, prostitutes living and working under extremely negative conditions are probably underrepresented in both of our samples.

Another important aspect in this context is the presence of ex-prostitutes in the first sample. Ex-prostitutes may have left the job exactly because of difficulties and not being able to keep up the work, thereby forming a group in which 'troubles' are overrepresented compared to women still working. On the other hand, one might argue that no longer working as a prostitute gives way to a more 'honest' report of the troublesome aspects of the work. This might result in a more accurate representation concerning well-being. Whatever the effect of the presence of ex-prostitutes is, in interpreting the findings the difference between the two samples in this respect must be acknowledged.

Unlike many of the studies reviewed in Chapter Two, the samples in our studies are comprised not only of street prostitutes, but of women working in other types of prostitution as well. This diversity of working places obviously improves the representativity of the samples in relation to the target population of prostitutes. The representativity of women working in different types of prostitution can be checked against the estimates by the National Center for the Fight against AIDS (Nationaal Centrum voor Aids Bestrijding -NCAB-, 1990). These comparisons are listed in Table 4.2.

Where women work.

Table 4.2: Different types of prostitution. Comparison of the two samples with the estimates of the National Center for the Fight against AIDS (NCAB); percentage of prostitutes

type of prostitution	NCAB estimate	coping and well-being-study	protective behavior-study
street	10	7	23
window	30	27	21
clubs and brothels	30	46	46
escort	15	5	4
own home	15	5	6

Since the percentage of street prostitutes in the total target population in The Netherlands is estimated at 10%, they are somewhat overrepresented in our second study. Window prostitutes are somewhat underrepresented. The representation of both street and window prostitutes seems quite appropriate in the first study. Compared to the NCAB estimates, club- and brothel prostitutes might be somewhat overrepresented in both studies, and both studies definitely show an underrepresentation of escort prostitutes and of women working in their own homes. By defining women working as escorts and in clubs and brothels as working in an organized context, and the others as working in an 'unorganized' setting, the first group is slightly overrepresented and the latter underrepresented in our studies, compared to the NCAB-estimates. However, it needs to be stressed that the NCAB-percentages are estimates (on the basis of expert information), and in the end, no definite or exact conclusion can be drawn as to the accuracy of representation of the different sorts of prostitutes. As for working as madam or manager, -

an aspect on which the NCAB does not give an estimate-, the 4% in the second study is probably a more accurate reflection of the actual situation than the 22% in the first one.

While migrant women are clearly underrepresented in the 'coping and well-being'-study, they are rather well represented in the 'protective behavior'-study compared to the estimate of thirty to sixty percent (depending on location) of female migrant prostitutes in The Netherlands (Brussa, 1989:231). Whereas migrant women in our second sample are predominantly German and Latin American, women from Southeast Asia and Africa are unfortunately absent. Eastern European and ex-Soviet Union women are underrepresented as well. Even though these were not as active in prostitution in The Netherlands at the time of our studies, their number has rapidly increased during the past year.

In both studies, the group of women working in the four big cities and the west of The Netherlands is large, even though there certainly is a concentration of prostitution in that area. However, women working in other parts of the country appear to be somewhat underrepresented.

The most problematic aspect of our prostitute samples, especially in the 'protective behavior'-study, may be the fact that women working under duress, living in abusive relationships or living under otherwise extremely burdensome conditions at the time of the interview, seem to be underrepresented. Findings regarding well-being and risk may therefore reveal a somewhat optimistic picture.

In general, with regard to the demographic properties of our samples, it is difficult to say anything conclusive about the extent to which these are representative of the population of prostitutes in The Netherlands because of the lack of knowledge about the characteristics of the total target population. On the other hand, it is remarkable that there is a high resemblance between the two prostitute samples in this respect. We are inclined to estimate that overall both our samples provide a reasonable reflection of the total population of women working in prostitution in The Netherlands. The same applies to their clients. One thing can be said about the sample of clients; non-white and migrant men are clearly underrepresented.

4.4: Instruments and operationalizations

In both studies, face-to-face interviews were chosen as the research instrument because a face-to-face situation was considered necessary to bring about enough trust for the respondents to open up to an outsider. Moreover, the face-to-face situation increases the validity of the findings because the interviewer has the opportunity to probe and have the respondents' statements clarified. Data were gathered qualitatively as well as quantitatively in a combination of open and limited choice questions.

In the 'coping and well-being'-study, the 60 interviews with (ex)prostitutes were divided equally amongst the three researchers engaged in the project. All (semi-structured) interviews were audiotaped and lasted an average 2.5 hours. They focussed successively on the following topics: demographic information;

working history, conditions and relations; physical complaints and drug use; psychosocial and emotional problems; experiences with violence and abuse; general coping responses; informal and formal support.

In the 'protective behavior'-study, the interviews (average length: 2.5 hours) were somewhat more structured and consisted of open and limited choice questions and a number of self-report questionnaires to be completed by the respondents. The interviews were conducted by nine trained female interviewers and the two researchers. Translations of the questionnaires were used for spanish-speaking subjects. One interviewer mastered the Spanish language. All interviews were audiotaped. The following topics were successively addressed: demographics and financial need; working history and conditions; job satisfaction; the use of alcohol and drugs while working; interaction with clients and experiences with violence while at work; causal attributions of unpleasant contacts with clients; sexual conduct and condom use with clients in the last year; STD-history, physical and emotional complaints; risk perception and fear of AIDS; general coping responses; meaning of (paid) sex and experiences with (sexual) violence in the private sphere; sexual conduct and condom use with steady and casual non-paying partners; and behavioral changes in protective behavior.

The clients were asked the same types of questions as the prostitutes in a comparable interview situation but they were not questioned about physical and emotional complaints, victimization, or coping behavior. The following topics were addressed: history, motivation and evaluations of visiting prostitutes; drug use; sexual conduct and condom use with prostitutes in the last year; evaluation of condoms; interaction with prostitutes; sexual conduct and condom use with steady and casual non-paid partners; STD history and attitudes towards AIDS; behavioral changes in protective behavior; and demographics.

Instruments used in both studies have been listed in Table 4.3. The main operationalizations will be shortly discussed further on.

Well-being and job satisfaction

In the first study, well-being was orally investigated on the basis of a list of complaints and problems, constructed by the researchers[2], whereas in the second one, it was measu-red by respondents' self-report to the standardized short version (Sandfort, 1985) of the Dutch translation (Arrindell and Ettema, 1987) of the Symptom Check List (SCL-90; Derogatis, 1977). Our preference was for the standardized questionnaire in the second study for the sake of the comparability of

---

[2] The items were orally presented to the respondent with the question 'Have you had trouble with this since the time you work(ed)?' The qualitative information thus gathered was quantified into data on frequencies by systematically urging the respondents to formulate an answer ranging from 'never' to 'hardly ever', thus constructing a 4-point scale for all the items discussed.

Complete description of t/ge

Table 4.3: Overview instruments and operationalizations in the two studies

	The 'coping and well-being' study		The 'protective behavior' study			
			Female prostitutes		**Male clients**	
instrument	semi-structured face-to-face interview		structured face-to-face interview		structured face-to-face interview	
well-being	questions on 23 complaints		short Symptom Check List (SCL)		not measured	
	psychosomatic complaints*	4 items	social insecurity*	15 items		
	work related physical complaints*	4 items	psychosomatic complaints*	16 items		
	depressive anxiousness*	7 items				
	inward/outward directed aggression*	4 items				
	social problems*	4 items				
job satisfaction	not measured		questions on 5 different aspects		not measured	
			at ease on the job	1 item		
			atmosphere with colleagues	1 item		
			freq. refusing clients	1 item		
			freq. undesirable course	1 item		
			stress because of work	1 item		
protective behavior	not measured		extensive questioning on condom use w. clients		ext. quest. on condom use with prostitutes	
			consistent protection style		consistent protection style	
			selective protection style		defaulting protection style	
			risk taking protection style		selective protection style	
					indifferent protection style	
					recalcitrant protection style	
victimization	questions on 17 experiences		questions on 7 experiences		not measured	
	force and violence by a partner*	7 items	violence private sphere*	3 items		
	violence by strangers/at work*	4 items	violence on the job*	2 items		
	youth violence*	4 items	childhood violence	2 items		
coping behavior	Utrecht Coping List (UCL)		list of coping behaviors (20 items)		not measured	
	problem solving*	6 items	dissociation*	8 items		
	depressed/palliative pattern*	7 items	problem solving*	6 items		
	avoiding*	4 items	seeking support*	4 items		
	seeking support*	5 items	denial*	2 items		
drug use	questions on the use of 6 drugs		questions on the use of drugs and alcohol		questions on the use of drugs and alcohol	
	drugs*	4 items	freq. drug use	1 item	freq. drug use	1 item
	alcohol	1 item	freq. alcohol use	1 item	freq. alcohol use	1 item
working conditions	apart from place of work and working position, no specific information gathered		questions on 5 different aspects		not applicable	
			place of work/position	1 item		
			av. no. of clients p. week	1 item		
			av. no. of working hours p.w.	1 item		
			av. duration client-contacts	1 item		
			av. earnings per client	1 item		

financial need	not measured	questions on 4 different aspects	not measured
		finan.resp. household — 1 item	
		other sources of income — 1 item	
		pr.rel.to drug dependency — 1 item	
		finan.resp.drug dependency other — 1 item	
Health Locus of Control	not measured	Health Locus of Control scale	Health Locus of Control scale
		fate* — 3 items	external control* — 5 items
		expert control* — 3 items	internal control* — 3 items
		external control AIDS* — 3 items	external control AIDS* — 3 items
		internal control* — 3 items	surroundings* — 1 item
AIDS-related cognitions	not measured	list of cognitions (3 items)	list of cognitions (3 items)
		seriousness AIDS — 1 item	seriousness AIDS — 1 item
		chance of getting AIDS — 1 item	chance getting AIDS — 1 item
		fear of AIDS — 1 item	fear of AIDS — 1 item
influence strategies	not measured	list of strategies used (31 items)	list of strategies used (31 items)
		manipulative negotiation* — 13 items	manipulation* — 7 items
		high pressure* — 10 items	rational strategies* — 5 items
		negative emotions* — 8 items	negotiation* — 4 items
		formal arguments* — 2 items	
attributions of undesirable contact proceedings	not measured	list of attributions (18 items)	not measured
		powerlessness/indifference* — 7 items	
		formal attributions* — 5 items	
		anxious helplessness* — 6 items	
evaluation of condoms	not measured	not measured	list of opinions (10 items)
			positive evaluation* — 4 items
			negative evaluation* — 4 items
			negative attitude* — 2 items
evaluation of prostitution visits	not applicable	not applicable	list of opinions (12 items)
			positive evaluation* — 5 items
			negative evaluation* — 3 items
			preference other sex* — 3 items
			neg.att.prostitutes* — 1 item

Note. All scales with an asterix have been constructed after factor-analyses. For references and information regarding the scales, see the text.

the findings with those in other samples. Because the whole questionnaire was rather time-consuming, we chose the short version. An important difference between the operationalizations of well-being in the two studies is, that in the 'coping and well-being'-study respondents reported on complaints and problems that they had (had) since they worked in prostitution, while in the 'protective behavior'-study, respondents reported on their present situation. The first method probably reveals a wider range of difficulties, while the second one may better reflect present well-being.

The subscales for well-being in both studies were constructed according to factor analysis[3]. In the 'coping and well-being'-study this resulted in five subscales, two on physical complaints and three on psychosocial and emotional problems. *Psychosomatic complaints* (e.g stomach aches and hyperventilation) have been distinguished from *work-related physical complaints* (e.g. STD's and gynecological complaints). In the psycho-social area, the distinction was made between *depressive anxiousness* (e.g. fears, anxieties, tension and depression), *aggression directed outward and inward* (distrust, aggression, suicide thoughts and nightmares), and *social problems* (e.g. shame and problems in relationships). Particularly the subscale *aggression directed outward and inward* may relate strongly to (unresolved) traumatic and violating experiences. For detailed information on the subscales' composition, the percentage of explained variance, their internal consistency and item factor loadings, and their mutual correlations, see Appendices 4.1 to 4.3.

In the 'protective behavior'-study two subscales were developed (see Appendices 4.9 and 4.10). The subscale *social insecurity* (comprised of items like 'feeling that others are unfriendly', 'feeling inferior to others' and 'feeling hurt quickly') seems to refer predominantly to problems in the social sphere, low self-confidence, and depression. Feelings of anxiety, tension and fear, taken separately in the first study, are also included in this subscale. *Psychosomatic complaints* as a subscale (comprised of items like 'painful muscles', 'tension in the neck', and 'stomach aches') is composed of somatic complaints known to have a psychological component and seems to relate predominantly to the somatizing of problematic emotions. The subscales correlate significantly with one another.

Job satisfaction was measured only in the 'protective behavior'-study. A scale was constructed to assess the degree to which the respondents feel comfortable in their work. The average sumscore on the following items was used as a measure: the degree in which one feels at ease on the job, perceived atmosphere with colleagues, frequency of confrontation with clients one refuses, frequency of undesirable course of contact, and stress because of the work. Cronbach's alpha

---

[3] In all factor analyses we used varimax rotation in order to get well-distinguished subscales. If the analysis with the default criterium (Eigenvalue > 1) did not result in a factor solution that was meaningful in its contents, another criterium was chosen and the procedure was repeated. Alternative criteria are indicated in the appendices.

for this scale is .61. *Job satisfaction* is negatively related to both *social insecurity* and *psychosomatic complaints* (see Appendix 4.10).

Protection behavior

In the 'protective behavior'-study, both prostitutes and clients were asked how often they used different sexual techniques with paid/paying partners and how often they used condoms with these different techniques. Apart from that, subjects were questioned extensively about their reasons for condom use or their abstention. Further, all respondents were asked to describe in detail their last commercial sexual contact and one contact that differed substantially from the first, preferably with regard to condom use. Both quantitative and qualitative analysis of these data resulted in different typologies regarding protective behavior for prostitutes and clients, referred to as *protection styles*.

Childhood trauma and victimizing life-events in adolescence and adulthood

In both studies the data concerning victimization were quantified by the researchers on the basis of qualitative information obtained through open questions about experiences with sexual and physical violence both on and off the job, about the experience of being forced into prostitution and about childhood and adolescent traumatic sexual experiences. The experiences which were questioned were, for example, 'unwanted sex with an acquaintance or family member before age 16', 'physical violence by a partner' or 'sexual violence by customers'. We probed for specific characteristics of the experiences and the way each respondent subjectively appraised them. A score of 1 was given by the researchers when there was no such experience, a score of 2 to an incidental, relatively mild experience, a score of 3 to experiences of moderate severity, and 4 to experiences of extreme severity.

In the first study, discussion of these experiences was much more extensive and more specific experiences were drawn out by the interviewers. The number of specific experiences had to be reduced from 17 to 7 items in the second study[4]. Respondents thus reported experiences with violence on only minimal invitation. This is clearly a disadvantage. Authorative researchers in the field of trauma and victimization like Russell in the United States and Draijer in The Netherlands, have stressed the fact that painful experiences have to be suggested extensively and in a detailed way in order for them to be reported by the respondents at all. This prerequisite has been better met in the 'coping and well-being'-study than in the 'protective behavior'-study. Since sexual risk behavior was the prime focus there, the interviewers were more specifically trained to discuss sex than to talk about trauma. There was a large amount of missing data on victimization as a

---

[4] The primary focus of this study was condom use and interaction between prostitutes and clients. Respondents were probed extensively about condom use and only secondarily asked about well-being and victimization.

result. Moreover, our results regarding the incidence as well as the severity of victimizing experiences in the 'protective behavior'-study probably only reflect the proverbial top of the iceberg.

Factor analyses on both sets of data clearly distinguished violence by acquaintances and partners (such as force into prostitution and sexual and physical violence by a partner) from that by strangers and clients. Although the composition of the subscales differs in the two studies (see Appendices 4.5 and 4.12), these two forms of victimization were distinguished in both the factor analyses. However, in both studies, they were also related to each other (see Appendices 4.6 and 4.12). *Force and violence by a partner* and *violence by strangers/at work* correlate significantly in the 'coping and well-being'-study; the same applies to *violence in the private sphere* and *violence on the job* in the 'protective behavior'-study.

Because the data on youth experiences in the 'protective behavior'-study show relatively many white spots (21.5% of subjects did not give sufficient information in this area), these variables were excluded from the factor analysis that was performed on the rest of the data. However, since the two items on unwanted sex before age 16 by strangers and by acquaintances or family members did correlate significantly (Pearson's r=.51, p<.001), they were used as a scale *childhood violence* in further analysis (Cronbach's alpha .67). This subscale *childhood violence* appears to correlate significantly with *violence in the private sphere*, but not with *violence on the job* (see Appendix 4.12). In the 'coping and well-being'-study, the data on childhood experiences had been comprised in the factor analysis where they appeared to group together in the factor *youth violence*. *Youth violence* as a subscale does not correlate significantly with the subscales for violence in adult life (see Appendix 4.6).

Coping behavior and drug use

Coping behavior was studied somewhat more extensively in the 'protective behavior'-study. In the 'coping and well-being' study, respondents answered to the short version of the Utrecht Coping List (UCL; Schreurs et al., 1988). The written questionnaire that was used in the 'protective behavior'-study consisted of several items from the UCL, selected because of their discriminative qualities in the first study. These were supplemented by some items which were self-constructed in line with frequent statements by respondents in that study. In addition, 5 items on dissociation were added which were a translation of strongly discriminating items in the dissociation scale of Sanders (1986). The latter formed an important extension in comparison to the UCL that was used in the 'coping and well-being'-study.

On the other hand, in the 'coping and well-being'-study, additional information on coping behavior was gathered orally. Questions like 'And what did you do then?' or 'How did you react?' were asked whenever problems were brought forward. These questions combined with the spontaneous statements of the respondents provided thorough qualitative information on the way respondents dealt with problems of divergent nature.

In the written questionnaires, in addition to the items on dissociation mentioned above, respondents in both studies were asked to state the frequency with which they generally reacted to problems by means of different specific coping reactions that were either problem focussed, palliative, denying or depressed, or referred to seeking social support, expression of emotions or using reassuring thoughts. In the 'protective behavior'-study, factor analysis on the data revealed strong clustering of particularly the items on *dissociation*, and also on *problem solving* and *seeking support*. The operationalization of *denial* by only two items must be considered less strong. Correlations between both *dissociation* and *denial* and between *dissociation* and *seeking support* are statistically significant. The relation between *dissociation* and *problem solving* is a negative one, but is not statistically significant (see Appendices 4.13 and 4.14).

The factor analysis in the 'coping and well-being'-study also revealed four factors, but here none of them were found to relate to each other significantly (see Appendices 4.7 and 4.8). The UCL used in the first study was also submitted to and completed by a (select) control group of 38 college students.

In the 'coping and well-being'-study a scale was used for the frequency of *drug use* (combining soft drugs, heroine, cocaine, and other hard drugs, such as poppers and amphetamines). In the 'protective behavior'-study one item asking for the frequency of drug use during work is used as a measure. Supplementary information showed that the respondents who did use drugs 'often' or 'always', used predominantly heroin, sometimes in combination with cocaine or other drugs. Of those who used drugs 'sometimes', most used soft-drugs, cocaine, or tranquilizers.

In both studies, the frequency of alcohol use was measured by one item. In the 'coping and well-being'-study we also asked about the use of tranquilizers. In neither of the studies, are drug and alcohol use related significantly (see Appendices 4.4, 4.8 and 4.14).

Working conditions and financial need

These variables were investigated in the 'protective behavior'-study only, although the place of work and working position were known in the 'coping and well-being'-study as well. The prostitutes were questioned about different aspects of working conditions, routine and earnings (see Table 4.3).

Financial need was operationalized by adding up the scores of several aspects that produce financial pressure for prostitutes, such as financial responsibility for a household, no other sources of income, and the necessity of prostitution work because of drug dependency (see Table 4.3).

Health Locus of Control and AIDS-related cognition

In the 'protective behavior'-study, prostitutes as well as clients completed a (standardized and validated) Dutch version (Pruyn et al., 1988) of the Health

Locus of Control Scale (Wallston et al., 1976). This scale measures the extent to which the respondent thinks his or her health is controlled either internally, by significant others, or by fate. The (three) items relating specifically to cancer in the list by Pruyn et al. were changed into items referring to AIDS. Factor analysis was used separately on the prostitutes' and clients' data. For both groups, there were four factors revealed, each with somewhat different composition (see Appendices 4.15 and 4.18). Among the prostitutes, the first and strongest factor was formed by the three items on *fate* and was distinguished from those on *expert control*. However, among the clients all these items group in the first factor which is called *external control*. The factors *internal control* and *external control over AIDS* are the same for both groups. In the prostitute sample, significant relations are found between *fate* and *expert control* (r=.23, p<.01) and between *fate* and *external control over AIDS* (r=.33, p<.001). *Internal control* is not associated with any of the external control scales.

Furthermore, three AIDS-related cognition were minimally measured all by one item, for both prostitutes and clients (see Table 4.3).

Interaction processes, influence strategies, perceived control

Interaction between prostitutes and clients was assessed in different ways. First, as already mentioned under 'protection behavior', all respondents were asked to describe in detail two recent commercial sexual contacts. Rich qualitative material was gathered in this way.

Next, clients as well as prostitutes completed a questionnaire on influence strategies used in commercial sexual contacts. The items were selected by the researchers on the basis of comparable instruments by Falbo and Peplau (1980), Howard, Blumstein and Schwartz (1986) and White and Roufail (1989). Prostitutes' and clients' data were factor-analyzed separately. With the clients, 13 items out of 31 hardly differentiated. The factor analysis was therefore used for the remaining 18 items only. As a result, different subscales were revealed for prostitutes and clients (Appendices 4.17 and 4.19).

For the prostitutes only, one additional instrument was used regarding attributions of undesirable contact proceedings. Again a factor analysis was performed to construct subscales (see Appendix 4.16). *Attributions of powerlessness and indifference* were distinguished from *formal attributions* and from *anxious helplessness*.

4.5: Conclusion

There were more variables studied in the 'protective behavior'-study than in the 'coping and well-being'-study. For those variables investigated in both studies there are differences in operationalization. This is due to differences in both focus and context of the studies. Some operationalizations in the second study are an improvement on those used in the 'coping and well-being'-study (e.g. the inclusion of dissociation in the operationalization of coping behavior), while others must be acknowledged to be qualitatively less (e.g. the limited operationalization of, and questioning about childhood trauma and victimizing life-events). In interpreting the findings in both studies these differences in the quality of the operationalizations must be taken into account.

Because well-being and protective behavior were studied from a multi-causal framework, many variables had to be investigated. We consider the incidental weaker operationalizations to be the unfortunate price to be paid in such a set-up. On the other hand, the combination of quantitative and qualitative data can be considered a strong point methodologically. The qualitative information is used to verify the quantitative findings and, in addition gives them more depth.

Chapter Five
WELL-BEING OF PROSTITUTES

Introduction
In this chapter the findings concerning well-being as they relate to the factors which were introduced in our theoretical framework will be presented and discussed. Alternately we draw upon quantitative and qualitative data that were gathered both in the 'coping and well-being'-study and in the 'protective behavior'-study.

In section 5.1 findings relating to the level of well-being of prostitutes are presented and compared to findings in non-prostitute samples. In sections 5.2 to 5.5 levels of well-being and job satisfaction will be related to demographic and context-related factors, the person-related factor Health Locus of Control, coping behavior and drug use, and childhood trauma and victimizing life events.

In section 5.6 some puzzling questions regarding coping behavior and victimization will be addressed with the help of the qualitative data. In section 5.7 the question of causality is raised analyzing the quantitative data. We will test our multi-causal theoretical model by means of a path-analysis. Additional qualitative insight is presented in the following section. In the final section 5.9, the findings are summarized and discussed in the light of the expectations formulated in Chapter Three.

5.1: Well-being
Incidence of physical complaints and emotional problems
A high number of respondents in the 'coping and well-being'-sample report complaints and problems (see Appendix 5.1). Nervousness is reported by almost all: more than nine out of ten women indicate having been troubled by it. The percentage of women who report feelings of depression, aggression, distrust and guilt is also high, varying from 75% to 80%. Even those complaints which relatively few women mention having suffered, are still reported often. For example, relatively few women experience agoraphobic anxieties; one in four women however reveals having suffered from them. Inflammation of the bladder, stomach ache and gynecological complaints are also relatively rare and/or mild and still 38% of the women studied have been bothered by gynecological difficulties.

It appears that all but nine women (N=60) say that they have been troubled by one or more of the physical complaints. All women report having been troubled by one or more emotional and psychosocial problems. Mean scores for the various subscales are presented in Table 5.1.

In the 'protective behavior'-study, there is also substantial report of complaints and problems (see Appendix 5.2). Head ache and low energy are the most mentioned: respectively 88% and 86% of the women report suffering from these complaints at least sometimes. Other high prevalence rates (at least 70% suffering from them) are: feeling misunderstood, being easily irritated, painful muscles, feeling easily hurt, concentration difficulties, self blame, and not being able to shake nasty thoughts. By the latter almost one in ten women says she is bothered 'very often' and it yields the highest percentage in that response category. Complaints mentioned by relatively few women (less than 30%) are: the body feeling numbed, constantly having to ask others what to do, and thinking of ending it all. Less than 40% suffer from palpitations, a tingling feeling in the body, inflammation of the bladder, and feeling inferior to others. Table 5.2 presents mean scores for the subscales in the 'protective behavior'-study.

Table 5.1: Subscales for well-being in the 'coping and well-being'-study (N=60); range, mean (SD) and mean item score.

subscale	range	mean (SD)	mean item score
psychosomatic complaints	4-16	6.8 (2.8)	1.7
work related phys. compl.	4-16	6.6 (2.3)	1.65
depressive anxiousness	7-28	13.8 (4.0)	2.0
outw./inw. dir. aggression	4-16	7.9 (2.4)	2.0
social problems	4-16	7.9 (2.4)	2.0

Note. Scores are on a 4-point scale, ranging from 1 (hardly ever) to 4 (very often)

Table 5.2: Subscales for well-being in the 'protective behavior'-study (N=106); range, mean (SD) and mean item score

subscale	range	mean (SD)	mean item score
short SCL	32-160	59.4 (15.7)	1.86
social insecurity	15- 75	28.3 (9.2)	1.89
psychosomatic complaints	16- 80	30.8 (9.0)	1.92

Note. Scores are on a 5-point scale, ranging from 1 (hardly ever) to 5 (very often)

Mean item scores thus are somewhat lower in the second study, taking into account the fact that here they were on a five-point scale as compared to a four-point scale in the first study. The frequency of complaints and problems seems to be slightly less in the second sample. However, there is not as much difference in prevalence and severity between the two studies as might be expected from the fact that in the first study, prostitutes reported on 'the time since they work(ed)' while in the second one, they reported on 'recent times'. It seems that prostitutes as a group are acquainted with a wide variety of complaints and problematic feelings, no matter which period they refer to.

In addition, the severity of complaints and problems was inversely related to job satisfaction (see Appendix 4.10). Women who are bothered by many complaints are feeling less at ease in their work.

Comparisons with the general population

We compared the incidence of some of the complaints amongst the prostitutes in the 'coping and well-being'-study with the scores of the general population of women in the same age-categories on similar items in the health-survey (1983/-1984) of the Central Bureau of Statistics (N=4000) and with the incidence of some complaints found by Draijer (1988) for the whole research sample of women between 20 and 40 years of age (N=1049). Results of Chi^2-tests are shown in Table 5.3. On all the complaints investigated, prostitutes as a group show a significantly higher incidence.

Table 5.3: Comparisons of incidence of some complaints among (ex)prostitutes (N=60) and representative samples of women; percentage of prostitutes cq. women, Chi^2

complaint	(ex)pro's	representative sample	Chi^2
insomnia[1]	47.4	23.0	18.5***
backache[1]	43.1	31.5	3.8*
headache[1]	53.4	36.6	7.1**
stomachache[1]	35.0	12.8	25.6***
nervousness[1]	56.7	28.5	30.7***
anxiety[2]	29.9	17.5	5.9*
aggression[2]	37.3	15.4	18.5***
depression[2]	39.0	19.1	13.1***
mistrust[2]	55.1	21.9	50.9***
nightmares[2]	26.3	9.3	18.3***

[1] Comparison with the CBS (1983/1984) sample (N=4000); scores 'sometimes', 'often' and 'very often' in our sample are compared with answers 'yes' in the CBS-study; with nervousness only '(very) often'-answers are counted, because of 'often' being a part of the item-formulation in the CBS-study.
[2] Comparison with the Draijer (1988) sample (N=1049); scores 'often' and 'very often' in our study are being compared with scores 'high' and 'very high' in Draijer's study.
*p<.05; **p<.01; ***p<.001.

In the 'protective behavior'-study, the average score of 59.4 (SD=15.7) on the short SCL has been compared to the average score on the same instrument found in another Dutch study by Schoemaker (1991). She found an average score of 68.7 (SD=22.3) for a group of women who had been severely sexually abused in childhood (N=100) and an average score of 48.4 (SD= 12.6) for the control group of non-traumatized women (N=35) and men (N=25). The difference in the average scores of prostitutes and the traumatized group is not statistically signifi-cant, but prostitutes have significantly more complaints and problems than the control group of non-traumatized women and men ($t=2.21$, $p<.05$). Among the prostitutes, only 27.2% have lower scores on the SCL than the average score of Schoemakers' control group. The scores of 23% of prostitutes are higher than the average score of Schoemakers' traumatized group of women.

It seems justified to conclude that our studies provide evidence that, as a group, prostitutes suffer from more (and more severe) physical complaints and psychosocial problems than other groups of (non-professionally specified) women. Of course, these differences can be related to other factors besides prostitution work, to demographic aspects or to the severity of victimizing experiences, for example.

5.2: Demographic and context-related factors

Several statistical tests have been performed to relate the scores on the subscales for well-being to demographic characteristics and context-related factors.

In the 'coping and well-being'-study, no significant differences were found for age, for the number of years of having worked as a prostitute. Working in the big cities or elsewhere does not make a difference either. Differences in educa-tional level show up in regard to work-related physical complaints: those with the highest educational level have the fewest complaints and the middle group (those who finished secondary school or/and a secondary vocational training) score highest on work-related physical complaints ($F=4.6$, $p<.05$). Those who have or had financial responsibilities for others have more psychosomatic complaints ($t=3.3$, $p<.01$) and social problems ($t=2.1$, $p<.05$) than those who do or did not.

Ex-prostitutes report more psychosomatic complaints ($t=2.1$, $p<.05$) and de-pressive anxiousness ($t=2.0$, $p<.05$) than women who are still working. There are several explanations for this. Ex-prostitutes may be less hesitant to admit pro-blems connected to the work or to acknowledge and face the full load of working as a prostitute. Another possibility is that by reporting relatively many complaints for the time since they worked, they legitimize the fact that they have quit prostitution. However, they may also have left prostitution exactly because they suffered too much from it. The possibility that ex-prostitutes really suffer more complaints must also be taken into account. One ex-prostitute said: 'It all comes down to you once you're out'.

Women who have worked as madams report more psychosomatic complaints than the others ($t=2.0$, $p<.05$), which may be connected to their having had more responsibility. Those working in an 'unorganized' context (on the street, in wind-ows, at home) also appear to have more psychosomatic complaints than those working in an organized setting ($t=2.1$, $p<.05$). Considering group-means for women in the different working sites, it appears that women working in their own homes, as escorts or in a combination of places, have more social problems ($F=3.8$, $p<.05$). This may be explained by the higher amount of social isolation in these working sites as compared to brothels and clubs.

In the 'protective behavior'-study, where variables were operationalized differently and other aspects were studied, we see a slightly different picture. Younger women report more psychosomatic complaints ($\underline{r}$=-.31, $\underline{p}$<.001) as well as more social insecurity ($\underline{r}$=-3.1, $\underline{p}$<.001). No differences were found between women with different levels of education on the complaints and problems measured here, which did not, however, include work-related physical complaints.

Job satisfaction appears to vary more on the investigated variables than the other subscales for well-being. To explain; job satisfaction is lower among women who work 'unorganized' ($\underline{t}$=6.0, $\underline{p}$<.001), earn less per client ($\underline{r}$=.24, $\underline{p}$<.01), with shorter client-contacts ($\underline{r}$=.36, $\underline{p}$<.001), whose financial need is higher ($\underline{r}$=-.31, $\underline{p}$<.001) and who were born outside The Netherlands ($\underline{t}$=2.1, $\underline{p}$<.05). Migrant women also report more complaints relating to social insecurity ($\underline{t}$=2.8, $\underline{p}$<.01).

In reference to the work place (F=8.1, $\underline{p}$<.001), it appears that women working in the street have the lowest job satisfaction, but those working in windows also appear to feel rather ill at ease on the job. Both groups suffer much social insecurity (F=3.2, $\underline{p}$<.05) which may, again, be due to the stronger social isolation of street and window prostitutes as compared to women working in clubs and brothels. Prostitutes who serve more clients report more psychosomatic complaints ($\underline{r}$=.25, $\underline{p}$<.01), but, strikingly, no relationship was found between other aspects of working routine and earnings on the one hand, and the level of well-being on the other.

Overall, most of the results from the two investigations support and supplement, rather than contradict each other. However, a remarkable inconsistency comes up regarding the relation between well-being and age. In the 'coping and well-being'-study, no relation was found between well-being and age, whereas younger women in the 'protective behavior'-study suffered significantly more psychosomatic complaints and social insecurity. We are inclined to interpret this difference as a sampling and/or operationalization effect. It may be seen as a sampling effect because of the presence of ex-prostitutes in the 'coping and well-being'-sample. These women are slightly older and, for reasons discussed above report relatively many complaints. Older women who were particularly bothered by the work and may therefore have decided to quit prostitution are not represented in the second sample. The older women in that group are possibly those who feel relatively at ease in the job as compared to the older ex-prostitutes in the first sample. Another explanation may relate to the differences in operationalizations: while the first study asked for complaints that have ever been experienced since working in prostitution, the second study asked only for present problems. In the first study, complaints that once existed, but are no longer present may have been reported as well. This effect would be most likely for ex-prostitutes who had started working a long time ago and were older at the time of the interview.

It is thus assumed that for different reasons the older women in the first sample reported relatively many complaints as compared to the older women in the second sample. If we want to consider women *in* prostitution and their present well-being, the findings from the second study on the relation between being younger and having more problems will have to be adhered to. The higher prevalence of complaints among younger women can not be explained directly by their working in prostitution for a shorter period because no significant relation was found between the duration of having worked and the level of well-being. Further analyses will have to shed more light on the matter of age and well-being.

5.3: Health Locus of Control
Respondents in the 'protective behavior'-study agree most with the Health Locus of Control items that refer to internal control (see Appendix 5.3). Almost three-quarters (strongly) agree with statements such as: 'I got my health in my own hand' and 'taking care of myself well will prevent illness'. Their average item score (after recoding) on that factor is 3.5, while 5 is the maximum. Lowest average item score (2.6) is on external control over AIDS. All in all it seems that an internal Health Locus of Control is more strongly present among prostitutes than is an external one.

Contrary to expectation, hardly any relations are found between Health Locus of Control and well-being or job satisfaction. Only expert control appears to relate significantly (although modestly) to social insecurity (r=.29, p<.01). The relation between expert control over health with insecurity in the social sphere seems a plausible one: ascribing much value to the judgement and role of others is charac-teristic of both phenomena.

5.4: Coping behavior and drug use
We will report the frequencies of different coping behaviors and drug use among prostitutes and compare them to those of a control group. Then we address our findings on the associations between coping and well-being. Finally, the relation between coping behavior and context-related factors will be discussed.

Coping behavior of prostitutes, compared to others
Considering the relative frequency of our respondents' employment of different coping behaviors, the data from the 'coping and well-being'-study show that the use of problem directed coping responses, such as 'looking at a problem from all sides' or 'thinking of different possibilities to solve a problem' is reported the most (see Appendices 5.4 and 5.5). However, palliative reactions, such as 'one way or another trying to feel better' and 'seeking diversion' and reassuring thoughts such as 'after rain comes sunshine' and 'others have much more difficult times' are also used by many. On the other hand, almost half of the respondents report hardly or never to 'feel incapable of doing something', and 'putting up with the course of things', 'asking for help', and 'being totally taken over by problems' are not very frequently mentioned as reactions either. A combination of problem solving and palliative reactions seems to be the favorite.

In the 'protective behavior'-study, problem solving reactions, such as 'thinking of different possibilities to solve a problem', 'purposeful action' and 'going through things' are also found to be used most often (see Appendices 5.6 and

5.7). Reactions reported least (more than 60% say they never experience them),
are some dissociative experiences, such as 'the feeling that I've lost contact with
reality' and 'the feeling as if I'm not in my own body' and some depressed ones,
such as 'being totally taken up by a problem'. Still, the mean item score on the
dissociative items is remarkably high (2.5 on a 5-point scale). Even if dissociation
seems to be a very extreme coping reaction, it is used relatively often by
prostitutes.

However, dissociation does not seem to exclude the use of problem directed
responses. As mentioned in the previous chapter, surprisingly, no negative relation
was found between problem directed and emotion directed coping responses (see
Appendices 4.8 and 4.14). It would seem that different reactions are used with
different sorts of stressful situations or events, and that a general 'coping-style' in
which one form of coping clearly and always dominates the other, does not exist.

Equally contrary to expectations, hardly any connection was found between
drug and alcohol use and emotion directed coping behavior (see Appendices 5.8,
4.8 and 4.14). In the 'protective behavior'-study about one quarter of the
prostitutes reported using hard-drugs during work (26%) and less than half (44%)
reported using alcohol while at work, but only a modest association was found
between drug abuse and denial, and none of the other subscales correlated
significantly.

It may be concluded that even though relatively high prevalence rates were
found for both problem and emotion directed coping behavior and for drug and
alcohol use these three forms of coping hardly appear to relate to each other.

Comparing the 'coping and well-being'-data on coping behavior with those
obtained from a control group of female college-students and university-
employees (N=37), no significant differences were found on the frequency of problem solving, but the women in the control group employed fewer emotion
directed responses. They scored lower on the depressive-palliative pattern (t=2.47,
p<.05) and lower on avoidance (t=2.98, p<.01). They also sought more social
support (t=4.13, p<.001). The fact that no difference in the frequency of problem
solving was found is all the more remarkable since the control sample consisted
largely of higher educated women, who are assumed to be more likely to use
problem solving strategies (see Chapter Three). However, prostitutes do rely on
manipulation of emotions more often and do not seek social support as much as
others.

Coping and well-being
As expected, a relation appears to exist between coping and well-being. The
strongest relations found in the 'coping and well-being'-study (see Table 5.4) are
those between the depressed/palliative pattern of coping and emotional and
psychosocial problems. Furthermore, psychosomatic complaints as well as out-
ward/inward directed aggression are related to the use of alcohol. Work-related

physical complaints and outward/inward directed aggression are related to the use of tranquilizers.

Table 5.4: Coping behavior and drug use related to well-being in the 'coping and well-being'-study (N=60); Pearson's r

	well-being subscales				
coping subscales	psychosom. complaints	work rel. physical	depressive anxiousness	outw/inw aggression	social problems
problem solving	.12	-.33	-.11	-.01	.12
depressed/palliative pattern	.19	.21	.51**	.56**	.50**
avoiding	.18	.07	.16	.25	.24
seeking support	-.24	.19	-.05	-.10	-.16
use of alcohol	.41*	.12	.28	.33*	.10
use of drugs	.09	.14	.25	.22	.21
use of tranquilizers	.30	.43**	.25	.50**	.24

Note. Pairwise deletion of missing values; minimum pairwise N of cases is 27.
*p<.01; **p<.001

Table 5.5: Coping behavior and drug use related to well-being and job satisfaction in the 'protective behavior'-study (N=127); Pearson's r

	well-being subscales		
coping subscales	social insecurity	psychosomatic complaints	job satisfaction
dissociation	.66**	.62**	-.50**
problem solving	-.05	.07	.09
seeking support	.36**	.35**	-.29*
denial	.37**	.29**	-.31*
use of alcohol	.00	-.04	.33**
use of drugs	.20	.11	-.31**

Note. Pairwise deletion of missing values; minimum pairwise N of cases is 86.
*p<.01; **p<.001

In the 'protective behavior'-study correlations between the emotion directed coping responses (dissociation and denial) and complaints and problems are even more convincing (see Table 5.5). The relations between lower levels of well-being and job satisfaction on the one hand and dissociation on the other are particularly strong. It is remarkable, that seeking support, a form of coping behavior often associated with problem solving, is related to well-being and job satisfaction in much the same way as the emotion directed responses are. That problem solving itself is not related to any of the well-being subscales is also remarkable. Alcohol and drug abuse are both, although in a different direction, related to job satisfaction. Remarkably, again, drug abuse is not directly associated with complaints and problems.

Context-related factors and coping
If we investigate how demographic aspects and context-related variables are associated with the coping behavior of prostitutes, we find fewer significant correlations than expected. In the 'coping and well-being'-study, only a slightly more frequent employment of the depressed/palliative pattern is found for employees as compared to madams (t=2.4, p<.05), for women working in the big cities as compared to the others (t=2.3, p<.05) and for women working as escorts or in a combination of places (F=2.8, p<.05).

In the 'protective behavior'-study, a slightly more frequent employment of problem solving behavior is found for women working in an organized setting as compared to those working 'unorganized' (t=2.1, p<.05), for women who work more hours per week (r=.25, p<.05), and for women at the middle educational level (F=4.0, p<.05). Problem solving is done least by the lower educated women. Denial appears to be stronger when financial need is higher (r=.27, p<.05) and/or one is not born in The Netherlands (t=2.0, p<.05).

Strong relations, however, are found between the use of dissociation and being younger (r=-.46, p<.001) and having worked in prostitution for a shorter period (r=-.25, p<.01). Undoubtedly, taking the strong relation between coping and well-being into account, there is a connection here with the higher prevalence of complaints and problems among younger women. It is interesting that although no relation was found between the level of well-being and the period having worked in prostitution, having worked for a shorter period is now found to be related to more dissociation. It is possible that the connection between working shorter and coping 'less healthily' explains in part the higher incidence of complaints and problems among younger women. This line of thinking would imply a causal relation between coping and well-being, in the sense that (unhealthy) coping causes problems, more than the other way around. We will come back to this matter.

Our data give evidence that drug and alcohol use differ with different demographic and context-related aspects, although in the 'coping and well-being'-study only ex-prostitutes were found to use somewhat more tranquilizers than women who were still working (t=2.1, p<.05) (which may be connected to their reporting more complaints and problems). Women with a middle educational level were found to use more alcohol than those with a low or high level (F=3.6, p<.05). This is a finding that is hard to interpret.

However, in the 'protective behavior'-study, relatively strong differences are found for alcohol and drug use: women who earn more per client (r=.21, p<.05), have fewer clients (r=-.25, p<.05), and who work in an organized setting (t=6.1, p<.001) use more alcohol, while women who work 'unorganized' use more drugs (t=3.9, p<.001). In part, this may not have to do as much with different ways of coping as with the work setting itself: the use of alcohol is a much more common phenomenon (and often part of the work) in the organized setting. In clubs and brothels the work routine is more relaxed and earnings are higher per client than on the street and in the windows. The use of drugs, particularly heroin, is forbidden in many clubs and brothels. Heroin use may drive women into the 'unorganized' forms of working, where routines are less relaxed and earnings per client are lower.

All in all, the most meaningful context-related factors in coping behavior appear to be age and the period having worked: the younger the woman and the shorter the time in prostitution, the more dissociation is used as a coping behavior. Drug and alcohol use seem to be predominantly related to work setting.

One final observation regarding coping behavior concerns the relation with Health Locus of Control. The expected association between internal HLoC and problem solving coping responses is not supported by the data, nor is its opposite; an external locus of control would be associated with emotion-directed strategies. None of the correlations between the coping subscales and drug use on the one hand, and the subscales for Health Locus of Control on the other hand, were found to be statistically significant. Coping behavior of prostitutes does not seem to be related to opinions of being either internally or externally controlled in health matters.

5.5: Childhood trauma and victimizing life-events

Again, we will first report the prevalence and severity of trauma and victimization among prostitutes, compared to others. Then we address the relations with well-being and coping. Finally, the relations with context-related factors will be discussed.

Prevalence of victimization among prostitutes, compared to others

The reported prevalence and severity of experiences with violence are high in the 'coping and well-being'-study (see Appendices 5.9 and 5.10). More than one in four women have left home before age 12, and more than four out of ten women have been either the victim of child physical abuse or of child sexual abuse or both. Again more than four out of ten women have been forced into prostitution and/or have been sexually abused by an acquaintance. More than half of the respondents have been physically abused by an acquaintance, which often accompanied being forced into prostitution. Physical and sexual violence by strangers or customers is experienced by six and four out of ten women respectively, while seven out of ten women have been verbally threatened. One quarter of the subjects have experienced sexual advances by helping agents, such as medical examiners or social workers.

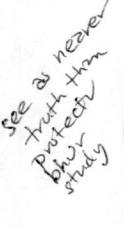

Only two women had experienced none of the 17 forms of violence that were put forward. Only 36% of the respondents had not experienced any burdening circumstances or violence in their childhood. Only 32% had not experienced any force and violence by a partner. Only 20% reported not having experienced any violence by strangers or at work. The mean item-score on this latter subscale is somewhat higher than on the other ones.

In the 'protective behavior'-study, the prevalence of victimizing experiences is lower (see Appendices 5.11 and 5.12). For example, 15% reported to have been abused sexually in childhood and almost three out of ten women reported having been forced into prostitution. The same figure applies to physical and sexual abuse in the private sphere, and a slightly higher number suffered violence on the job. Still, less than a quarter (23%) reported having experienced no violence at all. If we consider this figure as revealing only the top of the iceberg as the result of limited questioning (see Chapter Four), it is in fact again dramatic. The same applies if we consider only those respondents for whom no data on violence are missing (N=92). More than half (57%) reported violence on the job. More than half (55%) reported violence in the private sphere, either in their youth's or in their adult lives or both. 48% experienced one of those, and 8% were violated in their private lives in youth as well as in adulthood.

If we compare these data on the prevalence of victimizing events with those of Draijer's (1988, 1990) study of 'sexual abuse of girls by relatives' among a repre

Table 5.6: Prevalence of childhood sexual abuse by an acquaintance and physical violence by a partner among prostitutes, compared with prevalence in representative samples of women; percentage, Chi^2

	coping and well-being-study	representative sample	Chi^2
sexual abuse by an acquaintance < age 16	42.9	15.6	30.7**
physical violence ever by a partner	51.7	21.0	17.9**
repeated physical violence by a partner	41.4	11.4	44.3**
	protective beha-vior-study	representative sample	Chi^2
sexual abuse by an acquaintance < age 16	15.2	15.6	
multiple sexual abuse by an acq.< age 16	15.2	7.3	7.9*
physical violence ever by a partner	28.7	21.0	3.6
repeated physical violence by a partner	22.6	11.4	13.0**

Note. Representative samples are Draijer's (1988) in the case of childhood violence and Römkens' (1989) in the case of violence by a private partner.
*p<.01; **p<.001

sentative sample of Dutch women between ages 20 and 40 (N=1049), and to those of Römkens' (1989) study of 'violence against women in heterosexual relationships' among a representative sample of Dutch women (N=1036) between ages 20 and 60, we find what is shown in Table 5.6.

The prevalence rates of childhood sexual abuse by acquaintances and physical violence by partners in the 'coping and well-being'-study are all higher than among the representative samples. The comparison with the prevalence in the 'protective behavior'-study do not turn out to be statistically significant when the prevalence of abuse or violence is compared with the representative samples. However, all of the cases of child sexual abuse which were reported by our respondents were multiple and long lasting abuse. The comparison of the prevalence rates with those in Draijer's representative sample concerning experiences of being abused more than 5 times does turn out to be statistically significant. Repeated physical abuse by partners is also experienced significantly more often among prostitutes in the second sample.

In reference to the actual prevalence of childhood sexual abuse and physical violence by partners, we estimate the figures found in the 'coping and well-being'-study are nearer 'the truth' than those in the 'protective behavior'-study since the questioning in the former study was more adequate (see Chapter Four). These considerations do not detract from the conclusion: even on the basis of data from the second sample only, prostitutes compared to other women, have been the victims of prolonged childhood sexual abuse and repeated physical violence by partners more often. Their lower levels of well-being may be, at least partly, attributed to their more severe experiences of abuse and violence.

Trauma, victimization and well-being
Following our expectations, there is a strong relation found between victimization and well-being in both studies. In the 'coping and well-being'-study, both depressive anxiousness and outward/inward directed aggression are related to all three subscales for victimization (see Table 5.7).

Table 5.7: Victimization related to well-being in the 'coping and well-being'-study (N=60); Pearson's r

victimization subscales	well-being subscales				
	psychosom. complaints	work rel. physical	depressive anxiousness	outw/inw aggression	social problems
youth violence	.21	.49**	.37*	.50*	.09
violence by a private partner	.49*	.28	.59**	.36*	.04
violence by strangers/at work	.27	.35*	.55**	.64**	.19

Note. Pairwise deletion of missing values; minimum pairwise N of cases is 33.
*p<.01; **p<.001

Social problems, on the other hand, do not correlate significantly with any of the victimization subscales, which is remarkable since guilt and shame were comprised in this measure and are often associated with experienced violence. Possibly, in the case of prostitutes, feelings of guilt and shame are relatively strongly connected to the work itself, and less to specific victimizing life-events. Psychosomatic complaints, in addition, seem to be related to violence by a private partner, but surprisingly, not to violence experienced in youth or at work. Work-related physical complaints, despite their practical nature, appear to be related to both youth violence and violence at work.

In the 'protective behavior'-study, relations between lower levels of well-being and job satisfaction on the one hand and trauma and victimization or the other, are indeed almost all significant (see Table 5.8). Only the one between violence in the private sphere and social insecurity does not reach statistical significance.

Table 5.8: Victimization related to well-being and job satisfaction in the 'protective behavior'-study (N=127); Pearson's r

	well-being subscales		
victimization subscales	social insecurity	psychosomatic complaints	job satisfaction
childhood trauma	.26*	.43**	-.25*
violence in the private sphere	.18	.25*	-.29*
violence on the job	.39**	.26*	-.39**

Note. Pairwise deletion of missing values; minimum pairwise N of cases is 85.
*p<.01; **p<.001

In this study, according to expectations, psychosomatic complaints appear to be related to all subscales for victimization, and most strongly to childhood trauma. Lower levels of job satisfaction also appear to be related to all subscales for experienced violence, and not surprisingly, relatively stronger to violence on the job. Social insecurity is, aside from being related to childhood trauma, particularly strongly related to violence on the job. If one considers that various anxieties, fears, and tensions are part of the operationalization of social insecurity, this does not come as a surprise.

Again only a few associations are found with Health Locus of Control. However, the relation between expert control and violence on the job is modestly significant (r=.24, p<.01), indicating that the experience of being violated might negatively affect one's sense of control. An actual lack of control in contacts with clients may have been generalized to a perceived lack of control over health and well-being.

Trauma, victimization and coping

Overall, the relations between victimization and coping behavior are not as strong as we expected (see Appendices 5.13 and 5.14). In the 'coping and well-being'-study, alcohol use and drug use relate to violence by a private partner and violence at work, but none of the other subscales for coping associate substantially with those for victimization.

Stronger correlations are found in the 'protective behavior'-study. The use of dissociation relates significantly to both childhood violence and violence on the job, but not to violence in the private sphere. Denial relates to all three subscales for victimization. The link between victimizing life-events and emotion directed coping behavior appears to be supported by these findings. In addition, prostitutes' drug use is found to be related to violence in the private sphere and, most strongly to violence on the job. Problem solving and seeking support do not seem to be affected by experiences with violence.

Context-related factors and victimization

Considering the relationship of demographic and context-related factors to the different sorts of victimization, childhood violence does not seem to make a difference among prostitutes in neither of the studies. The exception was, women who had ever been a madam reported it more than employees ($t=2.7$, $p<.01$). This may be connected to the fact that madams also report more psychosomatic complaints than employees.

There is more violence in the private sphere reported by ex-prostitutes ($t=2.7$, $p<.05$), which apart from other reasons mentioned above may also be an explanation for them reporting more psychosomatic complaints and depressive anxiety. Moreover, in both studies, women with a high financial need/financial responsibility and those who work 'unorganized', as opposed to those who work in an organized setting, report having experienced more partner violence ($t=4.3$, $p<.001$; $r=.23$. $p<.01$ and $t=3.4$, $p<.01$; $t=2.1$, $p<.05$, respectively). Only in the 'coping and well-being'-study is a connection found between educational levels and violence by partners. It is experienced most by women at the lowest educational level and least by those with the highest educations ($F=4.3$, $p<.05$).

In both studies violence on the job is experienced most by those working 'unorganized' ($t=2.7$, $p<.01$; $t=3.1$, $p<.01$). When comparing group means we found that women working the street are the worst off ($F=11.5$, $p<.001$). However, the more specific characteristics of working conditions and routine do not seem to make a difference. In the first sample, violence on the job is experienced more the longer one works ($r=.42$, $p<.001$), but this finding is not replicated in the second sample. However, in the latter sample there is additional evidence that a high financial need and not having been born in The Netherlands relate to higher levels of violence experienced at work ($r=.39$, $p<.001$ and $t=2.7$, $p<.01$, respectively).

5.6: Some puzzling matters

The findings reported above leave us with some pressing questions. So far, the role of problem-directed coping behavior remains somewhat unclear. These forms of coping do not associate, as was expected, with higher levels of well-being, nor with lower levels of victimization, nor with less frequent use of emotion-directed coping behavior. The question then remains, when and how are problem-directed responses used, which after all was found to be done frequently.

The relation between victimization and coping is also somewhat puzzling. It was theoretically postulated that traumatic victimization is strongly related to internal coping strategies, but in the 'coping and well-being'-study, no such relations were found. In the 'protective behavior'-study, relations were found between childhood experiences and violence on the job on one hand, and dissociation and denial on the other. However, again relations between violence in the private sphere and internal coping strategies were weak. A possible explanation is that the connections are not rectilinear: relatively mild forms of violence may elicit anger and problem-directed responses, while emotion-directed responses become more likely when violence is more severe and long lasting. Moreover and in connection to this, the process of coping with victimization most certainly involves changes over time which can not be measured in the cross-sectional quantitative data as presented above. The qualitative material will be investigated for confirmation of these suppositions and for further exploration of the use of problem-directed coping responses.

Problem-directed coping responses: when are they used?

In order to find out when and where prostitutes use problem-directed coping responses, all sixty respondents in the 'coping and well-being'-study have been categorized according to their predominant ways of coping in four different sorts of problem areas. These are physical complaints, psychosocial and emotional problems, victimizing experiences, and business affairs. The different ways of coping are: predominantly problem-directed, predominantly emotion-directed, using both equally at the same time, or both but with a clear breaking point between the two. This represents a drastic change from predominantly emotion-directed to predominantly problem-directed behavior.

Reported behaviors such as thinking problems over, going to a General Practitioner (GP) or social worker, talking about a problem, raising difficulties with a boss, colleague or official agency, and trying to solve it one way or another have been categorized as problem-directed. Responses categorized as emotion-directed vary from conscious, partial redefinition of problems and emotions to manifestations of preconscious suppression or dissociation of negative feelings. Table 5.9 gives an overview of the division thus obtained.

In the areas of emotional problems and victimizing events, emotion-focussed responses dominate over problem-directed reactions, while in the area of business affairs (money, housing, other work), problem-directed reactions prevail. When dealing with physical complaints both approaches seem to be equally present.

Although problem-directed coping responses hardly seem to come into play in the dynamics that are controlled by the vicious circle of trauma, internal strategies, and emotional and psychosomatic problems, they may still fully be employed in reaction to physical complaints and business affairs. Moreover, in the areas of emotional problems and victimizing events, 17% and 15% of the respondents respectively, have at one point, clearly changed their coping behavior from predominantly emotion-directed to predominantly problem-directed.

Table 5.9: Predominant ways of coping in four problem areas in the 'coping and well-being'-study (N=60); percentage of women

	ways of coping			
problem area	predominantly problem-directed	predominantly emotion-directed	equally both	breaking point
physical complaints	28	35	37	-
emotional problems	3	45	35	17
victimizing events	8	45	32	15
business-like affairs	43	20	37	-

Some problem-directed reactions to physical complaints mentioned by the respondents are trying to control smoking and drinking and eating habits (such as keeping count of what has been consumed), exercising, taking saunas, having check-ups on STD's, getting physical therapy, and going to the doctor with complaints. A general 'body culture' (women taking care of their bodies) seems to be quite common among prostitutes. After all, 'their bodies are their business'.

More specific health complaints such as head aches and back aches, even if they are very well acknowledged, may not always be brought to the GP. Distortions and minimalizations are found to be quite common. One important rationalization brought forward by many respondents is 'I know what it is, it's only stress'. An important additional reason for not mentioning certain physical symptoms to a GP is the fact that only seven out of 59 women have ever told their doctors about their involvement in prostitution. When they have not, women often see it as useless to bring up a complaint which they perceive as work-connected. This seems to be even more true for emotional problems. This is based on the wide-spread belief that physical symptoms may always be treated, even if their context and background is unknown to the attending physician.

The problem-directed behavior mentioned in reference to business affairs and practical matters was: looking for another job and getting in touch with employment offices (as 29% of the women have done), raising money-question with employers, organizing child-care, getting benefits by contacting departments of social services, going to housing corporations and information services, or

organizing legal aid in cases of child guardianship or divorce. One woman says:
'Some things you don't do anything about because you're emotionally involved,
but as far as other things are concerned, I just as easily get at them. I've got a
subscription on lawyers.' All in all, as table 5.9 shows, practical, business problems are confronted most by problem-directed coping behavior.

An important reason that business problems are relatively often confronted
with concrete problem solving might be that they are considered more superable
than emotional problems. Practical problems in the area of earnings, child care,
etc., are often relatively isolated and calculable, and clearly circumscribed.
Emotional problems on the other hand, are often perceived as being part of a big
insuperable bundling of problematic conditions which can not be changed. This
would therefore call for emotion manipulation rather than trying to manipulate the
situation. In such a situation, minimalizing and softening considerations, in
combination with makeshift and palliative measures are relatively likely: 'When I
feel depressed, I try to put it away as fast as possible. When I feel depressed, it's
just because I see in what kind of a situation I've manoeuvred myself and I don't
know how to get out of it. But life goes on. There's always another day. It'll all
go down again. And then things will be better. I won't let it get to me. I just put
it aside.'

It must be noted that the employment of emotion-directed coping responses is
associated with an enormous buoyancy and stamina in the short run. Women
succeed keeping up morale by not letting themselves be overwhelmed by negative
emotions: 'I kept on putting things away, because I kept on believing in my pride.
That's a thing that's kept me on my feet for so long'. In this way, women
maintain confidence in themselves and in the future and often because of this,
they find the strength to undertake steps towards recovery from trauma or structural changes for the better. It has been shown that emotion-directed behavior
does not necessarily undermine problem-focussed action in all areas. Manipulation
of emotions such as minimalization, rationalization and downward social comparison, certainly seems effective considering the way in which prostitutes stand their
ground in often very burdening circumstances. The subjective reality that is being
created is made manageable. Here Lazarus' (1985) statements applies: 'mental
health requires some self-deception'. While 'some self-deception' may be beneficial in the short run and be exemplary for an enormous emotional strength, strict
denial and dissociation are more likely as problems become more severe and last
longer. This is associated with lower levels of well-being in the long run.

Nevertheless, threats to physical health and business affairs particularly seem to
be areas in which problem-directed strategies are relatively likely to be reported.
It must however be noted here that our analysis did not cover the whole array of
possible problems or stressors. It is probable that problem-directed behavior is
also employed in response to other problematic situations. The interaction with
clients may be one of these areas. The way women 'cope' with clients will be
further examined in Chapter Seven.

Victimization and coping behavior: changes over time
As Table 5.9 shows, the employment of emotion manipulation and distancing clearly prevailed in reference to victimizing experiences and (connected) emotional problems. More than half (32) of all respondents only referred to reactions like 'burying one's head in the sand', 'not giving in to it', or 'putting it away' in this context. The connection between victimizing experiences and emotion-directed coping seems very strongly present in the qualitative material. Childhood trauma is often explicitly mentioned as an experience that still needs constant and ongoing 'burying efforts': 'These feelings you just banish, but they keep on nagging at you. Sometimes you see things on TV or outside, like a father hand in hand with his daughter, and something comes up. Or you read something in the newspaper. But these things I always omit. I never want to talk about them, about these things in the newspaper. These are things I have to suppress myself'.

For many women, forms of distancing and emotion manipulation used to react to problems in later life can also be traced back to childhood when these internal strategies were used in reaction to violence and abuse. This woman refers to 'going over the same ground': 'When I have problems I just put them away. It's the same thing I had to do with my father when I was a child, so that's a thing you have learned through the years and it's what I still do, otherwise it hurts too much'. These and other statements give evidence that internal strategies once learned in childhood may be transferred into adulthood and other areas. They support the finding that childhood trauma and dissociation as a coping behavior are statistically related. Being (sexually) traumatized in childhood can be a life-long sentence which also influences coping behavior. Other women refer to the fact that problematic experiences had been piling up through the years and emotion manipulation was constantly necessary to arm against both 'old' and 'new' stressful emotions, fears and confusions: 'I've had times that I thought of going and talk to someone but I never did. Because of the well known lid of the cesspool. I can not use a nervous breakdown at this moment.' Another woman said: 'I don't know if I can tread water long enough when that bucket gets dumped.' Clearly, the overwhelming nature of childhood trauma and the related severity of emotional problems in adult life, make internal survival strategies structurally more likely.

Statements regarding the generalization of coping behavior which was learned in childhood were strikingly absent in reference to victimization in adult life. Moreover in this context, there is evidence that patterns of coping can change dramatically over time. Nineteen women in this study report a drastic change in coping behavior from predominantly emotion-focussed, suppressing or denying, to expressing and confronting behavior. This change concerned either emotional problems in general or a specific victimizing situation. This was usually an abusive relationship with a partner. In some cases a change in circumstances made way for the change in coping behavior such as the death of a pimp-partner, getting out of prostitution, getting pregnant, or finding a new lover. One woman says: 'It's only with this man that I have learned how to cry. It's very difficult when you haven't done it for such a long time. Laughing doesn't cost anything, but a tear is the most valuable thing'. In other cases, women ended up in a crisis that eventually meant a turning point in their lives: 'I was sent to this shelter by people from the hospital I was at because I just did not know anymore what I did, I was drawn back, I did not eat anymore. I did not dare to go into the street anymore. I was totally worn out. And that's where things started to change'. For this woman the situation eventually turned to getting away from her abusive pimp. Other women in due time broke up with their abusive partners by getting a knife, coming to a shelter, or bringing in the justice system.

Inspiring stuff...

All the women in our sample, who in the past had been in an abusive relationship with a partner, were no longer in that relationship at the time of the interview. Moreover, their resigned, emotion-directed way of coping with their former situations had been changed into considering such a situation untenable by definition and making sure that they would never end up in a situation like that again. Of the 18 women in the 'coping and well-being'-study who had been in abusive relationships involving force into prostitution, eleven later returned back to work, elated with their renewed control and self-determination in 'working for themselves'. Breaking up with an abusive partner changes a woman's situation drastically and opens up new ways of dealing with problematic aspects and events. Apparently while an internal coping pattern developed as a consequence of childhood trauma seems able to last and generalize in adult life, internal coping behavior developed as a consequence of traumatization in adulthood does not necessarily generalize once one has gotten out of an abusive relationship. It seems as if the experience of 'getting out' had given these women an all the more fighting spirit. This may indeed be an explanation for why the quantitative data did not show significant relations between violence experienced in the private sphere and emotion-directed coping behavior[1].

However, it seems from the statements of several respondents who were drug-dependent (treated here as a coping behavior), that their starting with drugs was connected to force and violence by a male partner. These partners often were themselves addicted and forced the women to earn money in prostitution to pay for their habits. The women eventually became addicted themselves and got caught in the vicious circle of working in prostitution to support their own habits and using drugs to be able to work at all. This relation between violence in the private sphere and drug use was found in the quantitative data as well as in the qualitative material. Even if the relation between violence in the private sphere and coping behavior at the cognitive level was not found to be strong for reasons outlined above, drug use as a form of coping behavior appeared to be related to force and abuse by a private partner for many of the drug-addicted women. A

---

[1] Of course, women who have not yet succeeded in getting out of an abusive partner relationship might be much more inclined to manipulate their emotions instead of their situations. Such women were not present in our sample, though.

number of these women clearly developed their drug dependency in order to cope with violence in the private sphere. In addition, their drug dependency makes it more likely that they work on the streets rather than in more protected work settings. This again has consequences for their experiencing violence on the job. Drug use was indeed found to relate both to private violence and violence on the job and may be assumed a mediating variable between the two forms of violence.

Violence on the job was also found to relate to the other emotion-directed forms of coping, at least in the 'protective behavior'-study. The qualitative material gives evidence that the suppression and dissociation of problematic emotions in relation to the work is something that one has learned through time: 'I don't have heavy emotions anymore. I do think it a bit scary, but no. At first I used to cry my brains out. But then that was over. I've just run out of tears.' Emotion manipulation may be a necessary coping strategy as long as one works, as well as a strategy that then generalizes to other problem areas. On the other hand, it was found that dissociative experiences become less frequently mentioned the longer one works in prostitution. Apparently, the longer a women works the less problematic she finds the work and the less call she feels to manipulate the emotions connected to it. In any case, once out of the work, emotion-directed coping may be less likely. The presence of ex-prostitutes in the sample may thus be an explanation for the absence of a statistical relation between emotion-directed coping and violence at work in the 'coping and well-being'-study.

With this exploration of the relation between different forms of victimization and different forms of emotion-directed coping behavior, we have already touched upon causal interpretations of the data. In the following section, causality will be elaborated upon on the basis of a further analysis of the quantitative data.

5.7: The question of causality: path analysis

So far, it has been found that prostitutes in comparison to other women suffer relatively many complaints and problems, have been victimized relatively often, and relatively often employ emotion directed coping behaviors. Significant relations have been established between the subscale scores for psychosocial problems and psychosomatic complaints and emotion directed coping behavior, such as dissociation and denial; between all subscales for well-being and different forms of violence; and between childhood trauma, violence on the job, and, to a lesser extent, violence in the private sphere on the one hand and emotion directed coping behavior on the other. However, probably for reasons outlined above, the latter were not found to be statistically significant in the 'coping and well-being'-study. Few relations were found between well-being and the person-related factor Health Locus of Control, but expert Health Locus of Control was found to be related to social insecurity. The demographic and context-related factors found to relate to well-being were age (at least for the sample of prostitutes wherein they were all still working), financial need, migration and stressful working conditions.

Having established these relations at a correlational level does not give any insight into causality yet. However, in reference to causality, the proposed

theoretical model holds certain clear assumptions and has some apparent chronological implications. Rereading our theoretical model (see Figure 3.1) more or less
from left to right, and refining it with the evidence collected so far, the following
picture regarding causality and chronology emerges.

p 42

Childhood trauma 'comes first'. Violence in adulthood in the private sphere,
'coming second', is assumed to be dependent on childhood trauma, as well as on
the context- and person-related factors that have been found relevant but do not
by definition relate to prostitution work (age, migration, expert Health Locus of
Control). Next, drug use is assumed to be chronologically positioned in between
violence in the private sphere and work-related aspects, because the analyses at
this point shows that drug use is often a connecting factor between violence by a
partner and working in prostitution. Moreover, it was found that two thirds of the
drug using women, particularly those who use heroin, started using drugs before
they entered prostitution. Drug use is assumed to be a coping behavior in reaction
to violence by a private partner and thus to be causally dependent on it. Then,
violence on the job is assumed to be dependent on all the aspects previously
mentioned as well as on the work-related contextual factors financial need and
stressful working conditions. Emotion-directed coping behavior (dissociation and
denial) is positioned next in terms of causality and assumed to be 'closest' to
well-being. Ultimately, social insecurity, psychosomatic complaints and job
satisfaction are assumed to be dependent on all the aspects mentioned, including
coping behavior.

In order to see to what extent these assumptions regarding chronology and
causality are supported by the data and to what extent the different factors in our
theoretical model ultimately account for variations in well-being among prostitutes, a path-analysis has been performed. From that it can be seen which factor(s)
ultimately best settle the matter of the well-being of prostitutes. The path-analysis
has been performed on the 'protective behavior'-data, because more variables have
been measured in that study and because the sample is substantially larger. All
variables relating significantly to either the subscales for well-being, or to other
factors in the theoretical model have gradually been brought into the subsequent
equations according to the chronological and causal assumptions.

The first regression analysis on violence in the private sphere thus was
performed with the independent variables age, migration, expert Health Locus of
Control, and childhood trauma. In the next analysis on drug use, violence in the
private sphere was added. In the next step, for the regression equation on violence
on the job, drug use, financial need and working conditions[2] were linked. Finally

---

[2] A single measure for stressful working conditions has been computed, in which high,
middle and low scores on the number of clients, working routine (duration of client
contact), earnings per client, and working independently or in an organized context were
taken into account. The number of working hours has been left out here, because few
significant relations were found with that variable.

in the regression analyses on social insecurity, psychosomatic complaints and job satisfaction, we also took violence on the job and emotion-directed coping behavior[3] into account. The latter was taken into account last not only because of the causal assumptions, but also since the scores for coping behavior, like those for well-being, referred to the current situation. Results of this path-analysis[4] are shown in Table 5.10.

Table 5.10: Effects of independent variables on dependent variables in the 'protective behavior'-study (N=127); path analysis, multiple regression coefficient (beta)

independent variables	dependent variables						
	violence pr. sphere	drug use	violence on the job	dissociation /denial	social insecurity	psychosomatic complaints	job satisfaction
age				-.33**			
migration		.19*					
expert HLoC					.17**		
childhood trauma	.24**			.25**		.19**	
violence private sphere		.28**					
drug use			.48**				
financial need							
working conditions							-.34**
violence on the job				.23**			-.16*
dissociation/denial					.65**	.55**	-.34**
Adjusted R2	.05	.07	.28	.27	.47	.40	.32

Note. Method step; missing values mean substituted.
*p<.05; **p<.01.

[3] For pragmatic purposes we combined the scores on dissociation and denial into one score. This did not make much difference in the regression equations. When the two were brought into the equations separately, explained variances for the dependent variables were the same, but denial alone did not contribute significantly to the explanation of psychosomatic complaints. In the path-analysis, 25% of the variance was explained by dissociation alone, compared to 27% combining dissociation and denial. Of denial alone, 14% was explained by childhood violence and financial need.

[4] Regressions were performed step-wise and with mean substitution of the missing values because big differences in N of cases with pairwise deletion could have caused invalid findings. As regards contents, both procedures did not differ much, but when pairwise deletion was used, adjusted R^2's were somewhat higher.

The variance explained for the well-being subscales is high in all three cases. The independent, direct effects of expert Health Locus of Control and dissociation/denial together explain 47% of the variance in social insecurity. Childhood trauma and dissociation/denial both have an independent, direct effect on psychosomatic complaints: together they explain 40% of the variance. In the case of job satisfaction, the crucial direct effects spring from stressful working conditions, violence on the job, and, again, dissociation/denial: together they explain 32% of the variance. The independent and direct effects of all variables on other variables in the path-analysis as they were listed in Table 5.10 are graphically presented in Figure 5.1, which is a refined version of our theoretical model (see Figure 3.1).

Figure 5.1: Results of path-analysis: direct and indirect effects on the dependent well-being subscales in the 'protective behavior'-study (N=127); multiple regression coefficient (beta)

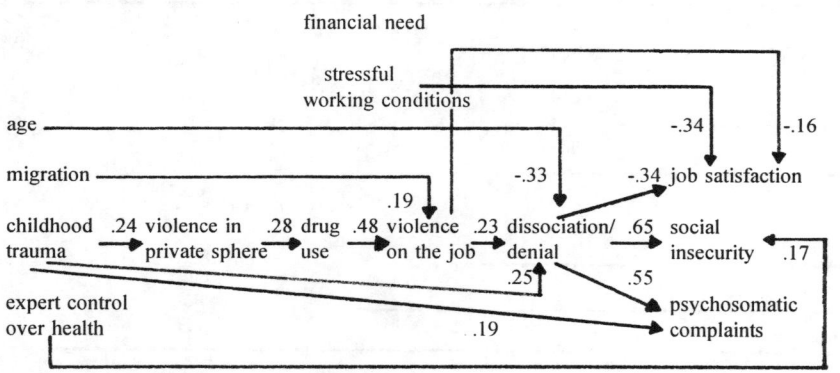

Apart from the direct effects referred to above, all factors brought into the analysis, except financial need[5], also have indirect effects on the dependent well-being subscales via their effect on other independent variables. The strength of these effects has been computed by multiplying all betas relating a factor to one of the dependent variables. Table 5.11 gives an overview of the sum of direct and indirect effects of the different variables on social insecurity, psychosomatic complaints, and job satisfaction.

The effects of emotion-directed coping on all three subscales for well-being is the strongest, although the effect of stressful working conditions on job satisfaction is as strong as the effect of dissociation/denial on job satisfaction. Other strong

---

[5] The effect of financial need on job satisfaction found at the correlational level may have been 'overruled' by the effects of migration and drug use.

effects are found for age, expert Health Locus of Control, childhood trauma and violence on the job in the case of social insecurity; for childhood trauma, age and violence on the job in the case of psychosomatic complaints; and for violence on the job, drug use and age in the case of job satisfaction. These are the factors that seem to matter most in relation to well-being.

Table 5.11: Effects of the independent factors on the dependent well-being subscales in the 'protective behavior'-study (N=127); sums of direct (beta) and indirect (multiplied beta) effects

independent variables	dependent well-being subscales		
	social insecurity	psychosomatic complaints	job satisfaction
childhood trauma	.17	.33	-.09
migration	.03	.02	-.02
age	-.21	-.18	.11
expert locus of control	.17	-	-
violence private sphere	.02	.02	-.03
drug use	.07	.06	-.12
financial need	-	-	-
stressful working conditions	-	-	-.34
violence on the job	.15	.13	-.24
dissociation/denial	.65	.55	-.34

Only in the case of social insecurity does the internal, person-related factor Health Locus of Control seem to play a role, but for all well-being measures, age as a person-related variable seems to settle a great deal of the matter. Younger women working in prostitution seem to be worse off than the older ones, and this seems to a large extent to be explained by the fact that they are more inclined to dissociate, deny and internally manipulate their emotions. The effects of violence on the job, migration, drug use, violence in the private sphere and childhood violence can also be partially traced back to the connected likelihood of emotion-directed coping behaviors.

However, childhood trauma also has an independent and direct effect on psychosomatic complaints. The direct and indirect effects of childhood trauma on psychosomatic complaints, and to a lesser extent, on social insecurity are all the more remarkable, since relatively many data were missing for childhood abuse and violence and prevalence rates found are considered to only show the top of the iceberg. If the data on childhood trauma had been more complete the effects we found would probably have been even stronger. These analyses give strong evidence that childhood trauma has a long term negative effect on the well-being of prostitutes.

Considering the variance explained and the strength of the effects found, it seems that the factors introduced in our theoretical model are indeed important to the well-being of prostitutes. The fact that the effect of dissociation/denial on the well-being subscales is strong and that many (although not all) of the other variables exert their effect via these emotion-directed strategies underscores the mediating role of the coping process in the relation between situation and events on the one hand, and well-being on the other. It also shows that strong emotion-directed behavior such as dissociation is indeed 'unhealthy'. Dissociation itself was found to be particularly more likely the younger one is, when one has been (more severely) traumatized in childhood, and when one has experienced (more) violence on the job. Together these factors explain 27% of the variance on dissociation (see Table 5.10). Even if this is a relatively high figure, it also shows that other factors which were not accounted for in our path-analysis must also play a role in the frequent use of dissociative coping strategies among prostitutes. It has already been pointed out that the severity, piling up, and overwhelming nature of complaints and problems themselves bring about a necessity for internal survival strategies. Low levels of well-being and internal coping responses thus must be considered reciprocally related. Moreover, the prostitution context itself may be of influence.

5.8: 'What good is a sad whore?'

The emotion manipulation and distancing found to be frequently employed by prostitutes, may be further illustrated by the following interpretations of statements frequently heard: minimalization ('it isn't so bad'), rationalization ('it's only stress'), downward social comparison ('others are worse off'), concentration on problems of others ('occupying myself with others and forget about my own problems'), splitting off of negative feelings ('these feelings you just banish' or 'I throw them behind a wall, close the door, I wipe them out, close another door if necessary') and role playing or switching -outward- personality ('I put up a big screen, nobody was to know who I was' or 'I hide behind aggressiveness').

The prostitution context seems to substantially add to the likelihood of emotion manipulation and connected complaints. In general, stigma and stressful working conditions which offer little protection may be assumed relevant. The physical and psychological strain caused by working in prostitution is often put forward as a background factor that 'simply cannot be changed'. An ex-prostitute states: 'I never talked about my complaints, they were so very much linked to the work at that time. So I can understand very well, that women working now also say: nothing will ever change. There seems to be so much self-evidence that everything is part of one and the same thing and that it's impossible to break through it all.' A lack of confidence in one's ability or possibility to change anything within the prostitution context often makes women take refuge in internal strategies.

More specific characteristics of the prostitution context and the work itself may be relevant as well. The prostitution subculture is very much a hidden world that invites hiding the experiences and emotions involved. Because of stigma and illegality, many women isolate their work from the rest of their lives. To a certain extent, all of the respondents led double lives. The separation between work and private life is sometimes brought about almost ritually, like in: 'Clothes I wear there I never wear in private, no ornaments, even if it's a little two quarter ring, I don't want it to be in touch with the body of that man, even if he is ever so clean'. Regularly changing names or using different names at the same time symbolizes (and stimulates) role playing and -temporary- distancing. Leading a double life is the pre-eminent soil for hiding away experiences and emotions and for their distortion, denial or dissociation.

It is because the work is kept silent that the experiences often stay diffuse. The lack of safe and supporting situations adds to this. Bringing the problematic sides of experiences up is often difficult in itself because 'people say very quickly that then you just should not do the work. As a result you are not so open about things'. The double lives prostitutes live and the necessary management of 'the secret' bring about ruptures in their social networks and social support systems. In our 'coping and well-being'-study, only 7% of the women live in relatively open social networks in which they move relatively freely since family and friends are acquainted with the fact that they work as a prostitute. The majority of subjects lives in narrow, closed social networks in which only a limited group of people are informed about her professional activities (see Groen, 1989). Leading a double life is not only a burden in itself, but brings about many social situations of limited affective quality, governed more by secrecy and fear than by openness and trust.

Acquaintances who know about the work or are part of the prostitution subculture themselves, often give support that is minimalizing, aimed at 'keeping it up and holding out'. Managers, pimps and madams often want to appease feelings that are problematical and advise prostitutes to 'not take them too heavily'. A respondent states: 'An emancipated whore is of no avail to nobody, because everybody wants to take advantage of her.' It seems that the social support prostitutes get is often of such a nature that it carries more costs than benefits. This may be an explanation for the fact that in the quantitative data, seeking support seems to be more related to emotion-directed coping behavior than to problem-directed behavior, although it is theoretically more strongly associated with the latter. Social support was also associated with lower levels of well-being: a social interaction burdened by the stigma on prostitution seems to bring more stress than relief. The prostitution context limits coping possibilities and resources and creates social support systems which offer little protection.

As far as the work itself is concerned, it seems that a certain skill in splitting off feelings ('switching over') is a precondition to keep on doing it. This is because of its intrusive nature and the heavy emotional burden that comes with it. One might even say that dissociative proficiency is the way to professionalism: 'You have to keep your head cool, you're there for it, you're turning tricks and you need to earn money. If you start thinking, you can't radiate anything. Pain and sorrow is not what the people come for. What good is a sad whore?' Some respondents emphasize the suitability of emotion-directed behavior for women in prostitution: 'It needs to be built in in a prostitute, that she always acts so as to be able to soothe herself immediately. Otherwise you're not a professional.' Others refer to a personal necessity: 'You cannot start talking about it [the work] otherwise you start to doubt.'

These statements indicate that the nature of prostitution work with its context of secrecy and stigma, and the burdening reality of leading a double life may be considered important reasons for the finding that prostitutes employ emotion-directed coping behavior relatively often. They also give evidence that the social support prostitutes get is often of a particularly minimalizing nature, partly because many people's interest in her 'keeping it up and holding out with the situation'. Seeking, and getting social support even more so, is thus likely to be associated more with emotion manipulation than with manipulation of the situation. The kind of support prostitutes get and the social interaction they get into seem to bring about even more psychological costs. They do not help to solve problems, but push the woman towards resignation and the consequently necessary internal coping.

5.9: Conclusion

The data uphold the expectation that prostitutes, as a group, fare less well than other women. Prostitutes suffer from more somatic complaints and psychosocial problems than women in representative samples, have been severely physically or sexually victimized more often, and use more internal coping strategies. Relatively severe traumatization and victimization and (connected) relatively frequent use of internal survival strategies in fact explain to a large extent the on average relatively low levels of well-being. In addition, women with more complaints and problems were found to have less job satisfaction.

However, these findings do not imply that all prostitutes are not faring well. Large differences were found regarding well-being between the women studied. Over a quarter of the women investigated are doing quite well, that is, even better than a control group of non-prostitute women on average. Another quarter approximately, have a large number of complaints and problems, even more than a control group of heavily traumatized, non-prostitute women on average. Half of the women studied fall in between those two extremes of well-being.

Many of the expectations formulated regarding the variations in levels of well-being are supported by the data. Generally speaking, our findings were concurrent with the other research findings of both prostitute and non-prostitute samples from which we derived our theoretical model (see Chapter Three).

It has been found that a prostitute fares less well and has lower job satisfaction when:

- she has been more severely victimized, whether in childhood, adult life, or on the job. Moreover, childhood trauma makes victimization in private life more likely and victimization in private life is related to victimization on the job. The results of path-analysis showed that childhood trauma explained more than one third of the variation in psychosomatic complaints, almost one fifth of the variation in social insecurity, and almost one tenth of the variation in job satisfaction. Having been traumatized in private life before entering prostitution seems to determine to a large extent how one fares in prostitution, particularly where psychosomatic complaints are concerned. Violence on the job explained about a quarter of the variation in job satisfaction, and 15% and 13% of the variation in social insecurity and in psychosomatic complaints respectively.

- she uses more internal, emotion directed coping strategies, such as dissociation and denial and a palliative/depressive coping pattern. This was found to be more likely the more severely victimized she has been, particularly in childhood or on the job. Victimization by a private partner in adulthood was found to have this effect to a lesser extent, at least for the women in our samples. They had all left these abusive relationships at the time they were interviewed and gave evidence of elation and a fighting spirit in connection to their renewed 'freedom'. However, victimization by a private partner in its turn was found to be related to the use of both alcohol and drugs. The latter was also strongly related to violence on the job. Drug abuse may be seen as a mediator between violence in the private sphere and violence on the job. The employment of emotion directed coping strategies can be seen as related to the nature of prostitution work and the context of secrecy and stigmatization and was also very closely related to various complaints and problems. In the path-analysis, variations in the use of dissociation and denial were found to explain 65%, 55%, and 34% of the variation in social insecurity, psychosomatic complaints and job satisfaction respectively. However, the relation between emotion manipulation and faring less well may also be considered as reciprocal. They may also both be seen as the outcome of the same reality: too much stress and too little protection.

- she seeks more social support. As opposed to the beneficial workings social support generally has, the social support prostitutes get is often minimalizing and stimulates suppression, 'keeping it up and holding out'. Therefore, support is more associated with the suppression of problematic feelings and brings along more psychological costs than it brings relief. No relations between well-being and (other forms of) problem-directed coping strategies were found. Problem solving coping behaviors were found to be employed primarily in areas such as dealing with physical complaints and practical matters.

- she has migrated. As expected, women who were not born in The Netherlands suffer more social insecurity and are less satisfied with their jobs. These effects appear to be mediated to a large extent by migrant women experiencing more violence on the job and (partly as a result) coping less 'healthily'. The situation migrant women find themselves in seems to be characterized by more stress and violence and less protection and support in comparison to the situation of women born in The Netherlands.

- she has a higher financial need. Financial need as an external factor was found to relate significantly to job satisfaction on a correlational level, but in the path-analysis was 'overruled' by the effects of migration, drug abuse, violence in the private sphere and violence on the job, to which it also related on a correlational level. Educational level as an other demographic variable was not found to be related to any of the well-being subscales.

- her working conditions are less favorable. Women serving a relatively high number of clients suffer from more severe psychosomatic complaints. Women working in windows and on the streets particularly suffer more social insecurity. Working conditions did seem to matter the most in relation to job satisfaction. Women working in an 'unorganized' setting (windows, streets, at home, as escorts) as opposed to in the organized sites (clubs and brothels), women who have a faster (as opposed to a more relaxed) working routine and women who earn less per client feel significantly less at ease on the job. Stressful working conditions as described above were found to have a large, direct and independent effect on job satisfaction. Thus, contrary to expectations, it was found that working in an organized context is less stressful than working 'unorganized'. To a large extent this can be explained by the fact that in the 'unorganized' forms the working routine is less relaxed, one serves more clients, earns less money per client, and one experiences more violence by clients. Moreover, women who had been victimized by a partner in their private lives were more likely to 'end up' in the 'unorganized', less protected working sites.

- she has a less strong external Health Locus of Control. A strong relation was found between external, more specifically expert, Health Locus of Control and social insecurity. The expert Locus of Control was even after dissociation and denial found to exert a strong direct and independent effect on social insecurity in the path analysis. A certain lack of perceived internal control may be due to more fear, anxiety, depression, and insecurity in the social sphere. However, the expert Locus of Control was not found to (negatively) relate to internal control, nor to childhood victimization, other victimizing life-events, or coping behavior. The other subscale scores for well-being, psychosomatic complaints and job satisfaction, did not relate to any of the Locus of Control subscales.

- she is younger. This was an unexpected finding: younger women suffer more severe social insecurity, more severe psychosomatic complaints, and employ more dissociation and denial. However, they were not found to have been victimized more often. It may be so that younger women are on the job for only a short period, are still relatively unprepared for it, and therefore feel more call to use internal coping strategies. Dissociation was found to be more likely in cases of shorter duration of time working in prostitution. The findings regarding age and dissociation coincide with findings among the population at large: dissociative experiences appear to decline with age (Ross et al., 1990). They may also be interpreted as a sampling effect: the older women in our samples may be exactly those who fare relatively well in prostitution and therefore stay in the work longer.

The findings presented here will be put further into context after our discussion of prostitutes' risk management and interaction with clients in the next two chapters.

Chapter Six
PROTECTION STYLES OF PROSTITUTES

Introduction
In Chapters Six and Seven, findings regarding protection behavior and the factors determining it will be presented and discussed. The theoretical model from which this has been studied has been described in Chapter Three. Protection behavior is considered an outcome of the dynamic relations between situation, person, and events and eventually occurs in interaction with clients. Interactional processes and clients will be discussed in the next chapter. This chapter focusses on the protection behavior of prostitutes and on its associations with context and person-related factors, childhood trauma and victimizing life-events, as well as coping behavior. In the first paragraph three different protection styles identified in female prostitutes on the basis of analyses of qualitative and quantitative data in the 'protective behavior'-study are described. In the second and third paragraph, associations found between protection style and the predictor variables on the basis of additional quantitative analyses are presented. In a final paragraph conclusions are drawn and discussed in the light of the expectations formulated.

6.1: Protection styles of female prostitutes
Eight of the 127 interviews with prostitutes were too incomplete to be analyzed properly. Three different protection styles have been distinguished for the remaining 119 prostitutes. Ninety three women in this sample (78%) used condoms consistently in vaginal or anal sex with clients (indicated as 'consistent protectors'). Of the others, 13 (11%) abstained from using the condom selectively and occasionally ('selective risk takers'); and another 13 (11%) regularly and unselectively worked without a condom ('risk takers').

Consistent protectors: 'a client is a client'
Consistent condom users (N=93) worked principally in clubs and private brothels, although window- and street-workers were also represented in this group. Seven of these women had a hard-drug dependency. Nine of them were Latin American.

When asked what their reasons for working in the sex industry were, virtually all of the consistent condom users said that even if debts and financial necessity had been the initial reasons for entering the work, they were now working for 'luxuries': 'to save, to buy clothes and jewelry and luxury items', 'to furnish my house' or 'to live better'. A large number of these women reported having a steady partner who also had an income (see Table 6.1). Compared to the risk takers, the financial need of these women was relatively low (Table 6.1). This also applied to the seven drug dependent women and the nine Latin American women in this group. The drug users reported having their dependency relatively under control, did not use much and infrequently and, as a rule, did not shoot-up. It is true that earnings were reported as being used to pay for the dependency, but there was no report of compulsive work-use-work-cycles because these women said that they could 'always get something from a friend' or 'get some on tick'. Besides, more frequently than among the addicted risk takers, these women had only begun to use drugs after they started working in prostitution and maintaining their drug habits had been their prime motivation less often.

The Latin American women among the consistent protectors also differed from their risk taking colleagues. Only one of them had worked in prostitution in her country of origin. Furthermore, these women had generally been in The Netherlands for a longer time than the risk taking Latin American women. More than half of them were permanent residents and seven out of nine had a Dutch partner. It seems that these women were, more so than the risk taking Latin American women, integrated into Dutch society. Because of this they had a different perspective on the future and a more long-term perspective on the work.

In general the whole group of consistent condom users can be said to have a fairly relaxed working routine. On average they worked the least number of hours (many worked part-time) and had the lowest number of clients (see Table 6.2). While their job satisfaction varied and was sometimes clearly ambivalent, positive evaluations were predominant: 'It is generally very enjoyable here in the club' or 'It is a terrific kick to be in the window'. Although one or two women stated that their own sexual enjoyment sometimes played a role while working, their relationship with the clients was reported as mainly detached and businesslike. There was no evidence of a far reaching client-friendliness among these women. Consistent condom users said they did not differentiate much between their clients: 'A client is a client'. More than three-quarters of the women in this group stated that they preferred not to have regular clients because 'then you get too involved'. They reported feeling little responsibility for their clients: 'If it's a disappointment, then it's a disappointment, there's nothing I can do about it'. This detachment was seen as a sign of being professional: 'A business woman must keep control of herself in her work' and 'A business woman is someone who sticks to the norms of the business, thus is not intimate and has a certain detachment'. Virtually all of these women saw prostitution as a profession ('social work, sexual problem department') and aimed at professionalism.

The desire to maintain (sexual) limits and to be seen as professional was therefore also a primary incentive to use condoms: 'Blow-jobs without a condom, screwing without a condom, then you have got it all wrong. They just see you as a hooker. You bring yourself down'. They talked in terms of rules and principles: 'It is a fixed rule, I work with a condom and if not... you can just forget it'.

For many of these women using a condom was, by definition, associated with the work. Some worked in a place where it is obligatory to use a condom: 'Without a condom, you're out'. For about ten percent of the group of 93 consistent users, such formal arguments were more important considerations for using a condom than AIDS: 'I don't think about AIDS, I just don't do it without a condom'. The symbolic value of the condom appeared to be high. The condom was not only reported to be the symbol of control and authority, but also played

Table 6.1: Protection style and demographic characteristics for prostitutes in the 'protective behavior'-study; mean score/percentage, F, N

demographic characteristic	consistent condom users	selective risk takers	risk takers	F	N
age	29	37	28	5.3**	119
educational level[1]	1.6	1.6	1.7	.1	119
% steady partner	69	23	30	6.7**	119
% child(ren)	48	62	46	.4	121
% born in The Netherlands	71	62	24	6.2**	119
financial need[2]	13	13	22	9.5***	121

Note. F-value: univariate analysis of variance.
[1]mean score; 1= primary school, 2= secondary education, 3= advanced study.
[2]For the operationalization of financial need see Chapter Four.
*p<.05; **p<.01; ***p<.001

Table 6.2: Protection style and work related features for prostitutes in the 'protective behavior'-study; mean score/percentage, F, N

work related feature	consistent condom users	selective risk takers	risk takers	F	N
age starting work	23	27	21	3.1*	119
number of years worked	6.2	9.5	7.5	1.4	119
% forced into prostitution[1]	17	0	7	1.6	119
% working organized context	59	39	0	9.5***	119
no. working hours per week	35	42	56	5.5**	119
no. clients per week	15	20	43	18.7***	119
earnings per client (Fl.)	97	114	45	1.8	118
no. minutes per client	40	45	18	1.7	116
general job stress[2]	6.6	7.1	10.8	12.4***	115
job satisfaction	22	23	18	10.8***	119

Note. F-value: univariate analysis of variance.
[1]Choice for prostitution was 'predominantly' or 'totally' someone elses.
[2]Average of high, middle and low scores on number of working hours, number of clients, work routine (duration of client-contact), earnings per client, and working 'unorganized'.
*p<.05; **p<.01; ***p<.001

Table 6.3: Protection style and AIDS-related features for prostitutes in the 'protective behavior'-study; mean score/percentage, F, N

	protection style				
AIDS-related feature	**consistent condom users**	**selective risk takers**	**risk takers**	**F**	**N**
perceived seriousness AIDS	4.9	4.7	4.5	11.7***	116
fear of AIDS	3.9	3.9	3.9	.0	116
risk perception AIDS	3.0	2.8	3.1	.7	116
no. STD-checks per year	12	13	2	2.6	119
% AIDS-test	56	62	92	3.3*	119
no. acquaintances HIV-positive	1	0	8	5.4**	115
% behavior change since AIDS	31	33	25	.0	109
% condom also contraception	24	8	18	.4	115
% condom with vaginal sex	100	85	76	56.7***	118
% condom with oral sex	88	41	64	17.0***	112

Note. F-value: univariate analysis of variance. *p<.05; **p<.01; ***p<.001

Table 6.4: Protection style and Health Locus of Control, coping behavior, well-being, and victimization for prostitutes in the 'protective behavior'-study; mean score subscales, F, N

	protection style				
subscale	**consistent condom users**	**selective risk takers**	**risk takers**	**F**	**N**
Health Locus of Control					
fate	9.1	9.5	8.9	.1	107
expert control	9.3	9.3	10.2	.5	109
external control over AIDS	7.9	8.2	7.4	.2	108
internal control	10.5	9.9	11.4	1.3	110
coping behavior					
dissociation	15.0	11.9	19.3	3.1*	101
problem solving	16.6	17.6	16.3	.2	99
seeking support	9.0	7.5	9.6	1.0	97
denial	4.2	3.1	5.1	2.6	100
use of alcohol	1.9	2.2	1.2	2.8	119
use of drugs	1.6	1.3	3.2	9.0***	119
well-being					
social insecurity	28.3	24.0	32.1	1.6	97
psychosomatic complaints	30.3	26.6	38.3	3.8*	97
victimization					
childhood trauma	2.4	2.0	3.4	3.8*	95
violence private sphere	4.3	4.1	5.8	3.3*	99
violence on the job	2.8	2.7	4.8	16.0***	109

Note. F-value: univariate analysis of variance. *p<.05; **p<.01; ***p<.001

an important role in setting the boundary between work and private life and created the desired distance from the client: 'Just the idea of it, that there's a piece of plastic all around makes me feel it's not so bad, it's less intimate'.

Furthermore, for many women hygienic considerations played a role in using condoms: 'Without one I think it's nasty, dirty and disgusting'. Many women say 'nasty' because they are referring to 'strangers' and to 'many different men'. Sperm also often evoked a great deal of disgust: 'All those squalid blokes, all that foul spunk' and 'I loathe sperm, the idea that you should get it between your teeth'. Many women stated that they found oral sex without a condom even more disgusting than vaginal intercourse. Only 12% of the oral sex contacts of the consistent condom users were unprotected (see Table 6.3). For a quarter of the consistent users the condom also had the function of a contraceptive. This was an extra incentive to use condoms. However the largest number of consistent users stated that 'protection against diseases' is the pre-eminent reason for using condoms.

Most of these women were well aware of the threat of AIDS and saw the necessity of protecting themselves against it: 'AIDS is a part of your life and you have to take account of it, just like eating and drinking, the prevention of AIDS is part of it'. The threat of other venereal diseases was perceived as high, particularly with oral sex: 'It's always a risk without [a condom]. With a blow-job maybe not for AIDS but certainly for other venereal diseases'. It is striking that many of these women said that it is in the interest of 'third parties' that they work safely. Primarily, they were referring to the steady partner which nearly 70% of these women have (Table 6.1). One woman said: 'It is a condition for doing this work, an agreement between me and my man, always to use a condom'; and another said: 'I am a whore and I don't want him to be able to say that it was me if he catches something'. Responsibility for children was also frequently mentioned as an argument. So was their obligation toward colleagues: 'It is detrimental to the other girls if you do it without'. On, as well as off the job consistent protectors seem to be, more than women in the other groups, embedded in stable social networks and to have more significant others who they knew could be affected by their behavior and for whom they felt responsible.

Consistent users can be said to be generally well aware how the AIDS virus is transmitted, even if only in broad terms: 'I don't know anything more than that it's via sex, that's it'. Still, many of these women were convinced that 'everything is dangerous'. Others doubted the infectiousness of oral sex and kissing: 'Shooting-up and to do with blood. And screwing without a condom and an ass-fuck and eating pussy - you can also get AIDS from I think, I am not really sure. And I also think from kissing, or is that wrong?'. Doubts and misunderstandings, such as the conviction that you die 'very quickly' or 'that you can also catch it from a glass' caused a few women a great deal of worry.

In general however, consistent users reported not to be worried about becoming infected: 'I don't do it without a condom, therefore I don't have to be worried'. Confidence in the efficacy of condoms was high. These women generally considered the chance of being infected by a client as low. 82% of the women in this group had never worked without a condom. Approximately half of them had begun to work in prostitution after AIDS awareness was already wide-spread. Many women, therefore, did not find an AIDS test necessary because 'what can really happen, you work safely here, then you have really got to do something stupid.' Others (56%) decided to have a test 'to be certain', sometimes as a result of unprotected sex with non-paying partners. Only nine women said they used condoms with their steady partner and, of the 32 women who had had casual partners in the past three years, 21 had not used a condom. None of them reported to be HIV-positive.

Selective risk takers: 'the old-fashioned attitude'

Three of the selective risk takers (N=13) were from Latin America and one was German, the only one in this group who used hard drugs. The Latin American women all worked as window prostitutes, the others mainly in clubs or at home. Although the percentage of women whose partner also had an income was lower in this group, their financial need was on average about as high as the consistent users' and significantly lower than the risk takers' (Table 6.1).

Particularly striking in the statements of these women, was their strong customer-friendly attitude. They stated having 'an old-fashioned attitude' towards their work, which may be related to the fact that all of them, on average, were older (Table 6.1) and had been in the business longer than the other respondents (Table 6.2). A typical statement was: 'I can't get along with these youngsters. They have a different attitude towards the customer. With me they still get a good service'. Major restrictions on services such as kissing and oral sex were said to be rejected because 'men then get very frustrated, you just can't do it'. The satisfaction of the customer was said to be the criterion for their professionalism: 'What you really see is that people are looking for some warmth, for a bit of attention and knowing this means I can do my job well'. In an occasional case this care went as far as visiting the client in the hospital or doing his shopping.

They expressed their preference for clients in terms of the relationship they had built up with them: 'The nicest clients are those with whom I have a really pleasant contact with, not one who comes in, heads straight for the bed and wham-bang is on top, in, out and away'. All of these women reported having a strong preference for 'regular clients with whom you get a special relationship' and 'you really like it when they come along'. Their job satisfaction was high, even somewhat higher than in the first group (Table 6.2). In reply to the question whether the work caused her stress one woman said: 'If you enjoy it, then it can't cause you any stress, can it?' Work routines appeared to be flexible. Contacts generally lasted the longest in this group. Most women were prepared to kiss and all of them were - selectively - prepared to have oral sex without a condom, which occurred most frequently in this group (Table 6.3). Professional considerations in combination with the appeal of the client or of sex itself sometimes made them decide to give a preferential treatment to some clients: 'How long it lasts, yes, that depends on how tasty they are' and: 'If he's an attractive, tasty, clean guy then I'll give him a blow job without. And yeah, a rubber in my mouth, no, because sucking also gets me going'.

Having these personal preferences does not mean that they were willing to have intercourse without a condom frequently. The risk of venereal disease was said to be the most important motivation for using a condom. It is noteworthy that considerations relating to the division between work and private life or the safety of their steady partner, like they were reported by the consistent protectors, were missing. These women had fewer non-paying steady (Table 6.1) and casual partners than the consistent users but, when they did they would have intercourse without using a condom with these men. Nor did these women raise considerations of hygiene. Despite this, on the job, most of them reported only making an exception regarding condom use for 'one or two regular clients'. Sometimes business factors such as customer relations were said to be the reason, but none of them was willing to indiscriminately not use a condom with whatever client, simply for financial reasons: 'You only allow it with some, but as far as possible you try and avoid it.'

In the short time they had been in Holland, the Latin American women were noteworthy for having one particular client become a 'friend'. It could be that the wish for a steady relationship (with all its perspectives) was the reason for this. In most cases this 'friend' was probably no more than a comforting bright spot in their loneliness and isolation, which should not be underestimated. A Venezuelan woman justified her occasional friendly contacts as follows: 'If you don't have anyone who cares for you, then this is the way you get'. Among the Dutch women the occasional exceptions were generally made for a regular client too, and, moreover, one with whom they -sometimes quite erroneously- judged the risk to be very low: 'He has had a prostate operation and does not produce any sperm' or 'He only visits me'.

If there were only a limited number of clients with whom they did it 'without', they saw these men as 'trustworthy': 'They are married men who can't afford to catch something' or 'This man has regular check-ups with the doctor'. One woman said the risk was low anyhow: 'It seems that it's difficult to get AIDS from vaginal contact. It is a 0.03% chance and then you have to have an AIDS patient'. The women who rarely made an exception seemed to have a fairly good knowledge of AIDS and their low risk assessment might be realistic.

Other women among the selective risk-takers reported to take risks with a (limited) number of clients. They often considered this as unavoidable: 'It is not always possible to use a condom. If you want to keep your clients, you can't get round it'. Particularly in the clubs, custom was said to play a role. If it was not obligatory to use a condom this was seen as an unsupportive social norm because of the competition with risk-taking colleagues. Additionally, virtually all of these women admitted that, with vaginal sex, their own sexual desires were also sometimes the motivation for not using a condom: 'Listen, when I am also in the mood, it is difficult to use a condom' or: 'I really enjoy making love with them. I don't have a man at home, so I use it for my own sexual satisfaction'.

Most of the women reported being well aware of the risks they run. They were generally well informed about AIDS and, within the limits of what is possible, regarded protection against AIDS as essential. At the same time they stated that running some risks in their occupation was unavoidable: 'If you carry on in this work, then you know that now and then you run a risk, so I accept it'. However, nearly a third of this group said that they had altered their behavior with their clients 'since AIDS' (Table 6.3). The change for these 'old stalwarts of the trade' has principally been their reducing the number of unprotected sexual contacts, and being more active in building up a regular clientele. Still, their personal risk perception was somewhat (but not significantly) higher than the other two groups (Table 6.3). None of them reported being HIV-positive.

Risk takers: 'wam, bam, in, out, and away'

Of the thirteen women identified as risk-takers seven used hard drugs (three of these were German) and the other six were from Latin America, principally Columbia. All the Latin American women had also worked in prostitution in their country of origin and had been in The Netherlands for only a short period of time. Having just arrived and planning to stay only a couple of months was bound to give them a more short-term perspective on working in prostitution in The Netherlands than their fellow country-women who were among the consistent users. They all worked as window prostitutes, whereas the women using drugs worked on the street. The drugs users all reported working exclusively for drugs. Financial need was an important motivation for not being able to use condoms consistently, and was significantly higher for these women than for those in both the other groups (see table 6.1).

Despite obvious differences in the backgrounds and behavior of the drug addicts and the Latin American women within the group of risk-takers, there were striking similarities. Job satisfaction for these women was significantly lower than in both the other groups (see Table 6.2). Statements such as 'It is only because I need the money, otherwise you would never catch me doing it', 'I never enjoy it' or 'I hate this work' were characteristic. High financial need was found to correlate with low job satisfaction (see Chapter Five). They said they had an attitude of resignation towards the work because 'there is no alternative'.

Even though most of them saw prostitution as a chance to earn some money and in this sense a profession, they did not regard themselves as professional prostitutes: 'I don't want to be a professional. I don't do it for the money, but for drugs'. There was no unequivocal, let alone positive, identification with the occupational group. All of these women saw their work mainly as something they had to do 'for the moment'. For the Latin American women, this feeling was strengthened by the fact that they were going to be in The Netherlands for only a short period of time: 'I have to work a lot because three months is nothing'.

The whole group reported to have relatively long work-weeks and a lot of clients that they 'finished off' relatively quickly (Table 6.2). Because these women had many more clients than either the selective risk-takers or the consistent condom users, they took risks much more often, even though the average percentage of unprotected intercourse was only 9% higher than the selective risk-takers (Table 6.3). In general the routine was: 'wam, bam, money, on top, in, out and away'. The quick work-tempo of these women was also dictated by the type of prostitution (street, window) in which they worked. A streetwalker said: 'And of course you are in the lowest class of prostitution where they don't pay very much; therefore you have to get more customers to get your money. You can't be so selective'. The need to work fast affected the proceedings of the contacts and the reasons for giving in to the wishes of the customer. The same applied to using condoms: 'If I see that [he] comes quicker without one, then I'll take it off because if they are on top of you too long, that's too much'. The quick routine determined their attitudes toward and the preference for certain types of clients. It was striking that except for two, all the Latin American women expressed a preference, though ambivalent, for Turkish and Moroccan men whom they call 'Arabs', who are often rejected by Dutch women: 'Arabs are quick. They pay less, but they are quicker'. Undoubtedly, this had to do with the risk-takers servicing significantly more 'Arab men' than the other groups (t=2.05, p<.05).

Both addicts and Latin American women in general claimed to have a real aversion to their clients; nobody spoke about them in positive terms other than 'quickly finished', 'clean' and 'not difficult'. Sex also carried many negative connotations for them. Many women associated this with a general disillusion with men or with male sexual violence. All but three of these thirteen women reported to have been raped or abused in childhood, or to have been beaten up and/or abandoned by former boyfriends. Risk takers reported both violence in private life and on the job significantly more often than both the consistent condom users and the selective risk takers (see Table 6.4).

In the remarks about the impossibility of using condoms consistently, there was an extreme sense of helplessness: 'It would be great if everyone would use a condom, but this work is not suited to it because so few men will use one'. Not being able to consistently use condoms was unanimously blamed on the clients: 'The problem is the man as he's the only one who can provide the solution'.

The customs at the work places of these women also made consistent use of condoms unlikely or impossible. The fact that all of them worked in places where they had to compete with other women working without condoms is crucial. Refusal to work without meant 'letting money go'; the customer always has the certainty of being able to go next door.

For the drug users the necessity of drugs at a particular moment overrode any other ideas: 'If you feel okay then you do it with a condom, if you feel bad then you do it without. You'll do anything for the money'. Others blamed their (apparent) indifference on a history of violence and misery: 'When I came here I couldn't care less. It didn't matter what happened.'

Health, health risks and long-term planning in terms of health appeared to be not very tangible concepts when 'your whole life's a misery and pain'. However, most of the women reported being somewhat selective in the sense that they would not do it without with just any customer: 'You do your best to see that he is clean, that he's not sick'. In particular the Latin American women 'checked' their clients for venereal disease and refused to do it without if they suspected anything. Most women (all except three) among the risk-takers were extremely scared of AIDS and were well aware of the risks they ran: 'I work and I shoot-up, those are the two dangers'. In general, the women in this group knew a significantly higher number of people who were HIV-infected or had AIDS (Table 6.3). For them, the threat of AIDS was not far from home.

More so than facing the risk, they reported the need 'to forget' it: 'I don't consider the risks, I don't think about them, just get back as quickly as possible and pick up another customer'. Possibly related to these attempts to distance themselves from the risk, was a limited knowledge of AIDS. There was an obvious lack of knowledge in three cases. Incomprehension and doubt seemed to lead to a sense of uncertainty and crippling of any feeling of their own efficacy to do something.

The only way to have a sense of control often appeared to be an AIDS test. The women in this group had themselves tested relatively often, certainly in relation to the low general frequency of STD-tests (Table 6.3). In the wish 'to know', concern for non-paying contacts also played a role: of the ten women who had had a regular partner in the past three years, only two used condoms, while none of the eight women with a casual partner in this period used one. As in the other groups, all the women tested reported being HIV-negative.

The combination of fear and lack of knowledge sometimes led to incompetent measures of risk reduction such as 'doing it quickly and washing myself'. Reassuring arguments and justifications were also used: 'I have not been a prostitute for a very long time so I don't think there's time to catch it' and 'I won't be ill, you've really got to be very bad to get it'. These women did not assess their chances of becoming infected as significantly higher than the other groups and perceived AIDS as being less serious (Table 6.3). Working as a prostitute was often seen as being synonymous with running risks; the perspective for a positive behavioral change in a work situation that was experienced as very negative, was often totally absent. However, a quarter of these women said that they had changed their behavior 'since AIDS' (Table 6.3). This meant mainly that they used condoms more often now, or 'had become more careful'. However, the optimistic illusion of a 'better future' seemed to be as important as behavior change. In the meantime there appeared to be nothing more to do than hope and pray that nothing would happen: 'I pray daily that the dangers will not catch up with me'.

From these quotes it seems that risk takers have a strongly diminished sense of control over their own health. This was not confirmed by the quantitative data. There were no significant differences between the three groups in their scores on 'fate', 'expert control' or 'external control over AIDS', nor on 'internal control' in reference to health (see Table 6.4).

6.2: Factors in risk taking

Considering the characteristics and mean scores on which the three groups with different protection styles significantly differ from one another (see Tables 6.1 to 6.4), the statistical 'effect' of protection style appears to be explained primarily by the extreme position of the risk takers. They were younger and started working at a younger age, were born outside The Netherlands more often and had the highest financial need. They worked least often in an organized setting, had the highest job stress and the lowest job satisfaction. They used the most drugs, had the most dissociative experiences and the most psycho-somatic complaints. They had experienced the most severe abuse and violence in childhood as well as in adult life, both off and on the job. Finally, they considered AIDS to be less serious than the women in the other two groups. Their scores on social insecurity were on average highest, but this difference does not reach statistical significance. The same is true for denial and seeking support. On both problem solving and alcohol use, selective risk takers scored highest, but these differences do not reach statistical significance either.

Discriminant analysis has been done on the variables found to significantly differentiate the three groups in order to find out what variables discriminate best between them. Results[1] are shown in Table 6.5.

Victimization on the job appears to matter most in relation to risk taking. The appraisal of the seriousness of AIDS matters least. Financial need and job satisfaction are also important. The exceptionally burdened situation of the risk takers is reflected in the results of this analysis: average group values for the discriminant function are 3.72 for risk takers, -.26 for consistent protectors, and -.98 for selective risk takers. As in the analyses reported in the previous paragraph, it seems that the selective risk takers are faring best.

Finally, we return to the comparisons with control groups. The whole research sample has been found to score significantly higher on average on the Symptom Check List (SCL) than Schoemaker's (1991) non-traumatized control group; to have been significantly more often the victim of multiple sexual abuse by an acquaintance before age 16 than Draijer's (1988) representative sample; and to have significantly more often been the victim of repeated physical abuse by a male partner than Römkens' (1989) representative sample (see Chapter Five). In table 6.6, comparisons between those control samples and the groups with different protection styles are reported.

---

[1] Unfortunately, all data necessary to perform this analysis, in which missing values can not be mean-substituted, were available for only 62 respondents. Results must be interpreted with caution.

Table 6.5: Main determinants of protection style of prostitutes (N=62); correlations of discriminating variables within discriminant function

determinant	correlation within function
violence on the job	.60[1]
financial need	.54[1]
job satisfaction	-.53[1]
violence in the private sphere	.41
psychosomatic complaints	.40[1]
job stress	.39[1]
childhood violence	.37[1]
dissociation	.34[1]
migration	.31[1]
age	-.21
seriousness AIDS	-.04

[1]These variables correlate significantly with the discriminant function that explains 94.4% of variance in protection style (Chi^2=49.4, p<.001). Correlation of the other variables was higher within the second discriminant function that explained not significantly, only 5.7% of variance in protection style.

Table 6.6: Comparisons on some well-being and victimization measures between control samples[1] (N=respectively 60, 1049, 1036) and the three groups of prostitutes with different protection styles in the 'protective behavior'-study; prevalence (test coefficients)

control samples	variable	consistent protectors	selective risk takers	risk takers
48.4	average SCL-score	58.3 (1.8)	52.6 (0.2)	73.5 (0.9)
7.3	multiple unwanted sex by acquaintance < age 16 (%)	14.4 (5.1)*	9.1 (0.1)	33.3 (9.9)**
11.4	repeated physical violence by a private partner (%)	15.8 (1.8)	25.0 (1.7)	58.4(29.6)**

Note. Test coefficients: Student's t for average SCL-score; Chi^2 for 'unwanted sex before age 16' and for 'physical violence by a partner'.
[1]Data from control samples are derived from Schoemaker (1991), Draijer (1988) and Römkens (1989) respectively.
*p<.05; **p<.01; ***p<.001.

The consistent protectors do not differ significantly on average from the control group in their average SCL-score. Neither do the selectives and the risk takers, but, in the case of risk takers, considering their much higher average score on the SCL, this must be due to the enormous difference in the sample size. Not surprisingly, significantly more risk takers than controls experienced multiple childhood sexual abuse, as well as repeated violence by a private partner. Among the consistent protectors also, more women experienced multiple childhood sexual abuse than among the controls.

Selective risk takers had been the victim of physical violence by a male partner more often compared to both the consistent protectors and the controls, although these differences do not reach statistical significance. Once more, it is stressed that all these abusive relationships were over at the time of the interview, and that all the women were now working exclusively 'for themselves'. Possibly, the noteworthy client-friendliness of the selective protectors, their generally faring well, and their high job satisfaction are manifestations of their satisfaction with their renewed self-determination in this changed situation.

6.3: The 'advantage' of privately victimized consistent protectors over privately victimized risk takers

The substantially higher prevalence of violence in the private sphere (in youth, as well as in adult life) among the risk takers may lead one to the adoption of views such as 'once a victim always a victim' or 'victimization leads to an inevitable, fatal piling up of consequent risks'. One must bear in mind though, that 43% of the consistent protectors had also been victimized sexually and/or physically in childhood and/or in a partner relation. What is the 'advantage' of these women over the privately victimized risk takers, so that at least in the area of professional HIV-risk, they seem to fare better?

To try and detect differences between the consistent protectors who have been privately victimized in childhood or by a partner or both, and the risk takers who have had comparable experiences, we conducted some t-tests. The two groups did not differ significantly with regard to the severity of the violence, even though the risk takers did, on average, report somewhat more severe childhood violence and violence in the private sphere. Neither were the differences regarding social insecurity and psychosomatic complaints significant. However, in spite of the comparable levels of well-being, significant differences were found on the subscale for general job stress: privately victimized risk takers worked under less comfortable conditions than privately victimized consistent protectors ($t=7.3$, $p<.001$). In connection to this, they experienced significantly more violence on the job ($t=4.5$, $p<.001$) and had lower job satisfaction ($t=4.2$, $p<.001$). They also worked under higher financial pressure ($t=3.6$, $p<.005$), dissociated more ($t=2.1$, $p<.05$), were more often born outside The Netherlands ($t=3.2$, $p<.005$), had stronger expert control over health ($t=2.6$, $p<.05$) and were more likely to use drugs ($t=3.7$, $p<.005$). Privately victimized consistent protectors, on the other hand used more alcohol ($t=2.2$, $p<.05$). No differences were found on perceived seriousness of AIDS, age, duration of the period of having worked in prostitution, or educational level.

It is shown here that the connection found between violence in childhood and violence in the private sphere, and less favorable working conditions (see Chapter

Five) does not apply to the same extent to all prostitutes who have been victimized before entering prostitution. Indeed, an important factor may be here, whether or not drug dependency was developed. Privately victimized women who managed to protect themselves consistently used fewer drugs than those who took risks. Abstaining from drugs must be considered a protecting factor in this context. The same holds true for more comfortable working conditions, a personal context of non-migration and lower financial need, as well as person-related factors such as Health Locus of Control and coping style. Along with the others factors found to differ significantly between the two groups, these factors 'protect' privately victimized consistent protectors from taking as many risks as the privately victimized risk takers.

6.4: Conclusion

Among the prostitutes studied regarding protection behavior, three different groups were identified: consistent protectors, selective risk takers, and risk takers. The risk takers differed particularly from the other two groups. An unselective risk taking protection style was found to be more likely in a prostitute when:

- she had experienced more abuse and victimization, be it in childhood, in adult private life, or on the job.
- she suffers from more severe complaints and problems, specifically more psychosomatic complaints, and has lower job satisfaction.
- she employs more dissociative coping strategies and uses more drugs. In addition, the qualitative material shows that risk takers take relatively great recourse to defensive cognition, such as reassuring thoughts and unrealistic optimism. There is evidence that risk takers do indeed cope in a more emotion-directed and more defensive way. There is no evidence of their coping in a less problem-directed way.
- she has higher financial need. Risk takers are also younger and have migrated more often. Contrary to expectation, educational level does not appear to differentiate the different protection styles.
- working conditions are less favorable. Risk takers more often work in an 'unorganized' context, work the most hours and serve the most clients. Their lower average earnings per client and the shorter duration of client contacts did not reach statistical significance.
- she experiences weaker norm-support regarding condom use. Risk takers more often work in those places where violence from customers is more likely and supportive social norms regarding condom use are generally less common.
- she appraises AIDS as a less serious disease. However, contrary to expectation, the 'choice' for one of the three protection styles was found to be related only marginally to AIDS-related knowledge, personal risk perception and the fear of AIDS. Nor did risk taking seem connected to Health Locus of Control. However, less expert Health Locus of Control was found to be one of the 'protective factors' differentiating privately victimized consistent protectors from privately victimized risk takers.

Both the protective and risk carrying conduct of prostitutes can be understood in the context of personal histories and the significance which the work has for them. Histories of violence, low well-being, and low job-satisfaction do not encourage the risk takers to abide by positively formulated professional codes, including consistent condom-use. In addition, as was found in earlier studies (see Chapter Three), risk taking often has an economic incentive.

AIDS-related cognition and attitudes play only a minor role in relation to condom use. For prostitutes, having risky sex is not primarily caused by a lack of health considerations.

Consistent condom use is most likely with a moderately positive, but businesslike attitude to the work and least likely with a very negative opinion of it and very low satisfaction. A positive attitude towards the work brings about an abundance of supportive (symbolic, hygienic) motivations for consistent condom use which relate to the wish to fit the work into positively formulated codes of behavior.

In contrast, when there is low job satisfaction (and severe financial need) another professional attitude prevails. Priorities are then more geared to (essential) earnings than to positive codes of behavior. Past and present situations are often so heavy and hard for risk takers that positive codes of behavior, particularly condom use, have become empty concepts.

Finally, consciously selective exceptions to using condoms were made chiefly by the women who felt highly friendly toward (preferably regular) clients and for whom their own sexual pleasure sometimes also played a role. Professionality was defined in terms of 'a good service' and 'flexibility' by the selectives, rather than in terms of 'a professional detachment' as was mostly done by the consistent protectors. The working conditions of selective risk takers and consistent condom users did not differ that much. On some of these, as well as on other factors, such as childhood violence and job satisfaction, selective risk takers seem to be somewhat better off than the consistent protectors. Their conscious choice to abstain from the condom with a few selected clients must be interpreted in the light of their positive attitudes toward sex and their pleasure in their work; traumatic histories or unfavorable working conditions do not seem to play a role here.

Having a negative or a positive attitude towards the work is to a large extent determined by the amount of aggression and violence experienced with customers. Moreover, discriminant analysis showed that victimization on the job in particular, contributes most to risk-taking. It is even more important than job satisfaction or financial need. Since clients and their violence seem to play a crucial role in the development of risk taking by prostitutes, it seems worthwhile to have a look at the clients and their interaction with prostitutes.

Chapter Seven
INTERACTION WITH CLIENTS

Introduction
In this chapter the interaction between prostitutes and clients will be investigated. The theoretical premises and empirical findings which show the importance of interaction regarding condom use in sexual encounters, have been described in Chapter Three.

We begin by considering different groups of clients' protection styles. The description of these different protection styles and the related subjective significance of prostitution sex and condoms, relies on qualitative as well as on quantitative data. The differences between consistent and inconsistent condom users will be discussed.

In section 7.2 we turn to the actual interaction. Different interaction scenarios are described on the basis of both prostitutes' and clients' reports of the purposes, preferences and proceedings of several commercial contacts. We have also gathered information on interaction by means of questionnaires about influence strategies and perceived control. These findings will be presented in section 7.3. Conclusions are drawn about the role of interaction in relation to the other factors found to associate with the protective behavior of prostitutes in the previous chapter.

7.1: Protection styles of prostitutes' clients
Five different groups of clients and their protection style have been identified on the basis of reported intentions and behavior towards condom use in both vaginal and anal sex with prostitutes[1]: consistent condom users, defaulting users, selective users, indifferent users, and recalcitrant users. Consistent and selective users have additionally been differentiated. Among consistent users who formed 75% of the total group of clients, distinctions have been made between a convinced, a guilty conscience, and an angst-ridden protection style. Selective users have been divided into maximum and minimum selectives. The rates of condom use in commercial sex for the different groups of clients are presented in Table 7.4. Descriptions of each group follow.

Convinced users: motivated sex consumers
These men who form almost half (46%) of the total study group can be defined as positively motivated sex consumers whose experiences with prostitutes are generally pleasurable. The motives given for commercial sex are: 'a pleasant

---

[1] Because oral sex seems to be less relevant to HIV-risk, it has been left out of consideration in determining the typology. This meant that four respondents who because of their preference (and not because of safety) did not have any vaginal or anal sex were not included in this analysis. The group of analyzed clients thus consists of 87 men.

hours relaxation', 'the change', 'the anonymity and lack of obligations', or a 'sexual pick-me-up'. For these men sexuality represents something positive. It adds to the quality of their lives. The positive control of events is characteristic for the group: 'If I don't find it okay then I don't do it'. On average they evaluate their prostitution visits the most positively of all men studied (see Table 7.2).

Convinced condom users see the threat of AIDS as absolutely relevant to their situation and are convinced of the necessity of using condoms: 'it's got to be', 'it's a bitter necessity'. Only in a few cases there is report of a behavioral change since the advent of AIDS. Most say they have used condoms 'always, as long as I've done it'. It is a 'matter-of-course' or has become 'a habit' and adds to the positive evaluation of commercial sex.

In evaluating condoms these men are relatively tolerant and have the least negative attitude toward condom use (see Table 7.4). They have faith in the protective nature of the condom. For those who find them a nuisance, the objections ('sometimes there is a hair in it' or 'they stink') are related mainly to details and not to the sexual experience as a whole.

Guilty conscience users: 'you should be able to resist it'
The ten men identified as guilty conscience users (11% of the study group) are, more than convinced users, motivated to consistent condom use by feelings of guilt, especially towards their partner, which eight of the ten men have. Other sources of guilt are religious beliefs and the money spent. In fact, they spend the least of all clients (see Table 7.1). Their guilt feelings make them more ambivalent toward their visits to prostitutes than the convinced users. In particular, they are less convinced about the legitimacy of their sexual desires; 'you should be able to resist it'.

Just as the convinced users do, these men see the use of a condom as a matter of fact in view of the risks of sexually transmitted diseases or AIDS. The condom has a protective purpose as well as a guilt-reducing one. As with other consistent users, their positive evaluation of the condom is high (see Table 7.4).

Nevertheless, these men are less convinced in their attitudes about condom use with non-commercial partners than those in the first group. Only one of the four men who had had casual sex with non-prostitutes in the past six months, had used a condom, as compared to six of the seven in the group of convinced users. The fact that sex with prostitutes particularly is guilt ridden is apparently a reason for using condoms with prostitutes more readily than with unpaid casual contacts.

Angst-ridden users: 'I hope I don't go on doing it'
There is also an association of risk and paid sex made by the angst-ridden users (11 men, 13% of the study group). They say that they visit prostitutes 'out of loneliness' and 'as an escape' or 'if they feel fed up and dissatisfied with themselves'. A 70-year old man in this group said: 'You try to escape by getting out onto the street. There are all sorts of figures whose lives are a complete mess'. Many of these men suffer from depression and emotional problems and are looking

more for comfort, contact and a 'nice chat' than for 'pure sex': 'I'd rather have a female companion that I could pay, with whom you can go out with and the like. I'm not that bothered about sex'. Some say that they are not happy with their visits to prostitutes because it symbolizes their problems and loneliness and because they generally do not find what they are looking for: 'You've got other expectations than the girls'. Their positive evaluation of prostitution visits is weak and their negative evaluation is strongest of all the men studied (see Table 7.2). Many of these men say that visiting prostitutes is an 'addiction' over which they do not have complete control: 'I would rather that it was over and done with again'; 'I hope that I don't go on doing it'.

Undoubtedly their fear of AIDS plays an important role in their negative evaluation. More importantly, it is the most important reason to use a condom, which they do consistently. These men find 'AIDS a gruesome subject'. They have the strongest sense of fear of AIDS and, compared to the other consistent users, see their own chances of becoming infected by the AIDS virus as much higher (see Table 7.3). Their high levels of fear can be related to their general despair: 'I don't want to think about the idea that I'll catch something on top of everything, as I wouldn't know what to do'.

Despite all the fear there is strong resistance to using condoms. Only two of the eleven men in this group say that it does not make much difference to them. Their most important objection to condoms lies in the fact that condoms can be seen as a symbol for 'the whole situation in which you have ended up'. In addition, they have doubts about the effectiveness of condoms: 'I use condoms, but you can never be sure'.

A strong fear and high risk assessment are combined with a full measure of defensive cognition. They often bring up ideas that minimalize the risks. The facts of having relatively little sex, or not belonging to a risk group are used as arguments: 'I don't have any homosexual desires and I believe that it comes from homos'. A combination of fear and defensiveness is also brought out as a reason for not having an AIDS test, which a relatively large number of men in this group have not done (see Table 7.3): 'I am afraid of the fatal answer' and 'I am afraid, imagine that I would have it'.

Defaulting users: the temptation of 'real sex'

The men's motivation and experience of prostitution sex in this group (6%) is very similar to the angst-ridden users. They too say that they start with the idea of 'an absence', 'wanting a bit of warmth and understanding' or 'a little love or such like'. In the light of these wishes it is understandable that the defaulting users also report great ambivalence and disappointment regarding their prostitution contacts because 'you can never get what you want' and 'it is just as if you are at the dentist or the doctor, there is no real contact'.

It is especially that temptation of 'real sex' and 'intense contact' that sometimes causes them to fail to use a condom, despite their intention to do so. They then give as reasons 'the high' and 'the heat of the play'. In contacts where

Table 7.1: Demographic and prostitution-related characteristics related to protection style for clients of prostitutes in the 'protective behavior'-study (N=91); mean score, comparison between consistent and non-consistent condom users (Student's t)

protection style	age	educational level[1]	freq.visits per year	no. years experience	money spent per month (Fl.)
convinced	45	2.9	30	21	387
guilty conscience	40	2.7	18	18	143
angst-ridden	44	2.5	24	9	238
defaulting	35	2.2	29	14	205
max. selective	56	1.9	17	16	246
min. selective	44	2.0	51	21	350
indifferent	54	2.3	14	11	150
recalcitrant	37	1.3	47	18	470
consistent	44	2.8	27	18	324
non-consistent	47	2.0	27	15	259
Student's t	0.9	3.1**	0.0	1.2	0.7

[1]Mean score for highest education: 1=lower; 2= secondary; 3= further; 4= advanced.
*p<.05; **p<.01.

Table 7.2: Evaluation of prostitution visits related to protection style for clients of prostitutes in the 'protective behavior'-study (N=91); mean score, comparison between consistent and non-consistent users (Student's t)

protection style	positive evaluation	negative evaluation	preference for other sexcont.	negative att. prostitutes	general evaluation[1]
convinced	20.6	5.6	8.3	1.1	3.1
guilty conscience	18.6	8.9	10.8	2.1	2.7
angst-ridden	16.6	9.6	12.1	1.5	1.5
defaulting	15.5	4.2	10.4	1.0	2.6
max. selective	19.2	7.3	9.3	2.1	3.3
min. selective	17.2	7.3	8.3	2.0	2.7
indifferent	19.2	7.4	7.8	1.2	3.2
recalcitrant	12.5	7.5	10.7	3.1	1.5
consistent	19.6	11.2	9.4	1.3	2.3
non-consistent	17.2	11.3	9.3	2.1	2.2
Student's t	2.2*	0.2	0.1	2.2*	0.2

Note. Averages computed for available N, varying from 83 to 91.
[1]Average score on a five-point scale, answering to the question 'Considering the last year, would you say you think visiting prostitutes is agreeable (score 5 or 4) or disagreeable (score 1 or 2)?'
*p<.05; **p<.01.

Table 7.3: AIDS-related cognitions and Health Locus of Control (HLoC) related to protection style for clients of prostitutes in the 'protective behavior'-study (N=91); mean score, comparison between consistent and non-consistent condom users (Student's t)

protection style	AIDS-related cognition and Health Locus of control							
	%AIDS test	fear of AIDS	risk percept.	seriousness AIDS	internal HLoC	external HLoC	external cont.	control sur-roun
convinced	40	3.4	2.8	4.9	9.4	14.3	7.0	3.0
guilty conscience	60	3.7	2.4	5.0	9.5	13.5	7.6	3.8
angst-ridden	18	4.5	3.5	4.9	8.8	12.6	7.5	3.7
defaulting	40	3.2	2.8	4.8	8.0	14.2	7.0	3.4
max. selective	14	3.3	3.4	4.7	9.3	18.0	7.6	3.6
min. selective	33	4.3	3.7	5.0	11.3	17.7	6.7	4.0
indifferent	0	2.2	3.0	4.5	8.8	14.7	6.5	3.3
recalcitrant	25	1.5	3.0	5.0	10.7	17.5	8.5	2.2
consistent	39	3.7	2.8	4.9	9.3	13.9	7.2	3.2
non-consistent	19	3.0	3.2	4.8	9.4	16.3	7.2	3.3
Student's t	1.8	2.4*	1.3	1.3	0.1	2.2*	0.1	0.3

Note. Averages computed for available N, varying from 83 to 86.
*$p<.05$; **$p<.01$.

Table 7.4: Condom use and condom evaluation related to protection style for clients of prostitutes in the 'protective behavior'-study (N=91); percentage/mean score, comparison between consistent and non-consistent condom users (Student's t)

protection style	condom use and condom evaluation					
	% condom use vaginal/anal sex	% condom oral sex	positive evaluation	negative eval.	negative attitudes	general evaluation[1]
convinced	100	87	17.3	9.4	5.9	2.2
guilty conscience	100	100	17.5	9.2	6.3	3.0
angst-ridden	100	86	17.5	12.3	6.8	1.9
defaulting	87	73	16.0	12.2	6.4	2.2
max. selective	10	22	16.3	10.4	7.4	2.3
min. selective	85	38	13.7	13.7	6.3	1.7
indifferent	70	28	15.2	10.0	6.8	2.3
recalcitrant	73	50	12.5	12.2	7.2	1.5
consistent	100	88	17.4	10.7	6.1	2.3
non-consistent	59	42	15.0	11.4	6.9	2.1
Student's t		5.4***	3.1**	0.8	1.6	0.8

[1]Average item score on a five-point scale, ranging from very irritating to highly pleasurable.
*$p<.05$; **$p<.01$; ***$p<.001$; '.' is printed when a value is not computed.

there was a failure to use a condom, they report having been 'taken by surprise' by a prostitute who worked without one: 'I just went in and was caught unawares'. Defaulting users think of themselves as victims of temptation, unable to resist the enticement of 'real sex'. Possibly the relatively young age of these men (see Table 7.1) plays a role. An ambivalent posture, an insecure attitude and a lack of control all seem to go together to bring about unprotected sex in spite of intentions to the contrary.

Maximum selective users: 'with others I always do it with'
These seven men (8%) are consistent in using condoms in paid sex, except during frequent visits to a regular prostitute. In general, they are happy about their visits to prostitutes (see Table 7.2). Their motives for visiting a prostitute are positive. Some of those mentioned are 'fascination', 'curiosity and adventure', 'a diversion' or 'things you can't do at home'. These men are not only after sex, but also looking for 'friendship' or 'a steady girl'. The difference between them and angst-ridden and defaulting users lies in the fact that they have succeeded in realizing a friendly contact with a prostitute. They have found a woman with whom 'it clicks' and with whom they regularly practice unsafe sex. These women work principally at home, as escorts or in private brothels.

None of these men are concerned or worried about the risks they run. Aspects that they bring up to illustrate the relative safety of the contact relate principally to the relationship they say they have with her: 'You have a base, a friendship, you trust the woman' The presence of trust and closeness is associated with safety. Four of the seven men within this group say that they are sure that they are the only one with whom she 'does it without'. They differentiate between themselves and her other clients and see themselves as the favorable exception to her rule.

Their low assessment of the risk is based partly on misunderstanding ('then I should already have got it'), partly on exaggerating other risks: 'You can go along for years always doing things by the book and then get run over by a tram' and 'I could catch it at work, in principle you can get it anywhere'. A trump card in this rationalization is 'with others I always do it with'. Also the fact that they 'often stay with the same' is a reassuring thought. Unsafe sex is often connected to 'doing it with a lot of different people'. In fact they are not particularly negative in their evaluation of condoms (see Table 7.4), but the attraction of 'without' is stronger: 'It's that bit of privacy that we have'.

Minimum selective users: 'absolutely uninhibited'
These three men (3%) want a great deal of sex (they show the greatest frequency in visiting prostitutes, see Table 7.1) and a lot of variation. Their sexual demands are high, whereas their demands concerning a personal tie with the prostitute are low. Above all, they are concerned with 'doing it as much as possible' or 'being deliciously kinky'.

For these 'hedonists' among prostitutes' clients sexual satisfaction, horniness and pleasure take precedence over safety. If they can consider the prostitute to be safe to some extent, condoms are not used 'from horniness'. Just about the only women with whom they say they always want to use a condom with, are 'the junkies', 'darkies' or 'old slags'. Because sex is so dominant for them and is represented by so many positive connotations (these men consider 'not finding anything dirty' and being 'absolutely uninhibited' of paramount importance), it is almost not possible for them to think of sex as carrying risks. That would be a serious invasion of their sexual (and male) identity.

The condom has a very negative connotation to them (see Table 7.4), because it detracts from the sexual experience as a whole: 'Can't do it with condoms' and 'I want to come in her'. They also doubt the benefits and effectiveness of condoms: 'Even with a condom you don't know for sure' and 'They often rip'. Yet, in their own words they are using them 'more and more' and assess their own frequency of using condoms with prostitutes as high (see Table 7.4). These men say they 'never think about AIDS a lot, no', but have the strongest perception of personal risk (see Table 7.3). At the same time there is a reassuring feeling of invulnerability in their statements: 'I don't have AIDS, I don't feel sick'. It seems that these men rationalize strongly and try to distance themselves from the risks they run. These risks, however, can be objectively assessed as relatively high considering the frequency of their visits to many different prostitutes.

Indifferent users: 'because she wants me to'

The motives of these seven men (8%) are principally 'loneliness', 'wanting physical contact' and 'holding and being held by someone'. Three are widowers and three handicapped or registered as disabled. Only two of them have (occasional) unpaid sex. Their attitude towards prostitution principally exudes gratitude and their evaluation is very positive. They have the lowest preference for other sex contacts of all the men studied (see Table 7.2). They feel grateful to prostitutes for giving them the opportunity to fulfill their wishes. Their sexual needs are low, although they do not have any negative feelings about sexual desires. In general, they think that they (still) have too little experience in that area: 'I want to discover everything about it'. They consider sex with prostitutes an important part of their 'sexual opening-up', 'learning', 'enjoying it while I still can': 'And then after it, I think that was a pleasant moment. In the end I am 61 and I have to hurry up if I still want to get something from life, otherwise it's finished'.

Because for them orgasm-oriented sex is of less consequence, most of them are relatively tolerant in their evaluation of the condom (see Table 7.4): 'It doesn't bother me', 'It suits me fine'. For all of them, the wishes of the prostitute are most important and the motivating force to use a condom is 'if she wants me to'. The importance of the relationship is the main thing: 'Otherwise you have lost another relationship while you are alone anyway'.

However, if the decision was left to them, none of them would find a condom necessary. This is primarily because of their assessment of low risk: 'The virus is not that virulent' and 'My contacts are healthy girls, I am convinced of that'. The fact that they do not have much sex and that it is often with the same 'safe woman' (a high proportion of whom are escorts) explains in part this low risk assessment. At the same time, most of them are aware that they are not immune to the virus. However, ideas like 'it's also dangerous on the street' and 'the risk is exaggerated' temper their fear, which they report to be low (see Table 7.3).

In addition, the possibility of being infected is put into a personal perspective. A 71-year old said: 'If I get it and die in 15 years then I am 85 and that's not bad'. A 63-year old: 'I have been at home for 26 years, registered as handicapped; why should I start getting worried about being ill?'. AIDS is not a threat for indifferent users, 'it is not important'. None of them have undergone an AIDS test (see Table 7.3). One man said jokingly: 'I am not registered with Chamber of Commerce, because I don't have a shop'.

Recalcitrant users: 'never satisfied with it'
These four men (5%) are similar to the indifferent users to the extent to which they are dependent on sex with prostitutes. Only one has a steady partner, with whom he hardly has sex anyway. None of them have casual partners. The big difference is that these men are specifically after sex, but have a very negative attitude to it which forms a striking paradox with their very high frequency of visiting prostitutes (see Table 7.1).

They find sex in general, and paid sex in particular, absolutely distasteful: 'I have never been satisfied with it, I don't know what there is to see in it. It is destructive. Inside, I still feel at ease, but once outside the door it is just as if a ton of concrete lands on me. That strange feeling, I still have it when I go to sleep and the blame lies in the fact that I have not got any satisfaction from what I have done'. They evaluate sex with prostitutes the least positively of all groups and think the most negatively about prostitutes (see Table 7.2): 'Nobody is good enough for me'. Reasons for still going are a kind of physical 'necessity' ('Otherwise you get a headache') or an element of 'addiction' ('It is just like being on drugs'). These men do not talk about sexual desire, but express themselves in terms of an uncontrollable urge, a necessary evil or 'something that's passed from father to son'.

In their evaluation of their contacts with prostitutes they talk of a lack of control on their own part and of the prostitute being too dominating. Protests against using condoms can be seen as a part of the ritual fight with themselves and with the prostitute. Furthermore, they have a weak positive and strong negative evaluation of condoms (see Table 7.4). Criticism of them expands to the whole experience of 'the deed'. Never, or hardly ever, is reference made to the protective value of a condom, or to the hygienic aspect. These men emphasize only the negative aspects of their experiences, with prostitutes as well as with condoms.

Recalcitrant users do not see the threat of AIDS as at all relevant to their own situations. First, this is related to their very poor knowledge about the disease itself and how one can be infected; this, in turn, seems to be related to their low levels of education (see Table 7.1). One of them asked: 'I ask myself, for example if you do it with a woman, how can a man catch AIDS? Does the woman have the disease in her body, that's a puzzle for me'. For one of them there is also a major misunderstanding: 'I still have my national service card and it says that my blood is negative, zero-negative'. Apparently, aside from a lack of knowledge these men also have a distorted view of their own invulnerability. In answer to the question as to whether he ever thought about AIDS, one man said: 'I never think about venereal disease, I am medically protected'. Another said: 'I can see it in a person, in the eyes, if she is healthy or not'. Yet another man is reassured by the 'low' frequency with which he has sex. While it was apparent that his mother is ignorant about his (frequent) visits to prostitutes he said: 'My mother says, you can't have AIDS, it's only those people who have too many sexual contacts'.

Consistent versus inconsistent users

From the foregone analysis it can be seen that the risk assessment by prostitutes' clients forms part of a larger number of cognition, attitudes and experiences in respect to their experience with prostitution. Negative aspects and benefits of condom use are evaluated and expressed in the context of behavior, priorities, desires and assessments, just as is the perception of risk.

In particular, the positive and self-controlled choice of paid sex and the appreciation of its specific characteristics appears to positively affect the use and evaluation of condoms. If clients, on the other hand, entertain strong romantic illusions, are after an intimate relationship with prostitutes or associate sex with 'letting everything go', then the condom is a symbol of an undesirable detachment and artificiality and they will waver. Men with either strong romantic desires or sexual desire that could be described as compulsive, appear to be more likely to use condoms inconsistently. Straightforward resistance to condom use in turn, appears to be associated with a highly negative evaluation of prostitution in which the issue is more one of struggle than of pleasure. Sexual compulsiveness, however, is as much present in these men as in those with more hedonistic motives.

In addition, low protection motivation seems to coincide with an unrealistic risk assessment which, in part, springs from a lack of knowledge and understanding as to how one can be infected. This may relate to the level of education. If, on the other hand, in addition to negative evaluation of prostitution, clients have a strong awareness and fear of AIDS, as is the case with the angst-ridden condom users, condoms are more likely to be used.

We have compared consistent condom users to inconsistent ones on several demographic, attitudinal and cognitive factors by means of t-tests (see Tables 7.1 to 7.4). It appears, that consistent condom using customers have higher educational levels than inconsistent condom users, but on the other demographic variables like age, number of visits, and the amount of money spent, no significant differences were found.

Even though the qualitative analysis showed a large diversity in the evaluation of prostitution among non-consistent condom users, overall they appear to have a less positive evaluation of their visits to prostitutes than do consistent users and a more negative attitude towards prostitutes (as exemplified in their stronger agreement with the statement 'basically I find prostitutes women of ill-repute').

They also, on average, have a less positive evaluation of condoms. Resistance to using condoms appears to be related to the fact that health considerations are not very prominent and the positive, protective qualities of the condom are not given their proper value. This is not only because of the dominance of considerations in reference to sexuality and intimacy, but also has to do with their Health Locus of Control. Inconsistent users have a stronger external Health Locus of Control. On the other subscales for Locus of Control, no differences are found. Placing control outside themselves (which for some non-consistent users applies as much to prostitution as to health) is not conducive to operating health considerations as motives for their own behavior.

In reference to other cognitive factors relating to AIDS, only fear of AIDS seems to be somewhat higher among consistent condom users. No differences were found on the appraisal of the seriousness of AIDS or their own chances of becoming infected.

It was concluded that among prostitutes external factors and their objective situation were important factors in condom use. Internal and cognitive factors seem to play a somewhat stronger role among the clients. Consistent condom users are better educated, have a less strong external Health Locus of Control, evaluate condoms and visiting prostitutes more positively, and the prostitutes themselves less negatively, and have somewhat more fear of AIDS.

The central aspects of these findings have been duplicated in a study sequel to this one which was carried out in order to verify these findings for a larger group of clients (De Graaf et al., in press). Telephone interviews with 559 male clients of prostitutes showed that in comparison to consistent condom users, inconsistent condom users had lower educational levels, visited prostitutes more often, visited 'steady' prostitutes more often, either had stronger emotional motives for visiting prostitutes or had a high need for sexual variation and a compulsive attitude towards sex, and had a more negative attitude toward prostitution in general and toward condoms in particular. Our typology indeed appears to have touched upon the central features of non-consistent users of condoms among the clients of prostitutes.

The findings that cognition, affects, attitudes and experiences of sex in prostitution for this group of men relate in a complex, but consistent way to their protection motivation is probably connected to the fact that visiting prostitutes is often a solitary and secret activity. Whereas in other groups (not in the least prostitutes themselves) social norms, communication and social support are influential in protection behavior, visiting prostitutes for most of these men remains a very individual and isolated experience about which they rarely talk with anyone. As far as their behavior in prostitution is concerned, the clients generally do not have to answer to anyone apart from the prostitute herself. Therefore, apart from the individual and attitudinal factors playing a role, the actual interaction with the prostitute seems to be an important moment for the sexual and protective behavior of customers to take form.

7.2: Interaction scenarios: variations of the game

Interaction between prostitute and client which results in unprotected sex may be considered deviation from the standard interaction scenario in prostitution encounters. We will speak of a *standard scenario,* when both prostitute and client are consistent protectors, or when the prostitute manages to get a client to use a condom in a businesslike way and without too much trouble. However, there are variations on the game. Alternative scenarios may arise when the prostitute is a (selective) risk taker and the client also has an inconsistent protection style, for example a defaulting, selective or indifferent one. We distinguish a *romantic* and a *friendship scenario*, in which the significance, self-presentation and mutual perception differ from those in a standard scenario. Furthermore, another scenario may develop between a prostitute and client with a recalcitrant protection style. This is characterized by many explicit attempts at influencing each other. Dependent on the prostitute and the course of interaction, either protected or unprotected sex takes place. This scenario is called a *fight scenario*. The various scenarios will be described below.

A standard scenario
More frequently than in unpaid sexual encounters, interactions in paid sexual encounters follow a standard scenario. The definition of the situation is clear up to a certain extent. In a prototypical prostitution encounter, both actors are aware that money will be exchanged for sex, time, intimacy and specific sexual techniques. If intercourse takes place, it is protypically done with a condom.

In this standard interactional script, minimal cues are sufficient to guide the actors. Often the basic conditions are communicated very quickly by the prostitute, and the customer can choose whether or not he wants to go along with them. For example, a client who comes to a window-prostitute will hear: '50 guilders for a fuck or a blowjob with a condom, 75 for both or for different positions'. The experienced customer will be aware that this kind of contact will not last longer than 10 or 15 minutes and that he will have to come up with more money if he wants to do it 'easy' (if the prostitute is willing to take her time at all). If the client is not experienced, he will learn quickly.

Of course the standard interactional scenario also has its 'white spots' or 'niches' which will be filled up or take shape only in the actual encounter. There are always some aspects on which a working consensus is not given from the very start, but will have to be established on the spot. Some examples are: what body parts may be touched; will the woman undress; will (french) kissing be allowed;

will a condom be used with oral sex; how much intimacy will be established, etcetera. As a rule in the standard script, more sex, more time or more intimacy means more money. The ultimate result of this negotiation is determined by time and place too, and differs of course substantially from one form of prostitution to another. But whether the prostitute works on the street, in a brothel or club, behind a window, as an escort girl or completely self-employed in her own house, and no matter how the details in the working consensus are filled in, in all cases the vast majority of her clients will have to answer to the dominant, businesslike script with its inherent limitations. Condom use as has been said, is an important component of this main scenario.

A large number of the clients consent whole-heartedly. They identify themselves as positively motivated sex consumers who know the game and are willing to play by the rules. Convinced condom users particularly have a positive consumer attitude. They acknowledge that a satisfactory encounter requires 'choosing with care' and 'choosing someone with whom you can't go wrong'. Occasional disappointments are considered 'a wrong choice' or 'a flop', but they are not blamed on the prostitute or on 'the game' itself because these men (even when they are not wholly enthusiastic) accept the practices and routines in the work situation. In their self-presentation and lines of action they make clear that they have no trouble defining the situation as a businesslike contact with all the freedoms and restrictions implied: 'There are certain things that you can not expect from a prostitute' and 'With a prostitute it is only about sex, you know that beforehand and are geared up to it'. These men accept not only the fact that they visit prostitutes, but also the responsibility for both the success and the safety of the contact. They know that they are 'merely' another client and they are as motivated to use a condom as the prostitute is.

Other men among the consistent protectors are not as positively convinced of the standard scenario as they are fearful of an alternative one. Angst-ridden clients are very meticulous in choosing prostitutes and avoiding hazardous practices: 'Quite often I just let them jack me off, sort of from a fear of what might go and happen'. Yet others are bothered by feelings of guilt and shame which make them 'at the very least' want to use a condom, or feel obligations towards their spouses, or often use condoms simply because they do not want to put pressure on the encounter. The indifferent protectors particularly appreciate the possibility of 'having a good time with her' and are inclined to statements such as 'I don't want to damage the relationship', or, with regard to the condom: 'It's a question of give and take, it's also a protection for the girls'. Selective clients will only want to go along with the standard scenario with some prostitutes, but not with others.

Irrespective of these differences, 70% of the clients in our study appear to be willing and capable of coming to terms with and sticking to the businesslike, standard scenario, use of condoms included. Others reject this dominant script and try to get the prostitute to comply with another scenario. If dealing with a woman for whom the use of condoms is an indispensable condition, they will not be successful in their ploy. A characteristic of consistent protective prostitutes is that they do not distinguish between clients regarding protection or 'safety' and will not be influenced by any argument. A customer will always be a customer, no matter how attractive or familiar. Prostitutes in paid encounters, as opposed to women in unpaid sexual encounters (see for instance Holland et al., 1990), do not, generally speaking, have to deal with a link between sex and love (or the incompatibility of the condom with romantic endeavors), nor with problematic communication about sex and sexual wishes. Besides, female preponderance in paid contacts is much more self-evident. Maintaining the control over the interaction is part of the consistent protective prostitutes' view of professionalism and they give in as little as possible in this respect.

Women use different ways to call a client to order regarding condom use. Strategies vary from confrontation ('just had three dicks in my mouth') to disguised and soothing ('come on, you won't feel it'), or competently businesslike ('let's put a little hat on, sir'). When condom use is obligatory in clubs, women have the extra punch to make customers comply. However generally speaking, consistently protective prostitutes do not waste much time trying to persuade unwilling clients. These women are in the (financial) position to work according to the principle of 'take it or leave it'. If a client does not want to go along with the standard scenario, he better 'go look for someone else'.

A romantic scenario

The description of a romantic scenario is predominantly based on the defaulting protectors: men who have the intention of using a condom when having sex with a prostitute, but who do not always succeed in doing so. Ambivalence about visiting prostitutes is characteristic for these men, because 'you can never get from a prostitute what you would really want'. In fact, these men feel that sex should be linked to love. They state that they 'would never visit prostitutes if they had a girl-friend or partner'. They consider prostitution to be a necessary evil which they only use because of lack of better. At the same time, they expect to be disappointed because a commercial encounter can never meet their romantic and emotional desires: 'You don't get the warmth and attention that you are looking for'. However, they do consider these desires essential to their sexual identity, and in contact with a prostitute, they will try to establish more intimacy than is common in the standard scenario. As far as the situation allows those men will try to manipulate the prostitutes' perception of them and the definition of the situation by presenting themselves with a need for friendship and intimacy: 'I always make her feel that I want more than just sex'.

If these men encounter a prostitute who is, either because of personal or business considerations, willing to give room to intimacy, and who furthermore is willing to refrain from condom use, these men can feel 'taken by surprise'. Their intentions to use a condom can get lost in the flush of perceived intimacy: 'I went and did it because at that moment there is no time for reflection, could I help it?'. Often, they mention french kissing, something many prostitutes refuse to do, as a trigger. One man says: 'All of a sudden she started to french kiss me and I felt so good about that; I found it incredibly arousing. I thought this kissing was something so striking. And then she went on, on the bed, and fucking without a condom, but it was the most beautiful thing, we were a little crazy for each other, she felt really good about it too, I just thought it was delicious, perfect.'

This 'all of a sudden' that they mention, might just as well be the prostitutes' indulgent answer to his self-presentation as 'different', as 'romantic and needing' and to his line of action in accordance with these needs. Some women also indicate, that they sometimes decide on a 'softer' treatment of drunken clients for example, in order to prevent problems. Registration of customers, or the wish to finish off a client quickly (romantically inclined customers, in particular, know how to take their time), can also be the reason for such a decision. Defaulting clients visit Latin American prostitutes relatively often, because they expect more 'warmth' with them. Because communication is predominantly non-verbal in these contacts, misunderstandings about the romantic quality of an encounter are relatively likely and can 'seduce' the defaulting clients into unprotected sex. Because these men do not really accept the limitations of the standard commercial contact, they are consciously or unconsciously, very sensitive to and defenseless against cues which give the illusion of real romance. Many prostitutes are very well trained in creating this illusion.

A prostitute may also have real, positive feelings toward a client and have reasons to bind this man in particular to her. Such an attitude has a strong appeal to the romantic desires of defaulting clients. If an opportunity arises where 'romance' can be enjoyed at the expense of safety, they have a relatively weak defense. Moreover defaulting, and angst-ridden protectors as well, are constantly struggling with their assessment of the risk and thus do not appear to have really consolidated the use of condoms when visiting prostitutes. At the moment when these men have intercourse without a condom in spite of their strong intention to use one, one might say that they are the victims of 'script confusion'. On the one hand they want to follow the standard scenario and use a condom, but on the other they long for a scenario that gives more room to emotionality and intimacy and that better represents 'real sex'. In contacts like the one mentioned, the 'safe script' looses its dominance to the advantage of the 'romantic script' which they also crave, perhaps less consciously or rationally than the standard script. The risk they run is often minimalized by yet another romantic argument: 'If she says she wants to do it without, then I presume that it's perfectly safe to do so. I assume that she does not do this with everyone'. Since we almost never spoke to prostitutes who described an initiative on their part to have sex without a condom, we have the feeling that this romantic script does not come about that often in prostitution. However, the clients' accounts show that it happens at least occasionally.

Once an unsafe contact like the one discussed has taken place, most of the failing protectors will decide not to visit this prostitute again because once at home, their fear of infection and their adherence to the standard, safe script will prevail again. Some men however, will try to overcome their fear and try to stick to this newly discovered definition of a prostitution contact and a friendship scenario may evolve.

A friendship scenario

A second situation in which something other than the standard script is dominant occurs when the participants have become familiar to each other. Commercial contacts differ in the extent to which this is the case. Clients may visit prostitutes only once or several times, but they can also choose to 'go steady' with a certain prostitute. Many clients with different protection styles claimed to have one or several 'steady' prostitutes, but this is true especially for men with either a selective or an indifferent protection style.

Some selective protectors select the prostitutes they think are safe (and thus can have unsafe sex with), on the basis of first appearances, her neatness, her hygienic standards, or other criteria: 'If I think she is healthy enough, looks clean' or 'If you get them via newspaper advertisements, then they don't have many clients'. Most of the selective protectors however, come to think that a prostitute is safe in the course of their getting to know her. For indifferent protectors, the reason for being unconcerned is very often exactly the fact, that they -for reasons other than safety- prefer to visit only women they know better and of whom they subsequently think do not carry any risk of infection.

Mutual perceptions and perception manipulation are crucial in the development of a friendship scenario. Many times, merely the feeling of proximity and closeness (whether this is justified or not), makes the client perceive the prostitute as being safe. A man said: 'When I go to a window-prostitute I always use a condom, because them I don't know, but with her (a woman working at home), it feels as if you live there, as if you're at home with your own wife.' In this case the mere perception of proximity, enhanced by the 'domesticity' of the home-situation becomes associated with safety. Other men question the prostitute more explicitly for facts about her situation and sexual practices which may give him the idea that she is safe. One man says: 'I'm sure she will be careful in other contacts, she's got a boyfriend and two little kids, I'm sure she'll take care'. These men like to think that they are an exception to the prostitutes' rule. Very often this is not so much correct as it is the result of an effective perception manipulation on the part of the prostitute.

The men figuring in a friendship scenario either perceive proximity and closeness in the relationship which makes them define the situation differently from the standard prostitution contact, or they consciously follow a line of action through which they try to establish a close relationship and mutual trust. Some strategies and resources that he might use in order to establish trust on her part so that she will agree to tango with him on his terms, are: presenting himself as an 'easy' client, as a serious and trustworthy man, as someone she would be glad to work with regularly; stressing his financial resources or high status as attractive; convincing the prostitute that he is safe and does not go without a condom with anyone else; showing great care for her and her pleasure and acting as a good, unselfish lover; and, last but not least, gradually presenting himself as someone with a special interest in her as a person and defining their encounter not as one between a prostitute and a client, but as one between acquaintances, friends or lovers.

These lines of action, no matter how convincing, will not be successful with most prostitutes. The majority of prostitutes are not sensitive to these strategies and do not want this kind of commitments. However, selective risk taking prostitutes sometimes want it. As described before, these women are generally very client-friendly, have 'the old-fashioned mentality', and consider a flexible working attitude as pre-eminently professional. As a result, they show more readiness to negotiate. Aside from this attitude toward professionalism, personal reasons can play a role: perceiving a client as attractive may give way to a more friendly, less businesslike position, in which the prostitutes' own sexual desires possibly play a role as well.

However, some sort of screening often precedes a prostitute calling a particular client her 'friend'. A Latin American prostitute reports: 'When my friend told me that I was his girl-friend now, and that he only did it with me, I started to ask around and I heard that indeed he always sticks to one woman that he calls his friend, and only then I trusted him'. If a line of action aimed at friendship is successful, the money paid then becomes sort of an extra, merely tradition, or a symbol of a friend financially supporting a friend: 'I see her not as a woman I am paying, I see her as a girlfriend who I just happen to give money to'. The significance and definition of the situation and situational identities have fundamentally changed. The standard script has changed into a script of friendship in which unprotected sex is more likely.

A fight scenario

A third situation which challenges the standard scenario is one where there is no familiarity, no mutual trust, nor an 'emotional' script, as was the case in the previous situations. The lines of action and influence strategies were largely implicit there and leaned heavily on mutual perception and situational identities. This third situation is one where the client uses many explicit negotiation strategies on all aspects of a working consensus, including condom use.

This is especially true in the case of recalcitrant protectors, men who have high resistance to condoms, including during commercial contacts. Recalcitrant protectors typically feel very negative about prostitution and are vindictive toward prostitutes. They not only feel bad about visiting prostitutes, but they also feel bad about prostitutes for doing the job: 'I think a lot of them are disgusting'. Recalcitrant clients very often feel taken for a ride or cheated and as a result they feel there is substantial reason for them to try and get it their own way: 'I don't like to stick to rules' and 'You have to go after it yourself, they don't do it for you'. Therefore they visit prostitutes feeling as if they have to fight a battle.

Characteristically, recalcitrant condom users do not want to play by the rules because they do not accept the game. They identify themselves as men who really do not want to visit prostitutes at all, but are driven to it by uncontrollable urges or have been led astray or seduced by prostitutes, and women in general. Thus they feel they have the legitimate right to fight the prostitution situation and the prostitute: 'If I want real sex, then I want to do it without a condom. Then I am absolutely insistent on doing it without a condom'. Of course, this is of no use with many prostitutes. The women who can allow themselves to be fastidious are particularly able to keep these men in harness with their trump card of 'take it or leave it'. Many women are thus able to keep control over the encounter or refuse entirely to enter into these battles.

However, women who work under severe financial pressure are often obliged to take on these men, if only because they are visited by them relatively often. Exactly because of their need for many clients and quick money they very often fail to subject these men to the standard scenario. These women regularly feel obliged to capitulate, on the use of a condom among other things. Some women in the study seemed tired of fighting and did not really call on clients to use condoms anymore. A Columbian woman reported: 'I asked him would you like a condom and he said no and I said okay'. A woman addicted to heroin said: 'If they wanted to pay some extra I would take them without [a condom], and if they did not, it all depended on how ill I was. But I did never go enter into discussions like wouldn't it be better to use a condom because that is just a waste of time'. These women accept the risks they run as a necessary evil about which they can do little or nothing. Their powerlessness adds to the low job satisfaction which characterizes risk takers. These women do not consider prostitution 'a nice trade' and they define the work and their goals rather negatively. A less positively defined situation is also more negative in its consequences.

Positive professional codes such as control over contact proceedings and condom use are less feasible for these women and because of their negative definitions of the situation, less a 'conditio sine qua non'. Professionalism is thought of in terms of quick money and a minimal guarding of the boundaries. This ambivalent working attitude also influences interaction with clients. It less automatically entails prevalence on the part of the prostitute who may feel obliged to indulge in this situation. On the other hand, the perceived ambivalence of both parties may set off a chain reaction of mutual influence attempts. Recalcitrant condom users among the clients of risk taking prostitutes try to seize their opportunity. The consequence is that these women have to expend a lot of effort to keep even their limited professional standards.

7.3: Influence strategies

We have investigated which influence strategies are used by prostitutes and clients and whether differences in the use of influence strategies exist between the groups whose protection styles are different.

As stated in Chapter Four, 'manipulation', 'rational strategies', 'negotiation' and 'formal arguments' were distinguished for clients. 'Manipulative negotiation', 'high pressure', and 'negative emotions' were distinguished among prostitutes.

Prostitutes as well as clients with different protection styles have significantly different scores on the strategies they use (respectively F=5.1, p<.01 and F=3.2, p<.05). A significant difference is also found in the frequency of employment of the different sorts of influence strategies (respectively F=43.1, p<.001 and F=8.5, p<.001).

In general, prostitutes appear to use manipulative negotiation (using temptation, charm and flattery as well as arguments) more than high pressure (getting angry, nasty or rude and using minor threats) or negative emotions (crying, begging, acting pitiful and using major threats). Contrary to expectation, risk taking prostitutes appear to use all sorts of strategies most frequently: in all possible ways they try to influence their clients the most. However, only their more frequent use of negative emotions turned out to be statistically significant in an analysis of variance on the data of the three groups (F=22.1; p<.001). Selective risk taking prostitutes use the three different kinds of strategies the least frequently. Apparently they have the lowest need to try and influence their clients. Even manipulative negotiation that was found on the whole to be used the most by prostitutes in general, is used less by the selectives than by the risk takers (t=2.4; p<.05). The use of high pressure strategies was the only area where the three groups showed no significant difference.

As a group, clients use manipulative strategies more frequently than the other strategies. Recalcitrant condom users are the ones who use all the various sorts of influence strategies most often, whether they are manipulative (flattery and temptation), rational (argumentation), negotiative (offering money and promises), or formal (referring to obligations). Indifferent protectors appear the least inclined to try to influence the prostitutes they visit. As with prostitutes, these findings coincide with the qualitative descriptions of protection styles and interaction scenarios.

Control over contact proceedings

Whereas recalcitrant condom users undertake the most explicit influence strategies, they also complain most about the lack of control they experience over the contact proceedings. Apparently they fail to influence prostitutes almost as often as they try to. Indeed it appears that compared to their greater effort to influence prostitutes, they have relatively little success on the matter of condom use. In the end, recalcitrant clients use condoms 73% of the time they have penetrative sex (see Table 7.4), while indifferent clients use them 70% of the time and use the fewest influence strategies. Maximum selective protectors use them in only 10% of their contacts, but this high rate of success is due to a large extent to the fact that they have sex with the same 'steady' prostitute many times.

This combination of high influence effort - low success on the matter of condom use is even more clearly demonstrated with non-penetrative sex. If we take the percentage of oral sex contacts which take place without a condom as a measure of the willingness of prostitutes to go along with the clients' wishes and thus accept an alternative script, we see that recalcitrant clients whose very explicit lines of action to try and influence them are less 'successful' on this point than others who do much less to get their way. In the end, they use condoms with non-penetrative sex in 50% of the cases while the score for indifferent users is 28%, and for maximum selective users only 22% (see Table 7.4).

As far as condom-use is concerned, it appears that a lot of explicit effort to have sex without one apparently elicits the most effective counter-strategies on the part of the prostitute. The more explicitly a client assumes power for himself, the more on the alert the prostitute will be and therefore the less likely he is to get his way. Thus, extreme recalcitrant clients may enter a vicious circle: the more they try to get their own way, the less likely the prostitute is willing to go along with his wishes, and the more cheated on and the more negative they will feel, the harder they will try, et cetera.

We also observe that the prostitutes who make the most use of explicit influence strategies (the risk takers), experience the least control over contact proceedings. Considering the data on the causal attributions of undesirable contact proceedings; risk takers, more often than either selectives or consistent condom users, blamed the unpleasant course of a contact on their own 'powerlessness and indifference' (referring to being incapable and giving in; $t=2.27$, $p<.05$ and $t=2.47$, $p<.05$) and 'anxious helplessness' (referring to being too fearful and not daring; $t=4.56$, $p<.001$ and $t=3.11$, $p<.001$). Consistent condom users scored higher than selective risk takers on 'anxious helplessness' ($t=3.60$, $p<.001$), which leads to the conclusion that selective risk takers seem to have the strongest feeling of control over client contacts.

7.4: The role of interaction as compared to the other factors

From the analyses presented above it seems that for both clients and prostitutes, differences in interaction relate strongly to employing different protection styles. Different attitudes to prostitution visits or work (and the connected various practices regarding condom use) apparently relate to taking different positions in the interaction. To investigate the role of interaction in relation to the other factors found to differentiate between prostitutes whose protection styles are different, a second discriminant analysis was performed (see Table 7.5; for the first one, see Table 6.5). This time, the interaction variables which were found to differ significantly between the three groups of prostitutes were also considered in the analysis: negative emotions as an influence strategy, attributing the cause of undesirable contact proceedings to powerlessness and indifference, and feelings of anxious helplessness.

It turns out that both negative emotions as an influence strategy and attributions of anxious helplessness, relate most strongly to the discriminant function which explains almost all variation between the protection styles. They appear to discriminate even more strongly between prostitutes with different protection styles than violence on the job (to which they are strongly related; Pearson's r is .43, $p<.001$ for attribution of helplessness and .33, $p<.001$ for negative emotions), financial need, or migration. The correlations with financial need are also significant: respectively r=.34, p<.001 and r=.29, p<.01. Again as expected, the exceptional position of the risk takers is illustrated by the group mean for the discriminant function: risk takers' mean score is -5.97, while for consistent protectors and selective risk takers this is .38 and 1.09 respectively.

Table 7.5: Determinants (incl. interaction variables) of protection style of prostitutes (N=57); correlation within discriminant function

variable	correlation within function
negative emotions as an influence strategy	.60[1]
attributions of anxious helplessness	.40[1]
violence on the job	.36[1]
financial need	.34[1]
migration	.27[1]
job satisfaction	.27[1]
stressful work conditions	.26
violence in the private sphere	.24[1]
childhood trauma	.19[1]
psychosomatic complaints	.19
attributions of helplessness and indifference	.17
dissociation	.16
age	.09
seriousness AIDS	.02

[1]Significant correlation within the discriminant function that explains 93% of variance between protection styles (Chi square 73.5, p<.001). The other variables correlate more significantly within the second discriminant function, that explains only 7%.

Even if these findings must be interpreted with caution since a complete data set was available from only 57 respondents, it seems legitimate to conclude that among prostitutes risk takers differ strongly from the others by the frustrating combination of powerless influence efforts and feelings of anxious helplessness in their interaction with clients.

7.5: Conclusion
The employment of different protection styles among both prostitutes and clients relates strongly to the nature of the interaction between them. A standard interaction scenario usually prevails in prostitution and by definition results in protected sex. Consistent protective prostitutes figure here, in principle with all categories of clients. In reference to condom use the outcome of this interaction is set and not to be changed, although on other aspects such as the level of intimacy and the range and type of sexual acts performed, variations are possible. Convinced condom users among the customers feel most at ease in this scenario: they feel positive about prostitution, accept their identity as a client as well as the

game which is to be played. Condom use in this context is just one of the self-evident rules of the game. Both actors may try to manipulate and negotiate, but too much pressure on the part of the client will result in either authorative and effective counter strategies or dismissal by the prostitute.

Different interactive scenarios can come about between selective or risk taking prostitutes on the one hand, and defaulting, selective, indifferent, or recalcitrant condom using clients on the other. In those alternative scripts, specific goals and self-presentations, mutual perceptions, and implicit and explicit mutual influence strategies, may play a decisive role in the resulting condom use.

It has been shown that selective risk taking prostitutes use relatively few explicit influence strategies and at the same time experience a high level of control in their interactions. Abstention from the condom is in agreement with the prostitute. It can be traced back to her perception of the clients as being safe, friendly, attractive or all of these. Doing it 'without' does not detract from her feeling of being in control. When selective or indifferent protecting clients manage to get her to not use a condom, they do this with relatively few explicit influence strategies. Being a friend and having established a relationship of mutual trust does the trick here. Maintenance of the dominant script which selective prostitutes mostly stick to also causes them relatively little trouble. A positive attitude towards the work appears to coincide with greater prevalence and a higher interaction flexibility on the part of the prostitute.

Risk taking prostitutes on the other hand, especially in interaction with recalcitrant condom users (who visit them relatively often), use many explicit influence strategies, but experience little control over contact proceedings. The same is true for the clients. Typically, recalcitrant users neither accept the prostitution game, nor the rules by which it is played. The fight scenario that they stage is deeply rooted in their self-image, in the significance commercial sex has for them, in the identity with which they present themselves and in the lines of action they take in the interaction. All in all, they put a lot of pressure on the prostitute.

We expected risky protection behavior by prostitutes to be more likely when they used fewer explicit influence strategies. On the contrary, we find that risk taking prostitutes use all kinds of strategies most, whether they are manipulative, pressuring, pitiful, or aggressive. However, both quantitative and qualitative data show that a certain amount of resignation and indifference may also characterize their attitude. Whatever their line of action, they feel, as expected, the most anxious, helpless and powerless in their interaction with clients. These feelings must be considered the result of pressure and violence on the part of the client, many ineffective counter strategies on the part of the prostitute and her having to comply with clients trespassing her limits too often.

Chapter Eight
CONCLUSIONS AND DISCUSSION

Introduction
In this book, we have investigated the well-being and risk management of prostitutes in The Netherlands. We set the stage by describing the position of prostitutes in The Netherlands in comparison to other countries and by reviewing the relevant theoretical and empirical social scientific literature (Chapters One and Two). Then, a multi-causal theoretical framework was developed to explain the differences in well-being and risk management (Chapter Three). Next, methods and procedures were discussed (Chapter Four). Most of the research expectations which were derived from the theoretical framework have been supported by the data. These findings were discussed in the previous chapters (Five, Six and Seven).

In this final chapter, we will combine the pictures arrived at in these respective chapters (8.1) and draw some general conclusions (8.2). We will also reflect upon their implications, for policy and intervention (8.3) as well as for theory and research on well-being and risk of prostitutes (8.4).

8.1: Large differences in well-being and risk
A twofold answer is in order to the question of how prostitutes are doing, physically and emotionally. As a group they appear to fare less well than a control group of other women. On average, prostitutes are troubled by more somatic complaints and psychosocial problems. However, despite their many complaints and problems, there are large differences among them. When it comes to well-being, 'the' prostitute does not exist.

On the basis of our analyses it seems that over a quarter of the women investigated are doing quite well, that is, even better than the average non-prostitute. This group mostly enjoys their work in prostitution. They feel and act like professionals. Among others, the women identified as selective risk takers are present in this group. The very few times that they abstain from using a condom at work if they do at all, they do so voluntarily and sometimes for their own pleasure.

Approximately another quarter of the women suffers very much. Their suffering was even greater than the average of the control group of heavily traumatized non-prostitute women. These women all have very negative feelings about the work. They are merely surviving and hardly see it as an enjoyable profession. Some of them run high risks by frequently, non-selectively and unwillingly abstaining from a condom in intercourse with clients.

Between those two extremes, a heterogeneous middle group (half of the women studied) fares, on average, only slightly less well than the average non-prostitute in terms of somatic complaints and psychosocial problems. They mostly have a businesslike, professional attitude towards the work. All manage to use condoms consistently with clients.

Where well-being, job satisfaction, and risk management are concerned, at least three totally different groups of prostitutes work in prostitution in The Netherlands. Our analyses have led us to the identification of five 'critical moments' that determine to a large extent how well a woman fares in prostitution. These are: childhood experiences, economic situation, working conditions, survival strategies, and interaction with clients. Below, these 'moments' and their effects on well-being and sexual risk management will be discussed separately, while at the same time their interdependence will be shown[1].

Childhood experiences

The women who reported childhood sexual trauma showed worse outcomes in adult physical and emotional health. In the 'protective behavior'-study, childhood trauma explains more than a third of the variation in the severity of psychosomatic complaints and almost a fifth of the variation in the severity of social insecurity. This latter is a subscale referring to insecurity in the social sphere, (low self-esteem, anxieties, fears, and depression.) In the 'coping and well-being'-study, negative childhood experiences relate to more severe depressive anxiousness and more aggression directed both inward and outward, i.e. feelings of aggression and mistrust, suicidal ideation and nightmares.

Women who report having been abused in childhood are physically or sexually victimized by private partners more often later in their life, including being forced into prostitution. This in its turn has a detrimental long-term effect on their present well-being. Risk taking, i.e. relatively often and non-selectively having work sex without a condom is more likely for those who suffered sexual abuse as a child. In line with Allers and Benjack (1991) we tend to conclude that the risk takers' patience as well as their powerlessness or indifference towards protection against HIV is related to early victimization.

Having been traumatized in private life before entering prostitution determines to a large extent how one fares once one works in prostitution, and accounts strongly for differences between prostitutes in that respect. The severity of psychosomatic complaints particularly is determined more strongly by traumatic experiences in childhood rather than by (victimizing) experiences in the work itself. We may conclude that where the long-term effects of childhood trauma on somatic and emotional well-being had already been found for the Dutch female population at large (Draijer, 1988, 1990), they are also present for this specific group of women working in prostitution.

Economic situation

The prostitutes in this study mostly represent a group of relatively low educated

---

[1] Since these results support a theoretical model that presupposes causality, we feel free to speak in terms of causal relations where these 'critical moments', well-being and risk are concerned.

women with little opportunity for economical gain. At the same time many of them have a large financial responsibility for their households, often with children. Dire economical need is brought about either by a large economic responsibility for children and families while no other sources of income are available, or by drug dependency. Women who were not born in The Netherlands are on average in a situation of more harsh economic need.

Our data show that increasing economic need is related to lower levels of well-being and job satisfaction as well as to working more often without a condom. The women with the lowest levels of well-being, the lowest job satisfaction, and the highest risk are those who would never do the work if it were not for financial need. Those women for whom strong economic necessity is the prime motive for working in prostitution, fare less well.

Financial need is remarkably often related to abuse by a private partner. Many Latin American women reported struggling with a total lack of means after breaking up with an abusive partner. Drug abuse also appeared to be more likely for women who had been in abusive relationships. The likelihood of histories of traumatization for drug addicted women in prostitution has also been noted in other studies (e.g. Karsten, 1993).

Grinding economic need, often in combination with experiences of abuse and partner violence, is attended by more somatic complaints and emotional problems and lower job satisfaction. It detracts from the ability to protect oneselve by means of consistent condom use.

Working conditions

Large differences in well-being, job satisfaction and risk management exist between women in different work settings and between women working under different conditions. Women serving a relatively high number of clients have more severe psychosomatic complaints. Women working on the streets and in windows, particularly, suffer more social insecurity. Women who have a faster working routine and earn less per client feel much less satisfied with their work.

On average, women working 'unorganized' (window, streets, and, to a lesser extent, at home) feel less at ease on the job than those working in an organized setting (clubs and brothels). Our interpretation of this finding is that an organized context provides a more or less stable social network and frame of reference and offers beneficial protection and support. Still, working in the organized forms of prostitution leaves much to be desired. Many prostitutes are extremely dissatisfied with the exploitative relations they have to deal with and with all the regulations put forward by the managers of clubs and brothels. Some see it as 'volunteer slavery'. It is our strong impression that if safer independent working sites were available, many women would prefer these.

A major benefit of working in the organized forms is the fact that women are usually better protected from violence by customers. The streets and windows are particularly dangerous working sites where women work in relative isolation. Similar to other studies we found physical and sexual harassment associated with more severe psychosomatic complaints and social insecurity, and lower job satisfaction. Customer violence is extremely psychologically stressful and burdening. Even more than in 'normal' rape situations, the woman is held responsible or the violence is underestimated as being 'no big deal'.

The 'choice' for the more dangerous sites is often linked to prior life histories and economic starting positions. Women who have been victimized by a private partner are more likely to end up in one of the 'unorganized', less protected working sites. This is also true for migrant women, drug addicted women and, in general, women with a higher financial need. Practical reasons may be that Latin American women are brought to the sites of window prostitution by their 'intermediaries'. Addicted women may not be accepted in other places, or are unable to submit to disciplines other than the street. However, we emphasize that almost all of the women with dire financial needs have been victimized in their private lives.

Probably a combination of lower well-being, self-esteem and job satisfaction is related to compliance with more stressful working conditions (lower earnings, more customers and danger). These women seem to be more willing to settle for anything they can get, although perhaps reluctantly. For these survivors, the negative effect of bad working conditions seem to be in line with the negative effect of their burdened life-histories.

Survival strategies

In general, the women in our study often rely on internal survival strategies and manipulate their emotions by means of denial, dissociation and palliative reasoning. There was a remarkably high reporting of dissociative experiences such as depersonalization ('feeling as if I'm not in my own body' or 'as if I'm not myself').

Strong internal coping is related to worse outcomes in well-being, job satisfaction and risk. Variation in the use of dissociation and denial as a survival strategy was found to explain 65%, 55% and 34% in the variation of social insecurity, psychosomatic complaints, and job satisfaction respectively. Risk taking was also found to be related to the use of dissociation and defensive ways of coping. One illustration of this is the fact that risk takers report they do not take AIDS as seriously as the other categories of prostitutes. Internal survival strategies, although certainly associated with an enormous buoyancy and stamina in the short run, are clearly connected to lower levels of well-being in the long run.

The nature of the work and the context of secrecy and stigmatization have been brought forward as an important explanatory factor in the use of internal survival strategies. It seems as if a certain dissociative 'proficiency' is called for to be able to work professionally or at all. Although this also holds true for other professions like service occupations, house work, police work, working as a surgeon, or stressful occupations in general, it holds pre-eminently true for prostitution. Not only is the work of an extremely intrusive character, calling for the 'switching off' of certain kinds of awareness and consciousness, but it is also 'emotion work' as referred to by Hochschild (1979, 1988). Prostitution is a kind of labour where one has to act in a way that is known to be false or that actually transforms one's feelings. Prostitution work is to a certain extent built up from fake behavior and untrue emotions on the part of prostitutes: they *play* the whore, they are *on the game*. In this context it is extremely likely that problem feelings of all kinds are being split off, denied and dissociated. In addition, stigma and secrecy are an excellent soil for internal coping. A lack of alternative coping resources and supportive social structures add to this. These features can be said to more or less hold true for all women in prostitution. But there are differences.

Women with histories of violence who work on the more dangerous sites, report the most dissociative experiences. Childhood sexual trauma particularly was found to relate strongly to dissociation and denial. When these forms of coping behavior have been acquired in response to extremely stressful circumstances in childhood, they appear to generalize into adulthood and become an obvious survival strategy in all sorts of stressful situations. Those who have a less strong sense of self and more identity confusion because of severe victimization may be more negatively affected by 'playing the whore'. They find it more difficult to separate their identities and their work. In addition, victimization in private life increases the likelihood of experiencing violence on the job. This in turn exacerbates the frequency of dissociation and 'doing away' with feelings of depression and anguish.

The more prevalent use of internal coping strategies and the connected high prevalence of victimizing experiences, in fact explain to a large extent why prostitutes as a group fare less well than other women. Surprisingly, in this vicious circle (victimization - emotion manipulation - problems and complaints) in which more prostitutes than other women seem to be caught, even the relatively frequent use of problem-directed coping strategies does not seem to be able to turn the tide. Problem solving strategies were found to be used predominantly in other areas, such as in dealing with physical complaints and practical matters.

Age showed up as another factor related to dissociation and connected well-being. Younger women were found to have more dissociative experiences and lower levels of well-being. Dissociative experiences also appear to decline with age in the general population (Ross et al., 1990). Dissociation is more common among younger people. However, the relation found here between age and dissociation and well-being may also be interpreted as a sample-effect. Older women who feel ill at ease on the job, dissociating more and experiencing more complaints and problems, may already have left the work and not be represented in our sample. It may also be that younger women are less up to the demands of prostitution work and need more stringent internal survival techniques which are detrimental to their health.

Interaction with clients

The differences between prostitutes in terms of well-being and job satisfaction and the connected features of their lives and work as discussed above, find their ultimate and strongest expression in differences in the way they interact with clients. Attributions of helplessness and powerlessness in interaction with clients were related to increased psychosomatic complaints. Particularly in relation to risk taking, these appeared to be a factor of prime importance. Inter-action with clients, in particular feelings of helplessness and prostitutes' use of negative emotions as an influence tactic towards clients, turned out be the strongest discriminating factor between the group of risk taking prostitutes and the other, less risk taking ones.

Risk takers work on the more dangerous sites and are visited relatively often by the most troublesome and recalcitrant customers. Their interaction with them is characterized by extreme powerlessness and a lack of grip on the situation they find themselves in. They try in all possible ways to make contacts proceed the way they prefer; they fight and cry and beg for their customers to go along with their wishes, but, at the same time, they find themselves with a lack of authority or control over them. We tend to see this lack of control over clients as another manifestation of the lack of grip they have on their own lives; we consider this to be the consequence of learned helplessness as a result of their extremely burdened life histories and an ongoing decreasing capacity to shape their lives according to their own wishes. The risk taking prostitutes in our study are standing with their backs against the wall. The negative attitudes of a certain group of clients towards sex in general, as well as towards prostitution constitute a working context in which particularly the more vulnerable women do not succeed in making a stand. They are caught in a vicious circle of unhappiness and the inability to do something about it.

Risk taking by prostitutes, at least when done regularly and non-selectively must be understood against the background of generally risky lives, negative life experiences, strong external demands, dangerous working sites and few supportive coping resources. Risk taking in itself is in turn frustrating and stressful, calls for emotion-directed coping strategies and detracts from well-being, job satisfaction, and feelings of control.

Risk takers and recalcitrant clients often engage in fight scenarios (see Chapter Seven). These are most likely to occur when the situation is negatively loaded for both participants. Contact with stigmatized individuals often triggers feelings of ambivalence and aggression (Katz, 1981). These feelings are probably more poignant when the prostitution situation is defined negatively by those concerned. This involves a strong, mutual condemnation of the prostitute by the client and of the client by the prostitute.

8.2: Cumulating benefits and cumulating burdens

We identified a vicious circle of traumatic experiences in childhood and/or adult private life, dire economic necessity, unfavorable working conditions, internal survival strategies, powerless interaction with (violent) customers, and a low level of well-being and job satisfaction for about a quarter of the women in our study. Differences in well-being among prostitutes appear to depend to a very large extent on conditions and experiences that precede working in prostitution. Moreover, these factors seem to also influence the conditions under which a woman eventually works in prostitution. A series of down-slope stepping stones has been described, that -at least for some women- leads to low levels of well-being while working in prostitution. For others, these downward stepping stones are mostly absent.

The prostitutes who fare well and feel at ease at the job are likely to have been born in The Netherlands, not to have been sexually abused as children, not to have been in a violent private relationship or forced into prostitution, and not to work strictly out of economic necessity. As a consequence they feel relatively less inclined to use strict internal coping strategies and are less likely to have developed drug dependencies. In connection to all this, they are more likely to eventually work in the better protected, less socially isolated forms of prostitution, to have a more relaxed working routine, to serve fewer clients, to earn more per client and to experience less violence on the job. They feel in control over clients and over contact proceedings and are not to be trifled with. The price of stigma for these professionals is, to a certain extent, compensated by their relatively high earnings.

Women at the opposite extreme who have the weakest starting positions, fare worse. Earnings for these women are relatively low and the stigma of prostitution work is hardly compensated by anything[2]. Survivors in prostitution have fewer possibilities to break away from the negative consequences of stigma. The women at the lowest end of the well-being scale are exactly the ones whom one would wish never to have become dependent on such demanding and high-priced work as prostitution obviously is. Those women, who have the most burdened histories, the weakest sense of self and self-worth, and the least supportive networks to fall back on, also happen to be the hardest pressed. It seems that the women who are least fortunate at the start, who are in

---

[2] Considering the fact that women working under force or living in abusive relationships at the time of the interview were not present in our samples and that we considered severely troubled women to be under-represented, we estimate that the group of prostitutes suffering severe problems is somewhat larger for the whole population of prostitutes than the 23% found in our study. We estimate the group of 'survivors' to be about a third of all women working in prostitution in The Netherlands. For that matter, also the 27% who were found to fare well might be higher in reality. Women with top earnings and luxurious working positions may also be under-represented, although perhaps for other reasons.

fact the least fit to do the work, have the most burdening conditions which keep
piling up.

    This sad phenomenon reflects a more general process of increasing social
division and inequality and has for other spheres been described as the 'Matthew effect'[3] (e.g. by Merton, 1988, for science; by Engbersen, 1990, for
people living on welfare; by Komter and Schuyt, 1993, for the social consequences of informal giving). The 'Matthew effect' may be interpreted as the
result of an either fortunate or fatal interaction between an individual and his or
her surroundings. Women in more favorable economic conditions will settle less
quickly for uncomfortable working conditions or low earnings, but will be
inclined to set high prices and to safeguard themselves from an all too burdening invasion and trespassing of their physical or psychic limits. As a result,
they may not so easily be perceived as 'cheap', and may be treated with more
respect. This in turn will enhance their sense of self-worth, positive self-
identity, feelings of control and ability to stick to their demands, etc. etc.

    On the other hand, women with a high financial need may be more willing
to settle for relatively low earnings and bad working conditions. Even rather
uncomfortable working conditions may often not be perceived as too stressful
by them, compared to their previous working and living conditions (cf. Brussa,
1992). They are probably more easily looked down on as being 'cheap',
especially by those clients having ambivalent feelings about prostitution and
about spending money on it. As a result of obvious market mechanisms they
are relatively often visited by this type of client. The difficult interaction with
them may further detract from their well-being, their feelings of self-worth, and
their money-making options. Women with unstable identities are constantly
under pressure and the burdens keep on accumulating.

    In the 'Matthew-effect', sociological and psychological phenomena
reinforce each other mutually. Particularly the psychological consequences of
sexual traumatization in childhood and the feedback loops provided by the
surroundings are important factors in the effect. Traumatized people may be
'deprived of the psychological mechanisms that allow others to cope with the
small injuries of life' (Van der Kolk, 1987:4). They have a heightened sense of
vulnerability and rage and have difficulty controlling their anxious and aggressive feelings (Van der Kolk, 1987). They have lost their sense of basic safety.
They may be more inclined to subject themselves to other burdening and further victimizing experiences and circumstances. In explaining the likelihood of
revictimization and the accumulation of trauma, several explanations have been
brought forward (see also Draijer, 1988:107). Traumatized people may repeat
the trauma and re-engage in burdening situations, hoping to be able to control

---

[3] St. Matthew wrote: 'For unto everyone that hath shall be given, and he shall
abundance; but from him that hath not shall be taken away even that which he hath'
(cited in Merton, 1988: 332).

them this time. They may have acquired a 'learned helplessness' and have fewer possibilities to defend themselves. Childhood sexual trauma may make people feel less convinced of the fact that they matter as people and they may on a cognitive level feel less deserving of or entitled to comfort, fortune, protection and respect. As a result they may lower their standards for self-enhancement, whether emotionally, socially, or financially. Aversive stimuli may also have addictive-like qualities (Van der Kolk, 1989) or self-destructive behavior may be reassuring for victims of severe childhood abuse because it brings about a mental and emotional state that feels like 'back to normal' (cf. Schoemaker, 1991).

On the other hand, social reactions to victimization are often stigmatizing and demeaning in themselves and as such, lower self-esteem, self-worth and demands for respect. Women who are vulnerable in this sense are also the ones who are most taken advantage of by employers as well as clients. Their decreased capacity to protect themselves from further danger also supports the tendency of others to blame them for their misfortunes (Burgess and Holmstrom, 1979). In general, the social structures available to them are altogether less supportive and their external coping resources less broad. In terms of support, comfort, safety and respect they may expect less but they also get less. A fatal interaction between a less demanding individual and less sustaining surroundings manoeuvres the more vulnerable women down-slope.

However, there are exceptions to this rule. There is a relatively large group of women who suffer some of the negative conditions described, but not all. They grapple with burdening circumstances on the one hand, but experience other, more or less protective or rewarding conditions on the other. Most of these women succeed in having a businesslike, professional attitude towards the work, manage to stick to their own limits in their interaction with clients, and keep their heads above water.

Even though migration and drug use have been identified as risk factors for well-being, not all migrant women, nor all drug dependent women can be said to suffer extremely. Some of them belong to the middle group in terms of well-being. Some Latin American women in our sample were clearly doing quite well. An important difference with the less fortunate Latin American women is the fact, that the first group of women had been in The Netherlands for a longer period of time, often had a Dutch partner and were much more integrated into Dutch society. They were much less socially isolated and managed to arrange a somewhat stable social network to fall back on. These women have a more long-term perspective on working in prostitution and feel more positive about the work. The same is true for some drug dependent women who use less drugs than others, have more control over their dependency, and do not rely exclusively or desperately on prostitution to maintain their habits.

Protective factors may be present in the life and work of survivors of childhood sexual abuse as well. Depending on their experiences on the job, their coping styles and personality characteristics, and the quality of their social networks, some women who were traumatized in childhood clearly feel more at ease on the job than others. In the context of risk, a stronger internal Health Locus of Control, less drug use and working in an organized setting came up as protective factors to the privately victimized women who managed to use condoms consistently. Experiences with violence by a private partner in adult life, at least when such an abusive relationship has ended, seems even less to be a guaranteed passport to low well-being and job satisfaction. However, while differences in well-being between consistent condom users and risk takers were substantial on average, the well-being of the privately victimized women in these two groups was equally low.

These observations illustrate that the vicious circle described for some prostitutes is not a hard and fast rule for all of them and should not be viewed as a collective fate. However, unfavorable starting positions enhance the *likelihood* of further burdening conditions and experiences piling up, both on and off the job. The more this is the case, the more clear the need for a safety net offering protection and support. In prostitution, with its non-formalized working relations and law-of-the-jungle forms of organization, such safety nets are still insufficiently available.

8.3: Implications for policy and intervention: call for differentiation

From our analysis it can be concluded that any single, one-sided, political perspective on prostitution is inadequate. Differences among prostitutes are large and could become even larger in the future. At the one extreme, there are the prostitutes who feel and act like professionals and are relatively well off, and who will, hopefully successfully, continue to emancipate themselves and rise against the lack of professional recognition and workers' rights.

At the other extreme, there is the group who grapple with severe economic need or violent life histories, or both. These women will remain vulnerable to bad working conditions, exploitative employers, violent customers and HIV-infection. Moreover, as the world-wide prostitution mobility is increasing and the international commercial organization of sex is expanding, this unfortunate group may grow in size in the future.

Whereas for the former group professionalism is the keyword, surviving is the keyword for the latter. The distinction between professionals and survivors is not simply a question of migration, as is often assumed. It is a question of economical need, violent life histories and their burdening aftermaths.

Since prostitution has always been to a certain extent a self-regulating business which has often successfully escaped or countered interventions, governments have always been relatively powerless and ineffective. As international criminal networks seem increasingly able to control the sex business worldwide, effective interventions may become even more difficult in the future. Efforts to guarantee the well-being of prostitutes are as much the moral obligation of a caring state as they are a necessity in terms of public health. As we have shown here, the risk of infection in prostitution is higher as women fare worse. The ostrich-policy that most governments now adopt is not only detrimental to prostitutes, but to society as a whole.

However, professionals and survivors should not be looked at in the same way. Since prostitution is a differentiated phenomenon, differentiated policies and interventions are called for.

Policy toward professionals

There is no need to target the women whom we here call professionals on the basis of their presumed victimization and suffering. What these women need is intervention restricted to measures improving their position as workers which increase their safety and control over the organization of prostitution. Blunt refusal to interfere in the area of working relations with the argument that prostitution is morally rejectable is evading governmental responsibility.

Legalization, or the decriminalization of prostitution is indispensable to improve prostitutes' positions. The recent set-back in this process in The Netherlands (see Chapter One) must therefore be seen as potentially detrimental to the position of prostitutes. Law reform should be back on the political agenda as soon as possible. Governmental support for prostitutes' self-organization should continue or be even more generously provided. Support for prostitutes' self-organization would also serve the goal of supporting prostitutes' battle with employers whose power and dominance over their employees has remained highly invisible because of the illegality of their business.

Regulation of prostitution when formalized, should not only address hygiene, fire-department prescriptions, and the furnishings of clubs and brothels, but should also explicitly address labour relations. It is true that too strict regulation of labour relations could result in large-scale dodging and a subsequent illegal circuit. However, attempts to satisfactorily address the issue of exploitation should go further than just a declaration of intention (cf. Van Mens, 1992). Different types of agreements on the division of earnings, so that they are more to the employees' advantage than to the employers' might be one goal to strive for. One could think of prostitutes paying a set price for the room they hire instead of getting a percentage of what the client pays in the end. Preferential treatment of women in the provision of licenses to open a new business might be another example.

It almost goes without saying that legal and punitive measures should be used against those employers whose organizing activities involve deception, threats, extortion, or brutal force and violence toward women. Effective strategies against those criminal practices, possibly involving harsher punishment, should be developed on both national and international levels.

Policy toward survivors

As sad as the situation of survivors in prostitution sometimes is, repressive measures towards this group of women are not a viable option for 'saving' them, as many studies have now shown. Repression only results in a useless cat-and-mouse game between prostitutes and the police and a large hidden circuit where women are even worse off and even more vulnerable. In terms of their well-being the only effective measures for these women are those that aim at the installment of safety nets and at the strengthening of protective factors, both preceding their entry to and during their work in prostitution.

Intervention outside the direct sphere of prostitution should target the generally weaker circumstances of women, sexually and socially as well as economically. To the benefit of all women, these are the 'evils' to be fought against, not prostitution. As long as sexual violence against women and girls is a widespread social reality, which also affects prostitutes, provisions for surviving sexual trauma, aimed at overcoming the negative effects of (childhood) sexual abuse must be improved. One could think of more empowering projects in schools and youth clubs, more effective systems of detecting the abuse of children and adolescent women, and the development of more appropriate ways of intervening in abusive families. Victims should be assisted in finding supportive, alternative social networks which can offer them solace, recognition, and comfort. If in addition we develop possibilities and make more accessible the therapeutic process which might diminish the debilitating effects of sexual trauma, women might suffer less from its long-term consequences, including those eventually developed from prostitution work. Policies like these would not only benefit some of the women working in prostitution, but would benefit all victims of severe childhood trauma. We estimate that about nine out of ten of these women do *not* wind up in prostitution work.

Safety nets for women within the context of prostitution would also be advisable. Working sites where women work 'unorganized' (streets, windows) should be targeted for more protection. First of all, this means that at least in all larger cities, sites should be extended or provided where women can work without being chased by the police. Further interventions might involve the structural provision of easily accessible service agencies which give the opportunity to socialize, provide information and care, and develop training programs aimed at self-defence, empowerment or alternative careers. There are 'huiskamers' that function as a safe haven for street prostitutes which have already proven to be supportive for women working the streets in different places in The Netherlands (see Bovenkerk et al., 1993).

Concrete initiatives dealing with the financial need of the most vulnerable women are hardly feasible in the short term. To some extent, we have to rely on general emancipation processes and policies, which aim at strengthening women's social and economical position in the long run. However, particularly for those women whose drug dependence related financial necessity pushes them to work in prostitution, one concrete measure is rather obvious: free drug supply. Some experimental drug dispensing programs in Liverpool and Amsterdam have already proven feasible and successful when carried out under strict conditions (cf. Karsten, 1993). Denying addicted women with either moral or health arguments the easily distributable supply that could keep them off the streets and protect them from further pressure, violence and weakening is utterly irrational and short-sighted and can by no means be valued as a valid policy.

Policy toward clients

Perpetrators of sexual violence are relatively little looked at when making policy to fight sexual victimization. However, our study shows that their aggressive behavior is at the root of an interaction which is also in prostitution related strongly to women's low well-being and high risk.

This may get even worse in the future, if the developments (such as increasing violence from men towards women, in connection to an increasing sex addiction among men) suggested by Giddens (1992) and others (see Chapter One) are indeed taking place. On the supply side more and more prostitutes may work from relatively weak and vulnerable positions while on the demand side, more and more clients may be grappling with their male and sexual identity and work this out on prostitutes. A large number of prostitution encounters characterized by a fight scenario (see Chapter Seven) can be expected to take place in this context.

Clients should be targeted more for intervention, educating them both on their attitudes towards sexuality and prostitution and, more specifically, on condom use. Positive attitudes towards sex and prostitution are a prerequisite for 'playing the game by the rules', for respect towards prostitutes and for willingness to use a condom. Prevention messages for clients such as 'be welcome to it and have it safely' would aim at these different aspects and should be widely disseminated.

Intervention on the demand side of the market for commercial sex may indeed be more promising than intervention on the supply side. It most certainly holds true for prostitution that as long as there are clients who have extreme sexual demands or the need to exert power over women and/or who are willing to pay for unsafe sex, there will be women who, forced by circumstances, mangled by traumatic experiences, and weakened and undermined by their consequences, may be inclined to submit and answer to these demands.

8.4: Implications for theory and research on well-being and risk of prostitutes

Our research has shown that prostitutes are either doing well or not doing well, depending on certain conditions. Our multi-causal theoretical model has proven to be adequate to explain these differences. Differences in both well-being and risk can be explained to a large extent by differences in experiences of victimization and economic position before entering prostitution, and connected person-, context-, and interaction-related aspects of working routines once in the work. It has become clear that studying the well-being of women in prostitution merely from the angle of either personality characteristics, or victimization, or working conditions is reductionistic. These aspects are thoroughly intertwined.

Since the factors affecting prostitutes' health are to a large extent the same as those found affecting the health of the general population, it may also prove fruitful to study women's well-being in other forms of labour from this multi-causal perspective. The theoretical model may thus be more broadly validated.

From our findings it appears that prostitutes are on average faring some-what worse than other women, but the picture emerging for most prostitutes is by far not as grim as is portrayed in other, predominantly American or Canadi-an, studies (e.g. James, 1978; Silbert and Pines, 1981; Bagley and Young, 1987). In part, this may reflect differences between the countries. Considering the relatively mild legal restrictions put upon prostitutes in The Netherlands, prostitutes' working conditions in general may be worse under more repressive regimes. In the US women have more difficulty finding relatively safe working sites. There is less of a safety net for the already vulnerable groups of women. The percentage of women suffering from the negative consequences of unsafe and isolated working sites would be larger. Thus, prostitutes in The Netherlands may have a 'privileged' position compared to prostitutes in other countries who often work under more repressive regimes.

However, American and Canadian studies have often focussed exclusively on street prostitutes and in doing so, have predominantly investigated those prostitutes who are worse off. Indeed, our findings for the women working the street were comparable to those in the other studies. Our analyses have shown that a representative picture on the well-being of prostitutes can not be derived from the investigation of specific samples. In order to be able to say anything about the whole population of prostitutes, women working in all the various forms of prostitution will have to be taken into account in future research. From our study it has become clear that the vision of prostitution work as detrimental by definition or of itself, 'using up women in a very rough way' (Winick and Kinsey, 1971), can no longer be indiscriminately held. Prostitution work is only detrimental for certain groups of women and under certain conditions.

Particularly negative childhood sexual experiences have come to the fore as being crucial in well-being and risk. However, the prevalence rates we found were not as high as those found in other studies on prostitutes. Our 15% in the 'protective behavior'-study must be supposed to reflect only the proverbial top of the iceberg since that study did not focus on childhood trauma in the first place and the questioning concerning that topic was not entirely adequate (see Chapter Four). However, even the 43% found in the 'coping and well-being'-study is still substantially lower than the 60% and 73% found by Silbert and Pines (1981) and Bagley and Young (1987) respectively. There is no reason to believe that prevalence rates of childhood abuse are much higher among Ameri-can and Canadian prostitutes than among the Dutch. Again, the fact that the other studies focussed on very specific samples of prostitutes (street walkers) must be the reason for the enormously high prevalence rates. As for well-being in general, findings on childhood victimization of prostitutes can only be generalized to the total population if women working in different contexts of prostitution are taken into account.

Even if an all too stringent emphasis on victimizing experiences does not pay justice to all prostitutes, the study of prostitutes' well-being and risk as well as of the well-being of other groups of women, can not be done without considering sexual trauma. Only a limited number of studies on the mental health of prostitutes has explicitly done this (e.g. Bagley and Young, 1987). Particularly the study of risk behavior has hardly ever reckoned with this factor. This study shows that considering childhood trauma is a pre-requisite in future epidemiological enquiry of the determinants of risk-taking behavior, in commercial as well as in non-commercial sexual conduct.

Of equal importance for future research into prostitutes' well-being and risk is the study of the protective factors which may compensate for the negative effects of trauma. In our study, social integration and more stable social networks, either on or off the job, have come up as important protective forces. Further study of the role of possible protective factors will not only enhance insight, but may also offer more concrete recommendations for intervention.

More insight is also highly desirable in the area of exploitation and violence by customers and employers. Exactly by what strategies or tactics do clients and employers control prostitutes? What precisely can be done to prevent and counteract these? More research is needed to come up with useful recommendations in this area and to develop adequate training programs for and by prostitutes.

Research into the tactics of control are pre-eminently desirable in relation to the growth of international networks of prostitution organization. More insight into their working-methods is a prerequisite for the effective tracing and sanctioning of criminal practices.

The other side of the increasing international prostitution mobility also needs further inquiry. What are the starting positions of migrant women who are now entering prostitution in great numbers? What is the size of this group? What are their economical conditions? What are their histories of violence? How do they function in prostitution? And what can be done to enhance their well-being?

In the social scientific study of prostitutes their mental health and life-histories have mostly been linked to their 'choices' for prostitution. Implicitly or explicitly, it has often been assumed that deciding on prostitution work is the ultimate illustration of having travelled a down-slope track and having reached an absolute low in life. As a consequence, relatively little interest has been shown in the lives of women once in prostitution, not to mention their later lives. Research into the lives and well-being of women after having worked in prostitution, in comparison to women in comparable conditions who did not work in prostitution, may provide additional insight into the way a prostitution career affects the well-being of women in the long term. Our study has shown that prostitution need not be the absolute low by definition, at all. However, for those who are already troubled, as a consequence of violent life-histories, economical sorrow, or both, prostitution work is often an extra burden. For them, prostitution work is an obviously risky business. Particularly these women need care and protection. Future scientific inquiry should focus especially on the way these women can be better protected, before, during, and after their working in prostitution.

SAMENVATTING

Dit boek gaat over het welzijn en het beschermingsgedrag van prostituées. Het doet verslag van twee empirische studies in Nederland, waarin gegevens zijn verzameld bij in totaal 187 prostituées en 91 klanten. De twee afhankelijke variabelen worden bestudeerd vanuit een multi-causaal theoretisch kader dat het mogelijk maakt te begrijpen onder welke condities prostituées verschillen in de mate van welbevinden en hun beschermingsgedrag.

In het eerste hoofdstuk wordt de 'prostitutie in Nederland' beschreven en vergeleken met omringende Europese landen en de Verenigde Staten. Er wordt aandacht besteed aan de wetgeving ten aanzien van prostitutie, aan attitudes bij het publiek en aan feministische standpunten. Nederland wordt vaak gezien als een bij uitstek liberaal land wat prostitutie betreft. Hier wordt geconcludeerd, dat de Nederlandse overheid weliswaar een minder repressieve politiek voert ten aanzien van prostitutie en dat de decriminaliseringsbeweging in Nederland sterk is, maar dat het morele en politieke klimaat in feite slechts gradueel en niet essentieel verschilt in vergelijking met andere landen. In het verlengde hiervan wordt beargumenteerd waarom een beter inzicht in het welbevinden van prostituées wenselijk is.

Hoofdstuk twee geeft een uitgebreid overzicht van (voornamelijk Europees en Amerikaans) sociaal wetenschappelijk empirisch onderzoek naar welbevinden en gezondheid van prostituées tot nu toe. Er wordt een historische ontwikkeling geschetst waarin, grofweg, achtereenvolgens de vragen 'Wie zijn ze?', 'Waarom komen ze in de prostitutie terecht?' en 'Hoe doen ze het?' centraal hebben gestaan. Het blijkt dat prostituées in eerste instantie vooral onderzocht werden in verband met hun vermeende pathologische persoonlijkheidskenmerken. Vervolgens kwam de nadruk vooral te liggen op traumatische jeugdervaringen en onfortuinlijke omstandigheden als een mogelijke verklaring voor hun 'keuze' voor prostitutie. Deze kwesties zijn ruimschoots aan bod geweest, zowel in psychologische als in sociologische onderzoekstradities. Meer recent worden prostituées vooral onderzocht in de context van AIDS en is er vooral aandacht voor HIV-prevalenties en beschermingsgedrag in termen van condoomgebruik. In het hoofdstuk wordt ingegaan op de verdiensten en de tekortkomingen van de verschillende benaderingswijzen. Opvallend is dat er vaak kleine, specifieke groepen zijn onderzocht en dat er in het algemeen weinig onderscheid is gemaakt tussen prostituées. Het is tevens opmerkelijk, dat er nog nauwelijks een integratie heeft plaatsgevonden van deze verschillende invalshoeken. Onderzoek naar de (geestelijke) gezondheid van prostituées besteedt veelal relatief weinig aandacht aan trauma en deze beide aspecten zijn nog nauwelijks in verband gebracht met beschermingsgedrag. De onderhavige studies proberen tot een coherenter beeld te komen. Aan het slot van dit hoofdstuk zijn de onderzoeksvragen geformuleerd.

In hoofdstuk drie wordt het multi-causale model geïntroduceerd met behulp waarvan (variaties in) welzijn en beschermingsgedrag verklaard kunnen worden. Zowel welzijn als beschermingsgedrag worden beschouwd als de uitkomst van een wederkerig en dynamisch interactieproces tussen persoon, ervaringen en omgeving. Op basis van de resultaten uit onderzoek op verschillende terreinen en onder uiteenlopende groepen, kunnen verschillende factoren van belang geacht worden als het gaat om het welzijn en beschermingsgedrag van prostituées. Achtereenvolgens worden voor beide afhankelijke variabelen besproken: copinggedrag als mediërende factor; context-gerelateerde factoren (demografische variabelen, migratie, financiële nood en werkomstandigheden); persoons-gerelateerde factoren (Health Locus of Control en andere cognities); en victimiserende ervaringen, zowel in de kindertijd als gedurende het volwassen leven. In het kader van beschermingsgedrag wordt bovendien de interactie met klanten beschouwd als een cruciale factor. De stigmatisering van prostituées wordt beschreven als de (welzijns-belastende) achtergrond waartegen dit alles zich afspeelt. Aan het eind van dit hoofdstuk zijn de onderzoeksverwachtingen geformuleerd.

In hoofdstuk vier worden voor beide gerapporteerde onderzoeken de methoden beschreven. Behandeld worden de procedures van werving, de kenmerken en de representativiteit van de onderzoeksgroepen, en het onderzoeksinstrumentarium cq. de operationalisaties van de relevante variabelen.

In hoofdstuk vijf worden de bevindingen ten aanzien van het welzijn van prostituées beschreven en in verband gebracht met de relevant geachte factoren. Het merendeel van de geformuleerde verwachtingen wordt bevestigd in het materiaal. Prostituées als groep rapporteren meer klachten en problemen dan de controlegroepen, zijn vaker en ernstiger getraumatiseerd en gebruiken vaker interne overlevingsstrategieën. Desondanks zijn er grote verschillen. Met ongeveer een kwart van de onderzochte vrouwen gaat het ronduit goed. Een ander kwart daarentegen rapporteert extreem veel klachten en problemen. Een heterogene middengroep zit daar tussen in wat welzijn betreft. Door middel van een padanalyse is gevonden welke factoren het meest uitmaken in relatie tot welzijn. Seksuele traumatisering in de jeugd, ervaringen met geweld op het werk, en het aan beide gekoppelde gebruik van interne copingstrategieën (in het bijzonder dissociatie en ontkenning) blijken de belangrijkste 'risicofactoren'. Bovendien blijken jongere vrouwen het in het algemeen moeilijker te hebben. Daarnaast blijkt een sterkere 'expert Health Locus of Control' als intern persoonlijkheidskenmerk te associëren met meer 'sociale onzekerheid' en een lage arbeidssatisfactie blijkt sterk samen te hangen met druggebruik. Probleemgericht copinggedrag blijkt vooral lichamelijke klachten en zakelijke aangelegenheden te gelden en lijkt in de vicieuze cirkel van ervaringen met geweld-manipulatie van emoties-verminderd welzijn, buiten spel te blijven. In het hoofdstuk zijn deze bevindingen, alsmede de significante verbanden met andere factoren zoals werkomstandigheden, financiële druk en migratie, bediscussieerd. Gezien het frequente gebruik van interne, 'ongezonde' oplossingen voor problemen door prostituées, zijn ten slotte de aard van het werk en de prostitutiecontext onderzocht als potentiële voedingsbodems voor de manipulatie van emoties.

In hoofdstuk zes worden de bevindingen met betrekking tot het beschermingsge-drag van prostituées beschreven en in verband gebracht met de onderzochte factoren (op dit punt nog m.u.v. de interactie met klanten). Drie groepen met verschillende beschermingsstijlen zijn geïdentificeerd: consequente beschermers, selectieve risiconemers en risiconemers. Vooral de risiconemers (11% van de onderzoeksgroep) wijken sterk af van de twee andere groepen. Met deze vrouwen gaat het in het algemeen minder goed, zowel wat betreft welzijn en arbeidssatis-factie, als wat betreft arbeids- en financiële omstandigheden. Risiconemers hebben in hun privéleven, zowel in de jeugd als later, meer (seksueel) geweld meege-maakt en gebruiken vaker drugs. Ook op de werkplek hebben ze vaker te maken met gewelddadige klanten. Met de selectieven daarentegen gaat het op alle fronten het best. Als zij (incidenteel) het condoom achterwege laten met een klant doen ze dat veelal in een context van vertrouwen en plezier. Consequente beschermers op hun beurt worden vooral gekenmerkt door een zakelijke werkhouding en vertonen onderling een grote verscheidenheid wat welzijn betreft. AIDS-gerelateerde cognities spelen in dit geheel slechts een marginale rol.

In hoofdstuk zeven zijn de beschermingsstijlen van klanten van prostituées en de interactie tussen prostituées en klanten besproken. Een positieve acceptatie van zowel de mogelijkheden als de beperkingen in de prostitutie blijkt condoomge-bruik door klanten positief te beïnvloeden. Als mannen daarentegen sterke romantische illusies koesteren, verlangen naar 'vaste' relaties met prostituées, of seks associëren met 'alles laten gaan', is het condoom symbool van ongewenste afstand en zakelijkheid en wordt (de wens tot) onbeschermde seks met prostituées waarschijnlijker. Regelrechte weerstand tegen het condoom blijkt geassocieerd te zijn met negatieve gevoelens over het prostitutiebezoek en over prostituées en met een seksualiteitsbeleving die gekenmerkt wordt door dwangmatigheid en een gebrek aan controle. Recalcitrante condoomgebruikers accepteren het spel niet en willen het niet volgens de regels spelen. Daarnaast wordt gevonden dat conse-quente condoomgebruikers meer angst voor AIDS hebben, een hogere opleiding hebben genoten en een minder sterke externe Health Locus of Control. Interactie-scenario's tussen prostituées en klanten die, in tegenstelling tot het standaard script in de prostitutie, leiden tot onbeschermde seks, worden vaak gekenmerkt door een (wederzijdse) perceptie van vertrouwen en vriendschap of romantiek. In een ander alternatief scenario is er eerder sprake van een gevecht en van veel wederzijdse, expliciete beïnvloedingspogingen. Risiconemers onder de prostituées proberen hun klanten het sterkst op allerlei manieren te beïnvloeden en hebben tegelijkertijd de sterkste gevoelens van onmacht en hulpeloosheid. Voor de selectieve risiconemers is dat precies andersom. Deze interactieve aspecten blijken uiteindelijk het sterkst van alle onderzochte factoren te associëren met het beschermingsgedrag van prostituées.

In hoofdstuk acht worden alle bevindingen integraal beschouwd. Het gehanteerde multi-causale model is adequaat gebleken in de zin dat de factoren die er in opgenomen zijn tezamen hoge percentages van de variatie in welzijn en beschermingsgedrag verklaren. Geconcludeerd wordt, dat als het gaat om welzijn en beschermingsgedrag van prostituées, er gesproken kan worden van een sneeuwbaleffect: diegenen met de betere uitgangsposities slagen er eerder in om het werk relatief comfortabel in te richten, 'gezonder' met problemen om te gaan en tot een positievere (en veiliger) interactie met klanten te komen. Voor prostituées wiens leven voorafgaand aan de prostitutie daarentegen gekenmerkt werd door traumatisering en geweld en een (vaak daarmee samenhangende) sterke economische nood lijken problematische condities zich te blijven opstapelen. Zij komen op de minder veilige werkplekken terecht, hebben een sterk belastende werkroutine, hebben meer te maken met gewelddadige klanten, en hanteren, samenhangend met hun condities, meer 'ongezonde' interne overlevingsstrategieën. De prostituées met wie het het slechtst gaat, komen, vanuit een verleden dat zich kenmerkt door geweld en deprivatie, vaak opnieuw in extreem zware omstandigheden terecht en zijn bovendien het minst opgewassen tegen de belasting die het werk (op die manier) met zich meebrengt. Deze bevinding is beschouwd met behulp van gelieerde sociologische en psychologische inzichten en geplaatst naast bevindingen uit eerder onderzoek naar het welzijn van prostituées. Tot slot zijn er aanbevelingen voor beleidsinterventies en voor verder onderzoek geformuleerd. Gezien de grote verschillen tussen prostituées zullen ook de interventies met betrekking tot de prostitutie gedifferentieerd moeten zijn en zo goed mogelijk op de verschillende groepen toegesneden moeten worden. Daarnaast lijkt onderzoek naar de beschermende factoren en adequate 'vangnetten' voor de kwetsbaarste groep in de toekomst het meest gewenst.

REFERENCES

Abernethy, V. (1975) Family dynamics of promiscuous girls. *Medical Aspects of Human Sexuality 9(2)*, 90.

Abraham, K. (1922) Manifestations of the female castration complex. *International Journal of Psycho-analysis 3*, 1-29.

Adler, P. (1955) *A house is not a home.* New York: Popular Library.

Agoston, T. (1945) Some psychological aspects of prostitution: the pseudo-personality. *International Journal of Psycho-analysis 26*, 62-67.

Ajzen, I. and Fishbein, M. (1977) Attitude-behavior relations: A theoretical analysis and review of empirical research. *Psychological Bulletin 84*, 888-918.

Ajzen, I. and Madden, T.J. (1986) Prediction of goal-directed behavior: Attitudes, intentions, and perceived behavioral control. *Journal of Experimental Social Psychology 22*, 453-474.

Alexander, P. (1982) *Working on prostitution.* National Prostitution Committee, a national committee of the National Organization for Women (NOW).

Alexander, P. (1993) *International survey of the status of prostitution.* Internal Report, World Health Oganization.

Allers, C.T. and Benjack, K.J. (1991) Connections between childhood abuse and HIV infection. *Journal of counseling and development 70*, 309-313.

Altink, S. (1989) Arbeidsvoorwaarden en Arbeidsomstandigheden. In: Vanwesenbeeck, I., S. Altink and M. Groen. *Hoe (ex)prostituées zich zelf redden.* Den Haag: Ministerie SoZaWe, 86-133.

Altink, S. (1993) *Dossier vrouwenhandel NL.* Amsterdam: SUA.

Armstrong, E. (1978) Massage parlors and their customers. *Archives of Sexual Behavior 7*, 117-125.

Arrindel, W.A. and Ettema, H. (1987) *Handleiding bij een multidimensionele psychopathologie-indicator.* Lisse: Swets & Zeitlinger.

Bagley, C. and Young, L. (1987) Juvenile prostitution and child sexual abuse: A controlled study. *Canadian Journal of Community Mental Health 6*, 5-26.

Barnett, R.C. Davidson, H. and Marshall, N.L. (1991) Physical symptoms and the interplay of work and family roles. *Health psychology 10(2)*, 94-102.

Barrows, S. and Novak, W. (1985) *Mayflower Madam. The Secret Life of Sidney Biddle Barrows.* New York: Arbor House.

Barry, K. (1979) *Female Sexual Slavery.* Englewood Cliffs, N.J.: Prentice Hall.

Basel, A.S. (1970) Why do married men visit prostitutes? *Medical Aspects of Human Sexuality 4(7)*, 84-88.

Baum, A. and Gatchel, R.J. (1981) Cognitive determinants of reactions to uncontrollable events: Development of reactance and learned helplessness. *Journal of Personality and Social Psychology 40(6)*, 1078-1089.

Becker, H.S. (1963) *Outsiders.* New York: Free Press.

Becker, M.H. and Joseph, J.G. (1988) AIDS and Behavioral Change to Reduce Risk: A Review. *American Journal of Public Health 78(4)*, 394-410.

Belderbos, F. and Visser, J.H. (red.) (1987) *Beroep: prostituée.* Utrecht: SWP.

Bell, L. (ed.) (1987) *Good girls/bad girls. Feminists and sex trade workers face to face.* Toronto: The Seal Press.

Berg, T. van der and Blom, M. (1987) *Tippelen voor dope. Levensverhalen van vrouwen in de heroïneprostitutie.* Amsterdam: Mr. A. de Graafstichting.

Bess, B. en Janus, S. (1975) Masochism of prostitutes. *Medical Aspects of Human Sexuality 9(2)*, 89.

Bloor, M.J., McKeganey, N.P., Finlay, A. and Barnard, M.A. (1992) The inappropriateness of psycho-social models of risk behaviour for understanding HIV-rekated risk practices among Glasgow male prostitutes. *AIDS CARE 4(2)*, 131-137.

Boggs, V.W. (1991) Prostitute's occupational continuum: A blueprint for research. *Nordisk Sexologi 9(1)*, 31-43.

Boon, S. and Draijer, N. (1993) *Multiple Personality Disorder in the Netherlands. A study on reliability and validity of the diagnosis.* Amsterdam/Lisse: Swets and Zeitlinger.

Bouchier, T. and de Jong, H. (1987) *Hoerenlopers, mannen op zoek naar intimiteit.* Groningen: Jan Mets.

Bour, D.S., Young, J.P. and Henningsen, R. (1984) A comparison of delinquent prostitutes and delinquent non-prostitutes on self-concept. *Journal of Offender Counseling, Services and Rehabilitation 9*, 71-87.

Bourdieu, P. (1989) *Opstellen over smaak, habitus en het veldbegrip.* Amsterdam: Van Gennep.

Boutellier, J.C.J. (1987) Enkele cijfers over prostitutie. *Justitiële Verkenningen 13(1)*, 36-45.

Boutellier, J.C.J. (1991) Prostitution, criminal law and morality in the Netherlands. *Crime, Law and Social Change 13*, 201-211.

Bovenkerk, F., Dankoor, M., Lichtvoet, P. et al. (1993) *Een veilige plek: 'huiskamers' voor straatprostituees.* Den Bosch: Werkgroep Vraag en Aanbod i.s.m. Mr.A.de Graafstichting en Willem Pompe Instituut.

Brandt, A. (1985) *No magic bullet. A social history of veneral disease in the United States since 1880.* New York/Oxford: Oxford University Press.

Brecher, E.M. (1975) How prostitutes guard against VD? *Medical Aspects of Human Sexuality 9(11)*, 133.

Brown, M. (1979) Teenage prostitution. *Adolescence 14*, 665-680.

Browne, A. and Finkelhor, D. (1986) Impact of child sexual abuse: A review of the research. *Psychological Bulletin 99*, 66-77.

Brownmiller, S. (1975) *Against Our Will: Men, Women and Rape.* New York: Bantam Books.

Brussa, L. (1989) Migrant prostitutes in the Netherlands. In: Pheterson, G. (ed.) *A Vindication of the Rights of Whores.* Seattle: Seal press, 227-239.

Brussa, L. (1992) *Gezondheid in de raamprostitutie.* Amsterdam: Mr.A.de Graafstichting.

Bryan, J.H. (1966) Occupational ideologies and individual attitude of call-girls. *Social Problems 13*, 441-450.

Buijs, H.W.J. and Verbraken, A.M. (1985) *Vrouwenhandel. Onderzoek naar aard, globale omvang en de kanalen waarlangs vrouwenhandel naar Nederland plaatsvindt.* Den Haag: Ministerie van Sociale Zaken.

Buijs, H.W.J. (1991) *Dutch prostitution policy and human rights. Memorandum for the seminar on action against traffic in women and forced prostitution.* Strasbourg: Counsil of Europe.

Bullough, V.L. (1964) *The history of prostitution.* New york: University Books.

Bullough, V.L. (1970) Why do married men visit prostitutes? *Medical Aspects of Human Sexuality 4(7)*, 93.

Bullough, V.L. en Bullough, B. (1977) *Sin, Sickness, & Sanity. A History of Sexual Attitudes.* New York/ London: Garland Publishing, Inc.

Bullough, V.L. and Bullough, B. (1978) *Prostitution: An illustrated social history.* New York: Crown Publishers.

Burgess, A.W. and Holmstrom, E. (1979) Adaptive strategies in recovery from rape. *American Journal of Psychiatry 136,* 1278-1282.

Campbell, C.A. (1991) Prostitution, AIDS, and preventive health behavior. *Social Science and Medicine 32(12),* 1367-1378.

Carballo, M. (1990) Psychosocial aspects of AIDS: policy implications. *AIDS 4(suppl 1),* S29-S33.

Carovano, K. (1991) More than mothers and whores: redefining the aidsprevention needs of women. *International Journal of Health Services 21(1),* 131-142.

Carter, A. (1979) *The Sadeian Woman: an exercise in cultural history.* London: Virago.

Catania, J.A., Dolcini, M.M., Coates, T.J. et al. (1989) Predictors of condom use and multiple partnered sex among sexually active adolescent women: implications for AIDS-related health interventions. *The Journal of Sex Research 26(4),* 514-524.

Cave, V.G. (1970) Why do married men visit prostitutes? *Medical Aspects of Human Sexuality 4(7),* 97.

Centraal Bureau voor de Statistiek (CBS). (1988) *Onderzoek gezinsvorming 1988.* Den Haag: SDU.

Centraal Bureau voor de Statistiek (CBS). (1991) *Enquête beroepsbevolking, 1990.* Den Haag: SDU.

Centraal Bureau voor de Statistiek (CBS). (1992) *Vrouwen en mannen naast elkaar.* Den Haag: SDU.

Centres for Disease Control (CDC). (1987) Antibody to human immunodeficiency virus in female prostitutes. *Morbidity and Mortality Weekly Report 36,* 157-161.

Chacón, L., Ortiz, M., Rodriguez, A., Gutiérrez, A.L. and Zamorra, A. (1992) *Soy una mujer de ambiente. Un análysis sobre prostitutión feminina, prevention y SIDA.* San José: Instituto de Investigationes Sociales, Universidad de Costa Rica.

Choisy, M. (1961) *Psychoanalysis of the Prostitute.* New York: Philosofical Library.

Coleman, E. (1989) The development of male prostitution activity among gay and bisexual adolescents. *Journal of Homosexuality 17(1),* 131-150.

Correspondent, A. (1990) India: prostitutes and the spread of AIDS. *Lancet 335,* 1332.

Cowie, J., Cowie, V. and Slater, E. (1968) *Delinquency in girls.* London: Heinemann.

Curran, F.J. and Levine, M. (1942) Body image study of prostitutes. *Journal of Criminology and Psychopathology 4,* 93-116.

Darrow, W.W., Bigler, W., Deppe, D., French, J., Gill, P. et al. (1988) *HIV-antibody in 640 U.S. prostitutes with no evidence of intravenous (IV) drug use.* Presented at the Fourth International Conference on AIDS, Stockholm, june 12-16.

Davis, K. (1937) The sociology of prostitution. *American Sociological Review 2,* 744-755.

Davis, N.J. (1971) The Prostitute: Developing a Deviant Identity. In: Henslin JM. (ed) *Studies in the Sociology of Sex.* New York: Appleton-Century Crofts, 297-322.

Davis, N.J. (Ed.) (1993) *Prostitution. An International Handbook on Trends, Problems and Policies.* Westport/London: Greenwood Press.

Day, S. (1988) Editorial review: Prostitute women and AIDS: anthropology. *AIDS 2*, 421-428.

Day, S. (1990) Prostitute women and the ideology of work in London. In: Feldman, D.A. (Ed.) *Culture and AIDS.* New York: Praeger Publishers.

Day, S., Ward, H. and Harris, J.R.W. (1988) Prostitute women and public health. *British Medical Journal 297*, 1585.

Delacoste, F. and Alexander, P. (1988) *Sex Work. Writings by Women in the Sex Industry.* London: Virago Press.

Delft, M. van (1991) *Sociale atlas van de vrouw. Deel I.* Rijswijk: Sociaal en Cultureel Planbureau.

Derogatis, L.R. and Clearly, P.A. (1977) Confirmation of the dimensional structure of the SCL-90: a study in construct validation. *Journal of Clinical Psychology 33*, 981-989.

DeSchampheleire, D. (1990) MMPI characteristics of professional prostitutes: A cross-cultural replication. *Journal of Personality Assessment 54(1&2)*, 343-350.

Deutsch, H. (1945) *The Psychology of Women: Psychoanalytic Interpretation. Vol. 2.* New York: Grune & Stratton.

Deutsch, H. (1947) *The Psychology of Women: Psychoanalytic Interpretation. Vol. 1.* London: Research Books Ltd.

Dominelli, L. (1986) The power of the powerless: prostitution and the reinforcement of submissive feminity. *Sociological Review 34(1)*, 65-92.

Dorfman, L.E., Derish, P.A. and Cohen, J.B. (1992) Hey Girlfriend: An Evaluation of AIDS Prevention among Women in the Sex Industry. *Health Education Quarterly 19(1)*, 25-40.

Draijer, N. (1988) *Seksueel misbruik van meisjes door verwanten.* Den Haag: Ministerie van Sociale Zaken en Werkgelegenheid.

Draijer, N. (1990) *Seksuele traumatisering in de jeugd. Gevolgen op lange termijn van seksueel misbruik van meisjes door verwanten.* Amsterdam: SUA.

DuBois, E.C. and Gordon, L. (1984) Seeking Ecstacy on the Battlefield: Danger and Pleasure in Nineteenth-century Feminist Sexual Thought. In: Vance, C.S. (ed.) *Pleasure and Danger. Exploring Female Sexuality.* Boston/ London/ Melbourne/ Henley: Routledge & Kegan Paul, 31-49.

Dunkel-Shetter, C., Folkman, S. and Lazarus, R.S. (1987) Correlates of social support. *Journal of Personality and Social Psychology 53(1)*, 71-80.

Dweck, C.S. and Goetz, T.E. (1978) Attributions and learned helplesness. In: J.H. Harvey, W. Ickes and R.F. Kidd (Eds.) *New directions in attribution research (part II).* Hillsdale N.J.: Erlbaum.

Dworkin, A. (1990) *Pornography: Men Possessing Women.* New York: Dutton.

Earls, C.M. and David, H. (1989) Male and female prostitution: A review. *Annals of sex research 2*, 5-28.

Earls, C.M. and David, H. (1990) Early family experiences of male and female prostitutes. *Canada's Mental Health 38(4)*, 7-11.

Eckenrode, J. (Ed.) (1991) *The social context of coping.* New York: Plenum Press.

Ellis, A. (1959) Why married men visit prostitutes? *Sexology 25*, 344-347.

Engbersen, G. (1990) *Publieke bijstandsgeheimen. Het ontstaan van een onderklasse in Nederland.* Leiden: Stenfert Kroese.

Estébanez, P., Fitch, K. and Nájera, R. (1993) HIV and female sex workers. *Bulletin of the World Health Organization 71(3/4),* 397-412.

European Working Group in HIV Infection in Female Prostitutes. (1993) HIV infection in European female sex workers: epidemiological link with use of petroleum-based lubricants. *AIDS 7,* 401-408.

Exner, J.E., Wylie, J., Leura, A., Parrill, T. (1977) Some Psychological Characteristics of Prostitutes. *Journal of Personality Assessment 41(5),* 474-485.

Falbo, T. and Peplau, L.A. (1980) Power Strategies in Intimate Relationships. *Journal of Personality and Social Psychology 38(4),* 618-628.

Ferracuti, F. (1972) Incest between father and daughter. In: Resnik, Wolfgang and Boston (Eds.) *Sexual behaviors: social, clinical and legal aspects.* Boston: Little Brown & Co., 169-183.

Fields, P.J. (1980) *Parent-child relationships, childhood sexual abuse and adult interpersonal behavior in female prostitutes.* Ph.D. dissertation, California School of Professional Psychology, Los Angeles.

Finkelhor, D. and Browne, A. (1988) Child sexual abuse: A review and conceptualization. In: G.T. Hotaling, D. Finkelhor, J.T. Kirkpatrick and M.A. Straus (Eds.) *Family abuse and its consequences: New directions in research.* Newbury Park, CA: Sage, 270-284.

Fisher, J.D. and Misovich, S.J. (1990) Social Influence and AIDS-preventive Behavior. 39-69.

Fiske, S.T. and Taylor, S.E. (1984) *Social cognition.* New York: Random House.

Foa, U.G. and Krieger, E. (1985) Perveived need for resources: some differences among groups. *Personality and Individual Differences 6(3),* 347-351.

Folkman, S. and Lazarus, R.S. (1988) Coping as a mediator of emotion. *Journal of Personality and Social Psychology 54,* 466-475.

Foucault, M. (1976) *Histoire de la sexualité. 1. La volonté de savoir.* Paris: Gallimard.

Francis, V. De (1969) *Protecting the Child Victims of Sex Crimes Committed by Adults.* Final Report, American Humane Association, Children's Division, Denver, 215.

Frankenhaeuser, M., Lundberg, U. and Chesney, M. (1991) *Women, work and health. Stress and opportunities.* New York/London: Plenum Press.

Friedman, H.S. (1992) Understanding hostility, coping and health. In: Friedman, H.S. (Ed.) *Hostility, coping and health.* Washington: American Psychological Association.

Fullilove, R.E., Fullilove, M., Gasch, H. and Smith, M. (1992) *Violent trauma and HIV-risk.* VIII Conference on AIDS, Amsterdam, PoC 4252.

Gebhard, P.H. (1969) Misconceptions of female prostitutes. *Medical Aspects of Human Sexuality 3(3),* 24-30.

Gelder, P. van and Van Roekel, A. (1989) *Baltsen en Banen.* Rotterdam: GGD.

Gemeente Den Haag. (1988) *In het kader van het leven. Naar een vergunningenstelsel voor de Haagse prostitutie.*

Gibbens, T. and Silverman, M. (1960) The Clients of Prostitutes. *Journal of Venereal Diseases 36,* 113-117.

Giddens, A. (1992) *The Transformation of Intimacy. Sexuality, Love and Eroticism in Modern Societies.* Cambridge: Polity Press.

Girelli, S.A., Resick, P.A., Marhoefer-Dvorak, S. and Hutter, C.K. (1986) Subjective distress and violence during rape: their effects on long-term fear. *Victims and Violence 1(1),* 35-46.

Girtler, R. (1984) [The prostitute and her clients.] *Kölner Zeitschrift für Soziologie und Sozialpsychologie 36(2),* 323-341.

Glover, E. (1943) The Psychopathology of Prostitution. In: *The roots of crime.* New York: International Universities Press, 244-267.

Goffman, E. (1963) *Stigma: notes on the management of spoiled identity.* Englewood Cliffs, N.J.: Prentice Hall.

Goffman, E. (1977) The arrangement between the sexes. *Theory & Society 4(3),* 301-331.

Goldstein, P.J. (1979) *Prostitution and drugs.* Lexington: Lexington Books.

Goodkin, K., Blaney, N.T., Feaster, D., Fletcher, M., Baum, M.K., Mantero-Atienza, E., Klimas, N.G., Millon, C., Szapocznik, J. and Eisdorfer, C. (1992) Active coping style is associated with natural killer cell cytotoxicity in asymptomatic HIV-1 seropositive homosexual men. *Journal of Psychosomatic Research 36(7),* 635-650.

Graaf, R. de, Vanwesenbeeck, I., Van Zessen, G., Straver, C.J. and Visser, J.H. (1992) Prostitutie, seksueel gedrag en de mogelijke verspreiding van HIV. *Tijdschrift voor Sociale Gezondheidszorg 70(5),* 280-287.

Graaf, R. de, I. Vanwesenbeeck, G. van Zessen, C.J. Straver and J.H. Visser. (1992) Condom use and sexual behaviour in heterosexual prostitution in the Netherlands [letter]. *AIDS 6,* 1223-1226.

Graaf, R. de, I. Vanwesenbeeck, G. van Zessen, C.J. Straver and J.H. Visser. (1992) Homo-prostitutie en de mogelijke verspreiding van HIV. *Tijdschrift voor Sociale Gezondheidszorg 70(10),* 599-604.

Graaf, R. de, Vanwesenbeeck, I., Van Zessen, G., Straver, C.J. and Visser, J.H. (1993) Alcohol- en druggebruik in hetero- en homoseksuele prostitutie-contacten, en het verband met onveilig seksueel gedrag. *Tijdschrift voor Sociale Gezondheidszorg (71)5,* 258-266.

Graaf, R. de, I. Vanwesenbeeck, G. van Zessen, C.J. Straver and J.H. Visser. (1993) The effectiveness of condom use in heterosexual prostitution in The Netherlands [short communication]. *AIDS 7,* 265-269.

Graaf, R. de, I. Vanwesenbeeck, G. van Zessen, C.J. Straver and J.H. Visser. (1993) Mannelijke prostitués en safe seks. *Maandblad Geestelijke volksgezondheid 48(3),* 259-276.

Graaf, R. de, G. van Zessen, I. Vanwesenbeeck, C.J. Straver and J.H. Visser (in press) Condoomgebruik door mannen met heteroseksuele commerciële contacten: determinanten en overwegingen. *Tijdschrift voor Sociale Gezondheidszorg.*

Gray, D. (1973) Turning out: A Study of Teenage Prostitution. *Urban Life and Culture,* january 1973, 401-425.

Greenwald, H. (1958) *The Call Girl: A social and psychoanalytic study.* New York: Ballantine.

Greenwald, H (1973) Are prostitutes sociopaths? *Medical Aspects of Human Sexuality 7(9),* 261-263.

Groen, M. (1987) *Hoerenboek. Tien vrouwen over het vak.* Amsterdam: Feministische Uitgeverij Sara.

Groen, M. (1989) Het vragen van hulp in de informele en formele sfeer. In: I. Vanwesenbeeck, S. Altink and M. Groen. *Hoe (ex)prostituées zich zelf redden.* Den Haag: Ministerie SoZaWe, 178-231.

Haastrecht, H.J.A. van, Fennema, F.S.A., Coutinho, R.A. and van den Hoek, J.A.R. (1992) *Low socio-economic status is a predictor of inconsistent condom use for both prostitutes and their clients in Amsterdam.* VIII International Conference on AIDS, Amsterdam. Abstract PoC4184.

Hanson, R.K. (1990) The psychological impact of sexual assault on women and children: A review. *Annals of Sex Research 3(2),* 187-232.

Herk, B. van (1985) Ga je mee schat? *Intermediair,* november 1985.

Herman, J.L. (1981) *Father-daughter incest.* Cambridge, MA: Harvard University Press.

Herman, J.L., Russell, D. and Trocki, K. (1986) Long term effects of incestuous abuse in childhood. *American Journal of Psychiatry 143,* 1293-1296.

Heyl, B.S. (1974) The madam as entrepreneur. *Sociological Symposium 11,* 61-83.

Heyl, B.S. (1977) Madam as teacher; the training of house prostitutes. *Social Problems 24,* 545-555.

Hirschi, T. (1962) The professional prostitute. *Berkely Journal of Sociology 7,* 33-49.

Hochschild, A.R. (1979) Emotion work, feeling rules, and social structure. *American Journal of Sociology 85(3),* 551-575.

Hochschild, A.R. (1988) The managed heart: Commercialization of human feeling. In: Clark, C. and Robboy, H. (Eds.) *Social Interaction. Readings in Sociology.* New York: St. Martin's Press.

Hoek, J.A.R. van der (1988) Prostitutie en seksueel overdraagbare aandoeningen (SOA). *Nederlands Tijdschrift voor de Geneeskunde 132(49),* 2264.

Holahan, C.J. and Moos, R.H. (1987) Personal and contextual determinants of coping strategies. *Journal of Personality and Social Psychology 52,* 946-955.

Holland, J., Ramazanoglu, C., Scott, S., Sharp, S. and Thomson, R. (1990) Sex, gender and power: young women's sexuality in the shadow of aids. *Sociology of Health and Illness 12,* 336-350.

Hollander, X. (1982) *The Happy Hooker.* Utrecht: Skarabee.

Hollender, M.H. (1961) Prostitution, the body and human relatedness. *International Journal of Psycho-analysis 42,* 404-413.

Holzman, H.R. and Pines, S. (1982) Buying sex: The phenomenology of being a 'john'. *Deviant behavior 4(1),* 89-116.

Hooghiemstra, B.T.J. and Niphuis-Nell, M. (1993) *Sociale atlas van de vrouw. Deel 2: Arbeid en inkomen.* Rijswijk: Sociaal en Cultureel Planbureau.

Hooijkaas, C., Van der Pligt, J., Van Doornum, G.J.J., Van der Linden, M.M.D., Coutinho, R.A. (1989) Heterosexuals at risk for HIV: Differences between private and commercial partners in sexual behaviour and condom use. *AIDS 3,* 525-532.

Howard, J.A., Blumstein, P. and Schwartz, P. (1986) Sex, Power, and Influence Tactics in Intimate Relationships. *Journal of Personality and Social Psychology 51(1),* 102-109.

Hunt, C.W. (1989) Migrant labor and sexually transmitted disease: AIDS in Africa. *Journal of Health and Social Behavior 30,* 353-373.

Ingham, R. and van Zessen, G. (1994) Towards an alternative model of sexual behaviour: from individual properties to interactional processes. In: Hubert, M. et al. (Eds.) *New*

Conceptual Perpectives for understanding sexual behaviour and the risk of HIV infection. Brussels: EC Concerted Action on Sexual behaviour and the Risks of HIV infection.

Jackman, N.H., O'Toole, R. and Geis, G. (1963) The self-image of the prostitute. *Sociogical Quarterly 4,* 150-161.

Jackson, L., Highcrest, A. and Coates, R.A. (1992) Varied potential risk of HIV infection among prostitutes. *Social Science and Medicine 35(3),* 281-286.

James, J. (1976) Motivations for entrance into prostitution. In L. Crites (Ed.) *The female offender.* Lexington: Lexington Books, 177-205.

James, J. (1977) Why married men see prostitutes? *Medical Aspects of Human Sexuality 11(6),* 17 & 99.

James, J. (1978) The prostitute as victim. In: Chapman, J.R. and Gates, M. *The Victimization of Women.* Beverly Hills / London: Sage, 175-201.

James, J. (1980) Self-destructive Behaviors and Adaptive Strategies in Female Prostitutes. In: *The many Faces of Suicide: Indirect Self-Destructive Behaviors.* New York: McGraw-Hill, 341-359.

James, J. and Davis, N.J. (1982) Contingencies in female sexual role deviance: The case of prostitution. *Human Organization 41,* 345-350.

James, J. and Meyerding, J. (1977) Early sexual experience as a factor in prostitution. *Archives of Sexual Behavior 7(1),* 31-42.

Janoff-Bulman, R. (1985) The aftermath of victimization: rebuilding shattered assumptions. In Figley, R. (Ed.) *Trauma and its wake, 1.* New-York: Brunner/Mazel, 15-35.

Janovsky, V. (1922) De prostitutie. In: Goudsmit BC. en Ter Kuile CPF. *De man en de vrouw in hunne onderlinge verhoudingen en in hunne betrekking tot de heedendaagsche maatschappij.* Amsterdam: N.V. Gebr. Graauw.

Janus, S. (1967) Prostitutes' emotional needs. *Medical Aspects of Human Sexuality 11(11),* 102.

Janus, S.S. and Janus, C.L. (1993) *The Janus report on sexual behavior.* New York: John Wiley & Sons, Inc.

Järvinen, M. (1993) Prostitution in Helsinki: A Dissapearing Social Problem? *Journal of the History of Sexuality 3(4),* 608-630.

Kane, S. (1990) AIDS, Addiction and Condom Use: Sources of Sexual Risk for Heterosexual Women. *Journal of Sex Research 27(3),* 427-444.

Kantha, S.S. (1991) *Prostitutes in medical literature. An annotated bibliography.* New york/Westport/London: Greenwood Press.

Karsten, C. (1993) *Female hard drug-users in crisis. Childhood traumas and survival strategies.* Utrecht: Nederlands Instituut voor Alcohol en Drugs (NIAD).

Katz, I. (1981) *Stigma: a social-psychological analysis.* Hillsdale N.J.: Erlbaum.

Kemp, T. (1936) *Prostitution: An investigation of its causes, especially with regard to hereditary factors.* Copenhagen: Levin & Munskgaard.

King, D. (1990) Prostitutes as pariah in the age of AIDS: A content analysis of coverage of women prostitutes in the New York Times and the Washington Post, sept.1985-apr.1988. *Women and Health 16(3-4),* 155-176.

Kleber, R.J., Brom, D. and Defares, P.B. (1986) *Traumatische ervaringen, gevolgen en verwerking.* Lisse: Swets & Zeitlinger.

Kleber, R.J. and Brom, D. (1992) *Coping with trauma.* Amsterdam/Lisse: Swets & Zeitlinger.

Klein, D. (1980) The etiology of female crime: A review of the literature. In: S.K. Datesman and F.R. Scarpitti (Eds.) *Women, Crime and Justice.* New York: Oxford University Press.

Kolk, B.A. van der (1987) *Psychological trauma.* Washington: American Psychiatric Press, Inc.

Kolk, B.A. van der (1989) The compulsion to repeat the trauma, re-enactment, revictimization, and masochism. Treatment of victims of sexual abuse. *Psychiatric Clinics of North America 12,* 389-411.

Komter, A.E. (1985) *De macht van de vanzelfsprekendheid. Relaties tussen vrouwen en mannen.* Den Haag: VUGA.

Komter, A.E. and Schuyt, C.J.M. (1993) Geschenken en relaties. *Beleid & Maatschappij 20(6),* 277-285.

Koss, M.P. and Harvey, M.R. (1991) *The Rape Victim: Clinical and Community Intervention.* London: Sage Publications.

Kreiss, J.K., Koech, D., Plummer, F.A., Holmes, K.K., Lightfoot, M., Piot, P., Ronald, A.R., Ndinya-Achola, J.O., D'Costa, L.J., Roberts, P., Ngugi, E.N. and Quinn, T.C. (1986) AIDS virus infection in Nairibi prostitutes: Spread of the epidemic to East Africa. *New England Journal of Medicine 314,* 414-418.

Kuhns, J.B. and Heide, K.M. (1992) AIDS-related issues among female prostitutes and female arrestees. *International Journal of Offender Therapy and Comparative Criminology 36(3),* 231-245.

Lagergren, M., Giesecke, J., Hallqvist, J., Lidman, K. and Olin, R. (1990) Anonymous inquiries in Sweden regarding the individual's motives for HIV-antibody testing autumn 1987 and 1988. *AIDS Education and Prevention 2,* 171-180.

Lampl de Groot, J. (1928) The evolution of the Oedipus complex in women. *International Journal of Psycho-analysis 9,* 322.

Lazarus, R.S. (1966) *Psychological stress and the coping process.* New York: McGraw-Hill Books Co.

Lazarus, R.S. (1985) The costs and benefits of denial. In: Monat, A. and Lazarus, R.S. (Eds.) *Stress and Coping: an anthology.* New York: Columbia University Press.

Lazarus, R.S. and Folkman, S. (1974) *Stress, appraisal and coping.* New York: Springer.

Lazarus, R.S., Averill, J.R. and Opton, E.M. (1974) The psychology of coping: Issues of research and assessment. In: Coelho, Hamburg and Adams (Eds.) *Coping and adaptation.* New York: Basic Books Inc.

Leigh, B.C. (1990) The relationship of substance use during sex to high-risk sexual behaviour. *Journal of Sex Research 27,* 199-213.

Lemert, E. (1951) *Social Pathology.* New York: McGraw-Hill.

Liss, M. (1981) *Prostitutes in perspective: A comparison of prostitutes and other working women.* Ph.D. dissertation, Northern Illinois University, Illinois.

Lowman, J. (1987) Taking young prostitutes seriously. *Canadian Review of Sociology and Anthropology 24(1),* 99-116.

Lukianowitz, H. (1972) Incest: I. Paternal incest. *British Journal of Psychiatry 120,* 301-313.

MacMillan, J. (1976) Rape and Prostitution. *Victimology 1(3)*, 414-420.

Maerov, A. (1965) Prostitution: A survey and review of 20 cases. *Psychiatric Quarterly 39*, 675-701.

Maiuro, R.D., Trupin, E.W. and James, J. (1983) Sex role differentiation in a female juvenile delinquent population: Prostitute vs. control samples. *American Journal of Orthopsychiatry 53(2)*, 345-352.

Mak, R.P. and Plum, J.R. (1991) Do prostitutes need more health education regarding sexually transmitted diseases and the HIV infection? Experience in a Belgium city. *Social Science and Medicine 33(8)*, 963-966.

Markos, A.R., Wade, A.A.H. and Walzman, M. (1992) The adolescent female prostitute and sexually transmitted diseases. Editorial review. *International Journal of STD & AIDS 3*, 92-95.

Marshall, N. and Hendtlass, J. (1986) Drugs and prostitution. *Journal of Drug Issues 16*, 237-248.

Mathis, J.L. (1974) Desire to enter prostitution. *Medical Aspects of Human Sexuality 8(6)*, 154.

McIntosh, M. (1978) Who needs prostitutes? The ideology of male sexual needs. In: Smart, C. and Smart, B. (Eds.) *Women, sexuality and social control*. London: Routledge & Keegan Paul.

McKeganey, N. (1992) Sexworkers, AIDS and HIV. Amsterdam summaries. *AIDS CARE 4(4)*, 443-445.

McLeod, E. (1982) *Women Working: Prostitution Now*. London: Croom Helm.

Mens, L. van (1992) *Prostitutie in bedrijf. Organisatie, Management en Arbeidsverhoudingen in Seksclubs en Privéhuizen*. Delft: Eburon.

Merrick, G.P. (1890) *Work Among the Fallen, as Seen in the Prison Cells*. London.

Merton, R.K. (1988) Het Mattheuseffect in de wetenschap (II). *Tijdschrift voor Sociale Wetenschappen 33(4)*, 325-355.

Miksik, O. (1976) On the personality profile of women with specific manifestations in sexual behavior. *Ceskoslovenska Psychiatrie 20(6)*, 495-513.

Miller, H.G., Turner, C.F. and Moses, L.E. (1990) *AIDS: The Second Decade*. Washington DC: National Academy Press.

Mooij, A. (1993) Aids en de machteloosheid van het oude moralisme. *Psychologie en Maatschappij 65*, 353-366.

Mors, E. ter (1978) *Zedenpolitie. Wie de goede zeden wil verdedigen is met de wet gebrekkig gewapend*. Eindscriptie politie-academie.

Muchinsky, P.M. (1993) *Psychology applied to work*. Pacific Grove, C.A.: Brooks/Cole.

Nationale Commissie AIDS Bestrijding (NCAB). (1990) *AIDS en Prostitutie 1990*. Amsterdam: NCAB.

Nedoma, K. and Sipova, J. (1972) [Heterosexual relations of prostitutes.] *Ceskoslovenska Psychiatrie 68(1)*, 23-26.

Nedoma, K. and Sipova, J. (1972) [Family setting and childhood in socially and sexually depraved women.] *Ceskolovenska Psychiatrie 68(3)*, 150-153.

Nedoma, K. and Sipova, J. (1983) Gynaecological and health profile of prostitutes. *Ceskoslovenska Gynekologie 38*, 425-427.

Newburn, T. (1992) *Law and Morals in Post-War Britain*. London/New York: Routledge.

Newman, F. and Cohen, E. with Tobin, P. and MacPherson, G. (1985) Historical perspectives on the study of female prostitution. *International Journal of Women's studies 8(1),* 80-86.

Nicolai, N. (1990) Seksueel misbruik en psychiatrische stoornissen. Een orienterend onderzoek op een gesloten afdeling van een psychiatrisch ziekenhuis. *Maandblad Geestelijke volksgezondheid 9,* 908-923.

Nolimal, D. and Crowley, T.J. (1989) HIV-risk behavior: Antisocial personality disorder, drug use patterns, and sexual behavior among methadone maintenance admissions. *National Institute on Drug Abuse Research Monograph Series, Mono 95,* 401-402.

Otis, L.L. (1985) *Prostitution in Medieval Society. The history of an urban institution in the Languedoc.* Chicago/London: The University of Chicago Press.

Otten, W. and Van der Pligt, J. (1991) *Risk and Behavior: The Mediating Role of Risk Appraisal.* Paper submitted for the proceedings of the Thirteenth Research Conference on Subjective Probability, Utility and Decision Making. Fribourg, Switzerland.

Overall, C. (1992) What's wrong with prostitution? Evaluating Sex Work. *Signs 17(4),* 705-724.

Padian, N.S. (1988) Editorial review: Prostitute women and AIDS: epidemiology. *AIDS 2,* 413-419.

Paglia, C. (1990) *Sexual Personae. Art and Decadence from Nefertiti to Emily Dickinson.* Yale University.

Parent-Duchalet (1857) *De la Prostitution dans la Ville de Paris.* Paris: Bailliere.

Paterson-Brown, S. and Finnerty, S.P. (1986) Problems of London prostitutes. *British Journal of Sexuality and Medicine 13(9),* 260-261.

Pearlin, L.I. and Schooler, C. (1978) The structure of coping. *Journal of Health and Social Behavior 19,* 2-21.

Perre, P. Van de, Carael, M., Robert-Guroff, M., Freyens, P., Gallo, R.C., Clumeck, N., Nzabihimana, E., DeMol, P., Butzler, J.P. and Kanyamupira, J.B. (1985) Female prostitution: A risk group for infection with Human T-Cell Lymphotropic Virus Type III. *Lancet 8454,* 524-527.

Peterson, C. and Seligman, M.E.P. (1983) Learned helplessness and victimization. *Journal of Social Issues 39(2),* 103-116.

Pheterson, G. (1986) *Vrouweneer en Mannenadel. Over het stigma Hoer.* Den Haag: Ministerie van Sociale Zaken en Werkgelegenheid.

Pheterson, G. (Ed.) (1989) *A Vindication of the Rights of Whores.* Seattle: Seal press.

Pheterson, G. (1990) The category 'prostitute' in scientific inquiry. *The Journal of Sex Research 27(3),* 397-407.

Philpot, C.R., Harcourt, C.L. and Edwards, J.M. (1989) Drug use by prostitutes in Sydney. *British Journal of Addiction 84(5),* 499-505.

Pickering, H., Quigley, M., Hayes, R.J., Todd, J. and Wilkins, A. (1993) Determinants of condom use in 24000 prostitute/client contacts in The Gambia. *AIDS 7,* 1093-1098.

Pillai, T.V. (1982) [Prostitution in India]. *Indian Journal of Social Work 43(3),* 313-320.

Piot, P., Plummer, F.A., Rey, M.A., Ngigi, E.N., Rouzioux, C., Ndinya-Achola, J.O., Veracauteren, G., D'Costa, L.J., Laga, M., Fransen, L., Haase, D., Ronald, A.R. and Brun-Vézinet, F. (1987) Retrospective serepidemiology of AIDS virus infection in Nairobi prostitutes. *Journal of Infectuous Diseases 155,* 1108-1112.

Pligt, J. van der (1991) Risicoperceptie, onrealistisch optimisme en AIDS-preventief gedrag. *Nederlands Tijdschrift voor de Psychologie 46,* 228-237.

Pligt J. van der, Otten, W. and Richard, R. (1992) Perceived risk of AIDS: Unrealistic optimism and self-protective action. In: Pryor, J.B. and Reeder, G. (Eds.) *The Social Psychology of HIV-infection.* Erlbaum N.J.

Pomeroy, W.B. (1965) Some aspects of prostitution. *Journal of Sex Research 1,* 177-187.

Potterat, J.J., Phillips, L., Rothenberg, R.B. and Darrow, W.W. (1985) On becoming a prostitute: An exploratory case-comparison study. *Journal of Sex Research 21,* 329-335.

Potterat, J.J., Woodhouse, D.E., Muth, J.B. and Muth, S.Q. (1990) Estimating the Prevalence and Career Longevity of Prostitute Women. *The Journal of Sex Research 27(2),* 233-243.

Pruyn, J.F.A., Van den Borne, H.W., De Reuver, R.S.M., Bosman, L.J., Ter Pelkwijk, M.A. and De Jong, P.C. (1988) De Locus of Controlschaal voor kankerpatienten. *Tijdschrift voor Sociale Gezondheidszorg 66(12),* 404-408.

Putte, B. van den (1993) *On the theory of reasoned action.* Proefschrift Universiteit van Amsterdam.

Quinn, T.C., Mann, J.M., Curran, J.W. and Piot, P. (1984) AIDS in Africa: An epidemiologic paradigm. *Science 234,* 955-963.

Rademakers, J. (1991) *Anticonceptie en interactie.* Utrecht: Dissertatie Rijks Universiteit Utrecht.

Rappard, M. van (1988) *Tot hier en niet verder. Verzet van mishandelde vrouwen.* Baarn: Ambo.

Richard, R., Van der Pligt, J. and De Vries, N. (1991) De invloed van gewoontes, persoonlijke effectiviteit, en gevoelsmatige reacties op condoomgebruik bij jongeren. *Gedrag & Gezondheid 19(2),* 65-76.

Ridder, D. de (1990) *Determinanten van psychische gezondheid.* Utrecht: Nederlands Centrum Geestelijke volksgezondheid (derde, gewijzigde druk).

Rim, Y. (1986) Ways of coping, personality, age, sex and family structural variables. *Personality and Individual Differences 7(1),* 113-116.

Rio, L.M. (1991) Psychological and Sociological Research and the Decriminalization or Legalization of Prostitution. *Archives of Sexual Behavior 20(2),* 205-218.

Roebuck, J. and McNamara, P. (1973) Ficheras and free lancers: Prostitution in a Mexican border city. *Archives of Sexual Behavior 2,* 131-144.

Roerink, A. and van der Vleuten, N. (1988) *Handel in illusies. Prostitutietoerisme in Thailand.* Nijmegen: Uitgeverij De Haktol.

Rogers, R.W. (1983) Cognitive and physiological processes in fear appeals and attitude change: A revised theory of protection motivation. In: J.T. Cacioppo and R.E. Petty (Eds.) *Social psychophysiology, a source book.* New York: Guilford, 153-176.

Römkens, R. (1989) *Geweld tegen vrouwen in heteroseksuele relaties.* Amsterdam: WOSG.

Rosenberg, M.J. and Weiner, J.N. (1988) Prostitutes and AIDS: a health department priority? *American Journal of Public Health 26,* 418-423.

Rosenblum, K.E. (1975) Female deviance and the female sex role: a preliminary investigation. *British Journal of Sociology 26,* 169-185.

Rosenstock, I.M. (1966) Why people use health services. *Milbank Memorial Fund Quarterly 44,* 94 ff.

Ross, M.W. (1988) Personality factors that differentiate homosexual men with positive and negative attitudes towards condom use. *New York State Journal of Medicine*, dec. 1988, 626-628.

Ross, C.A., Joski, S. and Currie, R. (1990) Dissociative Experiences in the General Population. *American Journal of Psychiatry 147(11)*, 1547-1552.

Ross, C.A., Anderson, G., Heber, S. and Norton, G.R. (1990) Dissociation and abuse among multiple-personality patients, prostitutes and exotic dancers. *Hosp. Commun. Psychiatr. 41(3)*, 328-330.

Rubenstein, R. (1990) Antecedents of prostitution: Flawed attachments and early sexual experiences. In: Pottharst K (Ed.) *Research explorations in adult attachment*. New York: Peter Lang Publishing.

Rubin, G. (1984) Thinking Sex: Notes for a Radical Theory of the Politics of Sexuality. In: Vance, C.S. (Ed.) *Pleasure and Danger. Exploring Female Sexuality*. Boston/ London/ Melbourne/ Henley: Routledge & Kegan Paul, 267-319.

Russell, D.E.H. (1984) *Sexual exploitation. Rape, Child Sexual Abuse and Workplace Harassment*. Beverly Hills: Sage Publications.

Sanders, S. (1986) The Perception Alteration Scale: a scale measuring dissociation. *American Journal of Clinical Hypnosis 29*, 95-102.

Sandfort, Th.G.M. (1985) *Verantwoording voor de meting van variabelen middels vooraf geconstrueerde schalen binnen het onderzoek naar seksuele ervaringen in de vroege jeugdjaren*. Utrecht: Werkgroep Seksuologie, Instituut voor Klinische Psychologie en Persoonlijkheidsleer.

Sandfort, Th.G.M., Vroome, E.M.M. de, Paalman, M.E.M. and Tielman, R.A.P. (1989) *Condooms in Nederland: determinanten van huidig en toekomstig gebruik*. Utrecht: SOA-stichting.

Savitz, L. and Rosen, L. (1988) The sexuality of prostitutes: sexual enjoyment reported by street walkers. *Journal of Sex Research 24*, 299-302.

Schaffer, B. and Deblassie, R.R. (1984) Adolescent prostitution. *Adolescence 19*, 689-696.

Schneider, B.E. (1992) AIDS and Class, Gender, and Race Relations. In: Huber, J. and Schneider, B.E. (Eds.) *The Social Context of AIDS*. Newbury Park: Sage Publications, 19-43.

Schoemaker, B. (1991) *Niet gehoord en niet gezien. Verwerking van seksuele trauma's bij vrouwen en mannen*. Amsterdam/Lisse: Swets & Zeitlinger.

Schreurs, P., Van de Willige, G., Tellegen, B. and Brosschot, J. (1988) *De Utrechtse Copinglijst: UCL handleiding*. Lisse: Swets & Zeitlinger.

Schur, E.M. (1984) *Labeling women deviant. Gender, stigma and social control*. New York: Random House.

Seng, M.J. (1989) Child sexual abuse and adolescent prostitution: A comparative analysis. *Adolescence 24(95)*, 665-675.

Shameem, S. (1993) Victims, Liberated Glamour Girls and Dregs of the Earth: Countering the Counter-hegemonic Discourse of 'Prostitute'. *Feminism & Psychology 3(1)*, 135-138.

Shoham, S.G., Rahav, G., Markovski, R., Ber, I., Chard, F., Rachamin, Y. and Bill, C. (1983) Family variables and stigma among prostitutes in Israël. *Journal of Social Psychology 120*, 57-62.

Shrage, L. (1989) Should Feminists Oppose Prostitution? *Ethics 99*, 347-361.

Sikka, K.D. (1984) Prostitution: Indian perspectives and realities. *Indian Journal of Social Work 45(2)*, 213-231.

Silbert, M.H. and Pines, A.M. (1981) Sexual child abuse as an antecedent to prostitution. *International Journal of Child Abuse and Neclect 5*, 407-411.

Silbert, M.H. and Pines, A.M. (1982) Victimization of Street Prostitutes. *Victimology 7(1-4)*, 122-133.

Silbert, M.H. and Pines, A.M. (1982) Entrance into prostitution. *Youth & Society 13*, 471-500.

Silbert, M.H. and Pines, A.M. (1983) Early sexual exploitation as an influence in prostitution. *Social Work 28*, 285-289.

Silbert, M.H. and Pines, A.M. (1984) Pornography and sexual abuse of women. *Sex Roles 10*, 857-868.

Silbert, M.H., Pines, A.M. and Lynch T. (1982) Substance abuse and prostitution. *Journal of Psychoactive Drugs 14*, 193-197.

Silver, R.L. and Wortman, C.B. (1980) Coping with undesirable life events. In: J. Garber and M.E.P. Seligman (Eds.) *Human Helplessness: Theory and Applications.* New York: Academic Press, 279-340.

Simons, R.L. and Whitbeck, L.B. (1991) Sexual Abuse as a Precursor to Prostitution and Victimization Among Adolescent and Adult Homeless Women. *Journal of Family Issues 12(3)*, 361-379.

Simpson, M. and Schill, T. (1977) Patrons of massage parlors: some facts and figures. *Archives of Sexual Behavior 6(6)*, 521-525.

Singh, S. and Singh, A. (1980) The relationship between early negative sexual experiences and prostitution. *Indian Journal of Criminology 8(2)*, 127-133.

Siraprapasiri, T., Thanprasertsuk, S., Rodklay, A., Srivanichakorn, S. et al. (1991) Risk factors for HIV among prostitutes in Chiangmai, Thailand. *AIDS 5(5)*, 579-582.

Sittitrai, W., Brown, T. and Sterns, J. (1990) Opportunities for overcoming the continuing restraints to behavior change and HIV risk reduction. *AIDS 4 (suppl 1)*, S269-S276.

Sloane, F. and Karpinsky, E. (1942) Effects of incest on the participants. *American Journal of Orthopsychiatry 12*, 666-673.

Snyder, C.R. and Ford, C.E. (Eds.) (1987) *Coping with negative life events: clinical and social psychological perspectives.* New York: Plenum Press.

Spalt, L. (1975) Sexual behavior and affective disorders. *Diseases of the Nervous System 36(12)*, 644-647.

Special Committee on Pornography and Prostitution. (1985) *Pornography and Prostitution in Canada.* Canadian Government Publishing Centre: Minister of Supply and Services Canada.

Spina, M., Serraino, D. and Tirelli, U. (1992) Condom use in high-risk sexual practices of female prostitutes in Italy. *AIDS 6(6)*, 601-602.

Stein, M. (1974) *Lovers, friends, slaves.* New York: Berkeley Medaillon Books.

Sterk, C.E. (1989) *Living the life: prostitutes and their health.* Rotterdam: Erasmus universiteits drukkerij.

Sterk-Elifson, C.E. and Campbell, C.A. (1993) The Netherlands. In: Davis, N.J. (Ed.) *Prostitution. An International Handbook on Trends, Problems and Policies.* Westport/London: Greenwood Press, 191-206.

Stiffman, A.R., Dore, P., Earls, F. and Cunningham, R. (1992) The influence of mental health problems on AIDS-related risk behaviors in young adults. *Journal of Nervous and Mental Disease 180(5),* 314-320.

Strickand, B.R. (1978) Internal-external expectancies and health related behaviors. *Journal of Consulting and Clinical Psychology 46,* 1192-1211.

Suls, J. and Fletcher, B. (1985) The relative efficacy of avoidant and non-avoidant copingstrategies: a meta-analysis. *Health Psychology 4(3),* 249-288.

Surawicz, F.G. (1976) Prostitutes' hearts of gold. *Medical Aspects of Human Sexuality 10(11),* 40.

Tabet, P. (1987) Du don ou tarif. Les relations sexuelles impliquant une compensation. *Les Temps Modernes 490,* 1-53.

Taylor, S.E. (1986) *Health Psychology.* New York: McGraw-Hill, Inc.

Taylor, S.E. and Brown, J.D. (1988) Illusion and well-being: a social psychological perspective on mental health. *Psychological Bulletin 103,* 193-210.

Terborg (1990) *AIDS en Prostitutie.* NAC/Ministerie Volksgezondheid Suriname.

Tiefer, L. (1991) Commentary on the Satus of Sex Research: Feminism, Sexuality and Sexology. *Journal of Psychology and Human Sexuality 4(3),* 5-42.

Thomas, R.M. et al. (1989) Risks of AIDS among workers in the 'sex industry': some initial results from a Scottish study. *British Medical Journal 299,* 148-149.

Tollison, C.D., Nesbitt, J.G. and Frey, J.D. (1977) Comparison of attitudes toward sexual intimacy in prostitutes and college coeds. *Journal of Social Psychology 101(2),* 319-320.

Truong, T. (1988) *Sex, money and morality. The political economy of prostitution and tourism in South East Asia.* Amsterdam: Faculteit der Politieke en Sociaal-culturele Wetenschappen.

Udegbe, I.B. and Fajimolu, O.O. (1992) Family structure, parental attachment, need for affiliation and autonomy as factors distinguishing between young prostitutes and non-prostitutes. *Indian Journal of Behaviour 16(1),* 20-27.

UNESCO/Coalition Against Trafficking in Women. (1991) *The Penn State Report. International meeting of experts on sexual exploitation, violence and prostitution.*

Vance, C.S. (1984) Pleasure and Danger: Toward a Politics of Sexuality. In: Vance CS. (ed.) *Pleasure and Danger. Exploring Female Sexuality.* Boston/London/Melbourne/Henley: Routledge & Kegan Paul, 1-27.

Vanwesenbeeck, I. (1986) *Wiens lijf eigenlijk? Een onderzoek naar dwang en geweld in de prostitutie.* Den Haag: Ministerie SoZaWe.

Vanwesenbeeck, I. (1987) In de prostitutie moet je dat er allemaal maar bijnemen. Prostitutie en (seksueel) geweld. *Justitiële Verkenningen 13(1),* 110-127.

Vanwesenbeeck, I., Altink, S. and Groen, M. (1989) *Hoe (ex)prostituées zich zelf redden. Een onderzoek naar (de afwezigheid van) hulpvragen.* Den Haag: Ministerie van Sociale Zaken en Werkgelegenheid.

Vanwesenbeeck, I.(1990) Wat hebben ze nou aan een verdrietige hoer? Een onderzoek naar zelfredzaamheid bij prostituées. *Maandblad Geestelijke volksgezondheid 3-90,* 235-249.

Vanwesenbeeck, I. (1991) Het raam, de straat en de club. Sekswerk als professionele zorgarbeid. *Lover 18(1)*, 27-31.

Vanwesenbeeck, I., De Graaf, R., Van Zessen, G., Straver C.J., Visser, J.H. (1992) Beschermingsstijlen van prostituanten: intenties, gedrag en overwegingen in verband met aids. *Gedrag en Gezondheid 20(2)*, 82-93.

Vanwesenbeeck, I., De Graaf, R., Van Zessen, G., Straver, C.J., Visser, J.H. (1992) Condoomgebruik door prostituées: gedrag, achtergronden en overwegingen. *Gedrag en Gezondheid 20(3)*, 145-158.

Vanwesenbeeck, I., and De Graaf, R. (1992) Het spel en de regels. Interactie en safe-seks in heteroseksuele prostitutiecontacten. *Psychologie en Maatschappij 59*, 144-155.

Vanwesenbeeck, I., R. de Graaf, G. van Zessen, C.J. Straver, J.H. Visser. (1993) Protection styles of prostitutes' clients. Intentions, behavior and considerations in relation to AIDS. *Journal of Sex Education and Therapy 19(2)*, 79-92.

Vanwesenbeeck, I., R. de Graaf, G. van Zessen, C.J. Straver, J.H. Visser. (1993) Condom use by female prostitutes. Behavior, factors and considerations. *Journal of Psychology and Human Sexuality 5(1)*, in press.

Vanwesenbeeck, I., R. de Graaf, G. van Zessen, C.J. Straver, J.H. Visser. (1993) Risky lives risky business? Aidsrisico van prostituées in het licht van geweldervaringen en welzijn. *Gedrag en Gezondheid 21(5)*, 219-226.

Vanwesenbeeck, I., R. de Graaf, G. van Zessen, C.J. Straver, J.H. Visser. (1993) Associations between professional HIV-risk and levels of well-being and victimization in female prostitutes in The Netherlands. *Archives of Sexual Behavior*, in press.

Velde, F.W. van der and Van der Pligt, J. (1991) AIDS-related Health Behavior: Coping, Protection Motivation, and Previous Behaviour. *Journal of Behavioral Medicine 14(5)*, 429-451.

Velten, D. and Kleiber, D. (1992) *Characteristics and Sexual Behavior of Clients of Female Prostitutes*. Poster presented at VIII International Conference on AIDS, Amsterdam.

Vennix, P. (1989) *Seks en Sekse*. Delft: Eburon.

Vereijken, I. and Bauduin, D. (1992) *Sociale klasse, sekse en psychische problemen*. Utrecht: Nederlands centrum Geestelijke volksgezondheid.

Vingerhoets, A.J.J.M. and Van Heck, G.L. (1990) Gender, coping and psychosomatic symptoms. *Psychological Medicine 20*, 125-135.

Visser, J.H. (in press) Prostitutiebeleid: terug bij af? In: *De Emancipatie van de prostitutie*. Utrecht: Humanistisch Studiecentrum Nederland.

Walker, L. (1984) *The battered women syndrome*. New York: Springer.

Walkowitz, J.R. (1980) *Prostitution and Victorian Society*. Cambridge/ London/ New York: Cambridge University press.

Wallston, B.S., Wallston, K.A. and Kaplan, G.D. (1976) Development and validation of the Health Locus of Control (HLC) Scale. *Journal of Consulting and Clinical psychology 44*, 580-585.

Weeks, J. (1985) *Sexuality and its discontents. Meanings, myths and modern sexualities*. London/Melbourne/Henley: Routledge & Kegan Paul.

Weisberg, D.K. (1985) *Children of the night: A study of adolescent prostitution*. Toronto: Lexington.

Wei, Y. and Wong, A. (1949) A study of 500 prostitutes in Shanghai. *International Journal of Sexology 2*, 234-238.

Weiner, I. (1964) On Incest: A survey. *Exerpta Criminologica 4*, 137-155.

Weinstein, N.D. (1982) Unrealistic Optimism About Susceptibility to Health Problems. *Journal of Behavioral Medicine 5(4)*, 441-460.

Weiss, S.M. (1991) *Health at work.* Hillsdale, N.J.: Erlbaum.

Weitzer, R. (1991) Prostitutes' Rights in the United States. The Failure of a Movement. *The Sociological Quarterly 32(1)*, 23-41.

Wethington, E. and Kessler, R.C. (1991) Situations and processes of coping. In: Eckenrode, J. (Ed.) *The social context of coping.* New York: Plenum Press.

White, J.W. and Roufail, M. (1989) Gender and influence strategies of first choice and last resort. *Psychology of Women Quarterly 13*, 175-189.

Wilson, D., Chiroro, P., Lavelle, S. and Mutero, C. (1989) Sex worker, client sex behaviour and condom use in Harare, Zimbabwe. *Aids Care 1(3)*, 269-280.

Wilson, D., Sibanda, B., Mboyi, L., Msimanga, S., et al. (1990) A pilot study for an HIV prevention programme among commercial sex workers in Bulawayo, Zimbabwe. *Social Science and Medicine 31(5)*, 609-618.

Wilson, D., Manual, A. and Lavelle, S. (1992) Personality characteristics of Zimbabwean men who visit prostitutes: Implications for AIDS prevention programmes. *Personality and Individual Differences 13(3)*, 275-279.

Winick, C. (1962) Prostitutes' clients' perception of the prostitutes and of themselves. *International Journal of Social Psychiatry 8*, 289-297.

Winick, C. and Kinsie, P.M. (1971) *The Lively Commerce: Prostitution in the United States.* Chicago: Quadrangle Books.

Winnubst and Schabracq (red.)(1992) *Handboek Arbeid en Gezondheids-psychologie.* Utrecht: Lemma.

De Wit, J.B.F., De Vroome, E.M.M., Sandfort, T.G.M., Van Griensven, G.J.P., Metselaar, C., Tielman, R.A.P. (1991) De relatie tussen coping-stijl, health locus of control en seksueel gedrag in een cohort homoseksuele mannen. *Gedrag en Gezondheid 19(2)*, 88-92.

Woolley, P.D., Bowman, C.A. and Kinghorn, C.R. (1988) Prostitution in Sheffield: differences between prostitutes. *Genitourin Medicine 64*, 391-393.

Worth, D. (1989) *Sexual decisionmaking and AIDS: why condom promotion among vulnarable women is likely to fail.* Paper drawn from a seminar presentation at the Population Counsil, Montefiore Medical Centre, New York.

Wortman, C.B. (1983) Coping with victimization: conclusions and implications for future research. *Journal of Social Issues 39(2)*, 195-221.

Wyatt, G.E. and Powel, G.J. (1988) *Lasting effects of child sexual abuse.* Beverly Hills: Sage Publications.

Zalduondo, B.O. de (1991) Prostitution Viewed Cross-Culturally: Towards Recontextualizing Sex Work in AIDS Intervention Research. *Journal of Sex Research 28(2)*, 223-248.

Zessen, G. van (1993) Over dwangmatige sexualiteit. *Tijdschrift voor sexuologie 17(4)*, 350-360.

Zessen, G. van and Sandfort, Th. (1991) *Seksualiteit in Nederland.* Amsterdam/Lisse: Swets & Zeitlinger.

APPENDICES

Appendix 4.1: Subscales for physical complaints in the 'coping and well-being'-study (N=60); reliability, items, factor loadings for items

subscale	No[a]	item	factorloading
psychosomatic complaints	6	stomach-aches	.85
(.73; 38%)[b]	8	hyperventilation	.70
	4	back-aches	.64
	5	head-aches	.60
work related physical complaints	1	Sexually Transmitted Diseases	.80
(.63; 18%)[b]	3	gynecological complaints	.79
	7	tiredness	.66
	2	inflammation of the bladder	.65

Note. PC-extraction, varimax rotation, and a criterium of 2 were used in the analysis. Correlation between the two subscales is not significant: Pearson's r .36
[a]Numbers refer to the order of presentation to the respondent.
[b]Cronbach's alpha for the subscale; percentage of variance explained.

Appendix 4.2: Subscales for emotional and psychosocial problems in the 'coping and well-being'-study (N=60); reliability, items, factor loadings for items

subscale	No[a]	item	factor loading
depressive anxiousness	2	feelings of anxiousness	.81
(.83; 35%)[b]	14	agoraphobia	.77
	7	feelings of loosing control	.76
	10	feelings of loneliness	.67
	3	problems concentrating	.62
	1	feeling tense and nervous	.58
	4	feeling depressed	.56
outward/inward directed aggression	6	feelings of mistrust	.85
(.67; 12%)[b]	5	feelings of aggression	.66
	15	suicide thoughts/attempts	.56
	13	nightmares	.49
social problems	9	feelings of shame	.75
(.64; 10%)[b]	12	problems with a 'double life'	.65
	8	feelings of guilt	.63
	11	problems in intimate relations	.59

Note. PC-extraction, varimax rotation, and a criterium of 3 were used in the analysis.
[a]Numbers refer to the order of presentation to the respondent.
[b]Cronbach's alpha for the subscale; percentage of variance explained.

Appendix 4.3: Correlations between subscales for physical complaints and psychosomatic problems in the 'coping and well-being'-study (N=60); Pearson's r

Subscales	1	2	3	4
1. psychosomatic complaints	-			
2. work related physical complaints	.36	-		
3. depressive anxiousness	.58**	.52**	-	
4. outward/inward directed aggression	.41*	.65**	.59**	-
5. social problems	.31	.15	.32	.34*

Note.Pairwise deletion of missing values; minimum pairwise N of cases is 33.
*p<.01; **p<.001.

Appendix 4.4: Subscales for drug use in the 'coping and well-being'-study (N=60); reliability, items, factor loadings for items

subscale	No[a]	item	factor loading
drugs	2	soft drugs	.86
(.71; 38%)[b]	5	poppers/amphetamines	.71
	4	heroin	.70
	3	cocaine	.57
other[c]	6	tranquilizers	.84
(.18; 19%)[b]	1	alcohol	.56

Note. PC-extraction, varimax rotation, and criterium Eigenvalue > 1 were used in the analysis.
[a]Numbers refer to the order of presentation to the respondent.
[b]Cronbach's alpha for the subscale; percentage of variance explained.
[c]Factor disqualified as a subscale because of low alpha; items will be used separately in further analyses.

Appendix 4.5: Subscales for victimization in the 'coping and well-being'-study (N=60); reliability, items, factor loadings for items

subscale	No[a]	item	factor loading
force and violence by a partner	15	held prison	.85
(.84; 32%)[b]	13	threats towards family or child	.77
	6	forced into prostitution	.75
	11	being blackmailed	.74
	7	physical violence by acquaintance/relative	.63
	14	forced marriage	.62
	9	sexual violence by acquaintance/relative	.54
violence by strangers/at work	8	physical violence by stranger	.71
(.71; 13%)[b]	5	sexual abuse by stranger before age 16	.66
	10	sexual violence by stranger	.66
	12	being threatened	.56
youth violence	1	left home before age 12	.86
(.57; 10%)[b]	2	bad experiences being institutionalized	.79
	3	physical abuse before age 16	.58
	4	sexual abuse by acquaintance/relative < age 16	.38
'rest'[c]	16	extreme negative social reactions	.82
(.41; .)[b]	17	harassment by helping agents	-.57

Note. PC-extraction, varimax rotation, and a criterium of 4 were used in the analysis.
[a]Numbers refer to the order of presentation to the respondent.
[b]Cronbach's alpha for the subscale; percentage of variance explained; '.' when a value is not computed.
[c]Factor disqualified as a subscale because of low alpha and lack of content.

Appendix 4.6: Correlations between subscales for victimization in the 'coping and well-being'-study (N=60); Pearson's r

subscales	1	2
1. youth violence	-	
2. violence by a private partner	.18	-
3. violence by strangers/at work	.24	.54**

Note. Pairwise deletion of missing values; minimum pairwise N of cases is 52.
*$p < .01$; **$p < .001$.

Appendix 4.7: Subscales for coping reactions in the 'coping and well-being'-study (N=60); reliability, items, factor loadings for items

subscale	No[a]	item	factor loading
problem solving	14	purposeful action to solve a problem	.81
(.80; 17%)[b]	11	looking at a problem from all sides	.78
	13	thinking of different possibilities to solve problems	.75
	17	going through things	.70
	7	direct intervention	.62
	8	seeing problems as a challenge	.59
	5	putting up with the course of things	-.57
depressed-palliative pattern	18	being totally taken over by problems	.78
(.78; 15%)[b]	2	seeing things gloomy	.75
	26	feeling incapable of doing anything	.71
	9	getting out in order to drive away my problems	.60
	22	thinking sunshine comes after rain	-.54
	20	one way or another trying to feel better	.53
	10	seeking diversion	.53
	15	worrying about the past	.53
	3	getting angry at the one responsible	-.26[c]
avoiding	12	avoiding difficult situations as much as possible	.81
(.62; 10%)[b]	4	giving in to avoid difficult situations	.79
	16	asking someone for help	-.49
	21	thinking that others have difficult times too	.48
	19	thinking of things that have not got to do with the problem	.40
seeking support	24	looking for comfort and understanding	.69
(.66; 9%)[b]	6	sharing my problems with someone	.66
	23	showing my feelings	.62
	25	showing that something is bothering me	.60
	1	showing my annoyance	.51

Note. PC-extraction, varimax rotation, and a criterium of 4 were used in the analysis.
[a]Numbers refer to the order of presentation to the respondent.
[b]Cronbach's alpha for the subscale; percentage of variance explained.
[c]Item not taken into account in the sumscore for the subscale because of low factor loading.

Appendix 4.8: Correlations between subscales for coping behavior and drug use in the 'coping and well-being'-study (N=60); Pearson's r

subscale	1	2	3	4	5	6
1. problem solving	-					
2. depressed/palliative	.10	-				
3. avoiding	.02	.30	-			
4. seeking support	-.10	-.02	-.06	-		
5. use of alcohol	.17	.11	.07	.16	-	
6. use of drugs	-.27	.24	.28	-.04	.19	-
7. use of tranquilizers	-.11	.14	-.09	-.11	.10	.19

Note. Pairwise deletion of missing values; minimum pairwise N of cases is 44.
*p<.01; **p<.001.

Appendix 4.9: Subscales for health complaints and psychosocial problems in the 'protective behavior'-study (N=127); reliability, items, factor loadings for items

subscale	No[a]	item	factor loading
social insecurity	19	feeling that others are unfriendly towards you	.78
(.88; 28%)[b]	20	feeling inferior to others	.76
	18	feeling hurt easily	.75
	16	feeling desperate about the future	.70
	4	feeling others don't like you	.70
	24	all the time having to ask others what to do	.61
	23	having to do things slowly to be sure they're okay	.58
	5	puzzling over a slovenliness	.56
	9	thinking of ending it all	.54
	3	not being able to shake nasty thoughts	.50
	22	feeling that others don't understand you	.50
	17	having difficulty concentrating	.49
	15	blaming oneself	.47
	11	having difficulty breathing	.43
	29	being troubled by insomnia	.37
psychosomatic complaints	10	painful muscles	.66
(.83; 9%)[b]	26	tension in the neck	.65
	29	stomach-aches	.63
	2	dizziness	.63
	13	explosions of anger you cannot control	.63
	30	tingling feeling in the body	.56
	12	nausea	.56
	25	lower back-ache	.55
	21	palpitations	.54
	7	having little energy	.54
	31	difficult digestion	.48
	6	feeling easily bored	.45
	27	feeling easily irritated	.43
	8	difficulty talking when angry or exited	.39
	14	benumbed feeling in the body	.38
	1	head-aches	.32
	32	inflammation of the bladder	.28[c]

Note. PC-extraction, varimax rotation, and a criterium of 2 were used in the analysis.
[a]Numbers refer to the order of presentation to the respondent.
[b]Cronbach's alpha for the subscale; percentage of variance explained.
[c]Item not taken into account in the sumscore for the subscale because of low factor loading.

Appendix 4.10: Correlations between subscales for well-being in the 'protective behavior'-study (N=127); Pearson's r

subscale	1	2
1. social insecurity	-	
2. psychosomatic complaints	.58**	-
3. job satisfaction	-.55**	-.42**

Note. Pairwise deletion of missing values; minimum pairwise N of cases is 88.
*p<.01; **:p<.001.

Appendix 4.11: Subscales for victimization in the 'protective behavior'-study (N=127); reliability, items, factor loadings[a] for items

subscale	item	factor loading
violence in the private sphere (.53; 37%)[b]	physical violence in the private sphere	.82
	forced into prostitution	.70
	sexual violence in the private sphere	.58
violence on the job (.63; 23%)[b]	sexual violence outside the private sphere	.88
	physical violence outside the private sphere	.79

Note. The two items on *'childhood violence'* (unwanted sex with relatives before age 16 and unwanted sex with non-relatives before age 16) were not used in the factor analysis because of missing data on those items for 21.5% of the respondents. They have been used as a subscale though: alpha is .67; Pearson's r is .51, p<.001
[a]PC-extraction, varimax rotation, and a criterium Eigenvalue > 1 were used in the analysis.
[b]Cronbach's alpha for the subscale; percentage of variance explained.

Appendix 4.12: Correlations between subscales for victimization in the 'protective behavior'-study (N=127); Pearson's r

subscales	1	2
1. childhood violence	-	
2. violence in the private sphere	.29*	-
3. violence on the job	.19	.27*

Note. Pairwise deletion of missing values; minimum pairwise N of cases is 94.
*p<.01; **p<.001.

Appendix 4.13: Subscales for coping reactions in the 'protective behavior'-study (N=127); reliability, items, factor loadings for items

subscale	No[a]	item	factor loading
dissociation	19	feeling as if I'm not in my own body	.80
(.83; 24%)[b]	1	feeling as if I'm not myself	.69
	5	feeling as if I'm looking from the outside at myself	.69
	10	feeling as if I've lost contact with reality	.63
	3	staring without being conscious of the time	.63
	6	seeing things somberly	.62
	4	seeking distraction	.61
	20	being totally taken over by problems	.56
problem solving	13	going through things	.74
(.73; 14%)[b]	9	purposeful action to solve a problem	.70
	17	thinking of different possibilities to solve problems	.67
	14	seeing problems as a challenge	.62
	11	just putting aside negative feelings	.58
	7	thinking that others have difficult times too	.37
seeking support	16	sharing my worries with someone	.71
(.69; 8%)[b]	2	asking someone for help	.68
	18	seeking comfort and understanding	.66
	8	showing that something is bothering me	.51
denial	15	trying to think about problems as little as possible	.70
(.56; 8%)[b]	12	feeling incapable of doing anything	.68

Note. PC-extraction, varimax rotation, and a criterium of 4 were used in the analysis.
[a]Numbers refer to the order of presentation to the respondent.
[b]Cronbach's alpha for the subscale; percentage of variance explained.

Appendix 4.14: Correlations between the subscales on coping behavior and drug use in the 'protective behavior'-study (N=127); Pearson's r

subscales	1	2	3	4	5
1. dissociation	-				
2. problem solving	-.02	-			
3. seeking support	.45**	.14	-		
4. denial	.33**	.04	.16	-	
5. use of alcohol	.00	.18	.04	.09	-
6. use of drugs	.14	-.21	-.09	.29*	-.07

Note. Pairwise deletion of missing values; minimum pairwise N of cases is 98.
*$p<.01$; **$p<.001$.

Appendix 4.15: Subscales for Health Locus of Control for prostitutes (N=127) in the 'protective behavior'-study (N=127); reliability, items, factor loadings for items

subscale	No[a]	item	factor loading
fate	1	if I'll be ill, I'll be ill, whatever I do	.77
(.72; 22%)[b]	9	if it's so destined I'll stay healthy	.70
	7	good health is a matter of luck	.66
expert control	3	always when I don't feel good I should check with a doctor	.86
(.59; 15%)[b]	2	the best way to prevent illness is regularly check with my GP	.74
	5	my surroundings matter a lot in my health or illness	.49
external control over AIDS	12	me getting AIDS would be my own fault	-.81
(.61; 12%)[b]	11	me getting AIDS would be to blame on others	.76
	10	me getting AIDS would be a coincidence	.54
internal control	6	if I get ill it's my own fault	.79
(.35; 10%)[b]	4	I got my health in my own hand	.67
	8	if I take care of myself I can prevent illness	.57

Note. PC-extraction, varimax rotation, and criterium Eigenvalue > 1 were used in the analysis.
[a]Numbers refer to the order of presentation to the respondent.
[b]Cronbach's alpha for the subscale; percentage of variance explained.

Appendix 4.16: Subscales for 'causal attributions of undesirable contact proceedings' in the 'protective behavior'-study (N=127); reliability, items, factor loadings for items

subscale	No[a]	item	factor loading
attributions of powerlessness			
and indifference	7	I'm incapable of doing something about it	.76
(.79; 32%)[b]	13	it happened before I spotted it	.67
	8	I didn't feel like being difficult	.64
	9	it happened to be like that under pressure of circumstances	.61
	6	I gave in too quickly	.57
	2	I really didn't care that much	.53
	4	I wasn't really paying attention	.50
formal attributions	15	otherwise my earnings aren't enough	.82
(.81; 13%)[b]	17	I need the money badly	.80
	16	those just happen to be the rules	.74
	18	these things are necessary to keep up competition	.73
	14	that is just part of the job	.56
anxious helplessness	11	I was too fearful in that contact	.76
(.75; 7%)[b]	10	I didn't dare propose something else	.65
	3	I didn't see a possibility to get out from under it	.63
	5	the client used violence	.59
	1	the client put me under pressure	.52
	12	I like to keep up with that client	.46

Note. PC-extraction, varimax rotation, and a criterium of 3 were used in the analysis.
[a]Numbers refer to the order of presentation to the respondent; items are answers to the question 'A contact with a client may take another course than I would like, because..'.
[b]Cronbach's alpha for the subscale; percentage of variance explained.

Appendix 4.17: Subscales for influence strategies of prostitutes in the 'protective behavior'-study (N=127); reliability, items, factor loadings for items

subscale	No[a]	item	factor loading
manipulative negotiation	3	I try to tempt him to the thing I want	.73
(.85; 25%)[b]	4	I try to convince him with arguments	.73
	17	I use all my charm to influence him	.68
	5	I tell him how important something is for me	.61
	1	I try to influence him with flattery	.61
	6	I talk him into it	.59
	7	I try to come to an agreement	.59
	11	I tell him I'll make it extra good if he'll do what I want	.57
	2	I try to divert his attention	.56
	9	I make suggestions and propositions	.53
	14	I tel him I know better what's good and nice for him	.50
	15	I tell him other prostitutes don't do that either	.41
	28	I stick to my demands	.36
high pressure	23	I get angry	.76
(.81; 11%)[b]	13	I threaten to call in someone else	.70
	12	I threaten to end it if he doesn't do what I want	.67
	19	I'm rude to him	.66
	20	I get sulky and nasty	.63
	24	I threaten to use violence	.62
	18	I tell him to go and look for someone else	.58
	31	I tell him he owes me things	.55
	21	I lie to him about what I'll do	.54
	30	I tell him those are the rules	.40
negative emotions	22	I go and act pitiful	.62
(.69; 8%)[b]	10	I start to cry	.61
	25	I threaten to blackmail him	.57
	27	I beg him to do as I want	.53
	16	I ask him a lot of money for what I prefer not to do	.53
	26	I try to bribe him	.48
	29	I reward him if he does what I want	.45
	8	I go and make promises	.41

Note. PC-extraction, varimax rotation, and a criterium of 3 were used in the analysis.
[a]Numbers refer to the order of presentation to the respondent.
[b]Cronbach's alpha for the subscale; percentage of variance explained.

Appendix 4.18: Subscales for Health Locus of Control of clients in the 'protective behavior'-study (N=91); reliability, items, factor loadings for items

subscale	No[a]	item	factor loading
external control	2	the best way to prevent illness is regularly check with my GP	.73
(.74; 23%)[b]	9	if it's so destined I'll stay healthy	.72
	3	when I don't feel good I should check with a doctor	.67
	1	if I'll be ill, I'll be ill, whatever I do	.67
	7	good health is a matter of luck	.66
internal control	8	if I take care of myself I can prevent illness	.82
(.67; 15%)[b]	4	I got my health in my own hand	.77
	6	if I get ill it's my own fault	.74
external control over AIDS	12	me getting AIDS would be my own fault	-.75
(.58; 13%)[b]	11	me getting AIDS would be to blame on others	.74
	10	me getting AIDS would be a coincidence	.62
surroundings	5	my surroundings matter a lot in my health or illness	.87
(. ; 9%)[b]			

Note. PC-extraction, varimax rotation, and a criterium Eigenvalue > 1 were used in the analysis.
[a]Numbers refer to the order of presentation to the respondent.
[b]Cronbach's alpha for the subscale; percentage of variance explained; '.' when a value could not be computed.

Appendix 4.19: Subscales for influence strategies of clients in the 'protective behavior'-study (N=91); reliability, items, factor loadings for items

subscale	No[a]	item	factor loading
manipulation	1	I try to influence her with flattery	.82
(.89; 42%)[b]	5	I tell her how important something is for me	.78
	17	I use all my charm to influence her	.75
	2	I try to divert her attention	.72
	3	I try to tempt her to the thing I want	.67
	4	I try to convince her with arguments	.66
	6	I talk to her into it	.55
rational strategies	28	I stick to my demands	.80
(.80; 12%)[b]	18	I tell her I will go to another prostitute	.74
	8	I go and make promises	.64
	15	I tell her other prostitutes do these things	.57
	9	I make suggestions and propositions	.38
negotiation	16	I offer her money	.85
(.81; 7%)[b]	7	I try to come to an agreement	.67
	29	I reward her if she does what I want	.65
	11	I promise her to be extra good if she does what I want	.63
formal arguments	30	I tell her that those are the rules	.88
(.73; 6%)[b]	31	I point out to her that she owes it to me	.60

Note. 13 items in the original questionnaire hardly differentiated and were excluded from the factor analysis. PC-extraction, varimax rotation, and a criterium Eigenvalue > 1 were used in the analysis.
[a]Numbers refer to the order of presentation to the respondent in the original questionnaire.
[b]Cronbach's alpha for the subscale; percentage of variance explained.

Appendix 4.20: Subscales for 'evaluation of condoms' by clients in the 'protective behavior'-study (N=91); reliability, items, factor loadings for items

subscale	No[a]	item	factor loading
positive evaluation of condoms	8	condoms protect against AIDS and venereal disease	.80
(.71; 29%)[b]	10	using condoms prevents fear	.79
	7	using condoms is more hygienic	.73
	9	intercourse is more relaxed with condoms because you do not have to be worried	.73
negative evaluation of condoms	4	with a condom the penis does not look nice	.83
(.78; 23%)[b]	5	condoms cause physical irritation	.83
	6	condoms postpone the orgasm	.77
	1	condoms diminish the sensitivity of the penis	.64
negative attitude condom use	2	using condoms is disturbing while having sex	.84
(.70; 13%)[b]	3	using condoms is unnatural	.63

Note. PC-extraction, varimax rotation, and a criterium Eigenvalue > 1 were used in the analysis.
[a]Numbers refer to the order of presentation to the respondent.
[b]Cronbach's alpha for the subscale; percentage of variance explained.

Appendix 4.21: Subscales for 'evaluation of prostitution visits' of clients in the 'protective behavior'-study (N=91); reliability, items, factor loadings for items

subscale	No[a]	item	factor loading
positive evaluation of			
prostitution visits	1	I feel relaxed after having visited a prostitute	.76
(.78; 33%)[b]	4	it is good for me that there are prostitutes	.74
	3	I find sex with prostitutes great	.72
	10	visiting prostitutes is a good way to add to my sex life	.71
	2	as far as sex goes I get exactly what I want from prostitutes	.63
negative evaluation of			
prostitution visits	11	I feel cheated when I have visited a prostitute	.85
(.65; 14%)[b]	12	I feel guilty over visiting prostitutes	.70
	9	I really think prostitutes are pitiful	.49
preference for other sex	6	I think sex should go with love	.76
(.65; 10%)[b]	8	I would rather have a good relationship than visit prostitutes	.75
	5	I would rather not visit prostitutes	.67
negative attitude			
towards prostitutes	7	I find prostitutes basically women of ill-repute	.80
(. ; 9%)[b]			

Note. PC-extraction, varimax rotation, and a criterium Eigenvalue > 1 were used in the analysis.
[a]Numbers refer to the order of presentation to the respondent.
[b]Cronbach's alpha for the subscale; percentage of variance explained; '.' when a value could not be computed.

Appendix 5.1: Frequency of being troubled by physical complaints and by emotional/psychosocial problems in the 'coping and well-being'-study; percentage of prostitutes (N=60)

complaints and problems	frequencies			
	hardly or never	some-times	often	very often
psychosomatic complaints				
stomachache	65	8	28	0
hyperventilation	56	13	22	9
backache	57	14	24	5
headache	47	12	37	5
work related physical complaints				
STD's	40	35	26	0
gynecological complaints	62	17	16	5
insomnia	53	27	19	2
inflammation of the bladder	69	11	18	2
depressive anxiousness				
anxiousness	32	39	28	2
agoraphobia	76	12	12	0
feeling out of control	41	40	19	0
loneliness	36	35	26	3
concentration problems	49	24	25	2
nervousness	8	33	47	10
depression	20	41	34	5
outward and inward directed aggression				
distrust	22	22	52	3
aggression	20	42	31	7
suicide thoughts/attempt	63	23	14	0
nightmares	49	25	23	4
social problems				
shame	48	31	21	0
problems with double life	36	31	27	7
guilt	25	39	37	0
problems with intimacy	43	25	32	0

Note. Percentages rounded off and valid for available N, varying from 54 to 60.

Appendix 5.2: Frequency of different health problems in the 'protective behavior'-study; percentage of prostitutes (N=127)

health problem	never	some-times	regu-larly	often	very often
social insecurity					
feeling others unfriendly	31.1	56.6	7.5	4.7	0
feeling inferior to others	61.3	31.1	4.7	2.8	0
feeling hurt easily	26.4	48.1	11.3	9.4	4.7
feeling desperate over future	46.2	35.8	5.7	7.5	4.7
feeling others do not like you	39.6	50.9	4.7	2.8	1.9
all the time having to ask others what to do	71.7	23.6	0.9	2.8	0.9
having to do something slowly to be sure it's okay	43.4	40.6	6.6	8.5	0.9
puzzle over a slovenliness	36.8	45.3	6.6	7.5	3.8
thinking of ending it all	75.0	15.4	1.9	5.8	1.9
not able to shake nasty thoughts	27.4	42.5	9.4	12.3	8.5
feeling misunderstood	21.0	57.1	10.5	9.5	1.9
concentration difficulties	27.4	50.0	11.3	6.6	4.7
blaming one self	27.4	51.9	11.3	4.7	4.7
difficulty breathing	53.8	25.5	14.2	4.7	1.9
insomnia	46.2	29.2	7.5	9.4	7.5
psychosomatic complaints					
painful muscles	24.5	44.3	17.9	9.4	3.8
neck tension	32.1	33.0	16.0	13.2	5.7
stomach-ache	52.8	28.3	8.5	5.7	4.7
dizziness	43.4	38.7	5.7	10.4	1.9
no control over anger	57.1	28.6	7.6	3.8	2.9
tingling feeling	69.5	21.0	1.0	4.8	3.8
nausea	40.6	46.2	7.5	5.7	0
lower back-ache	38.1	37.1	8.6	9.5	6.7
palpitations	61.3	24.5	6.6	5.7	1.9
little energy	14.2	61.3	14.2	6.6	3.8
difficulty with digestion	50.0	32.1	10.4	3.8	3.8
being easily bored	35.8	40.6	8.5	12.3	2.8
easily irritated	21.7	54.7	14.2	5.7	3.8
difficulty talking when mad or exited	41.5	35.8	8.5	8.5	5.7
benumbed feeling	75.5	16.0	5.7	2.8	0
head-ache	12.3	50.9	18.9	11.3	6.6
inflammation of the bladder	67.3	22.4	6.1	2.0	2.0

Note. Percentages valid for available N; minimum N of cases 106

Appendix 5.3: Degree of agreement with different statements on Health Locus of Control in the 'protective behavior'-study; percentage of prostitutes (N=127)

statements	strongly agree	agree	in be-tween	disagree	strongly disagree
fate					
if I'll be ill, I'll be ill,					
whatever I do	9.5	31.0	19.0	27.6	12.9
if it's so destined I'll stay healthy	10.6	42.5	15.0	22.1	9.7
good health is a matter of luck	7.8	30.4	16.5	37.4	7.8
expert control					
when I don't feel good I should					
check with a doctor	10.4	36.5	13.9	33.0	6.1
the best way to prevent illness is					
to regularly check with my GP	13.8	32.8	12.9	29.3	11.2
my surroundings matter a lot					
in health or illness	11.2	35.3	22.4	25.9	5.2
external control over AIDS					
me getting AIDS would be my own fault	12.2	13.0	19.1	37.4	18.3
me getting AIDS would be					
to blame on others	6.1	18.3	13.0	37.4	25.2
me getting AIDS would be a coincidence	13.0	30.4	13.9	23.5	19.1
internal control					
if I get ill it's my own fault	5.2	26.7	25.9	35.3	8.9
I got my health in my own hand	25.0	44.0	17.2	12.1	1.7
taking care well of myself 'll					
prevent illness	22.4	52.6	13.8	9.5	1.7

Note. Percentages valid for available N; minimum N of cases 106

Appendix 5.4: Frequency of coping reactions in the 'coping and well-being'-study; percentage of prostitutes (N=60)

coping reaction	hardly or never	some-times	often	very often
problem solving				
purposeful action to solve a problem	4.1	38.8	36.7	20.4
looking at a problem from all sides	2.0	32.0	36.0	30.0
thinking of different possibilities to solve a problem	2.0	26.0	42.0	30.0
going through things	6.4	31.9	44.7	17.0
direct intervention	10.2	40.8	36.7	12.2
seeing problems as a challenge	27.1	39.6	20.8	12.5
putting up with something	34.7	44.9	18.4	2.0
depressed-palliative pattern				
totally taken over by a problem	35.4	39.6	16.7	8.3
seeing things gloomy	22.9	54.2	18.8	4.2
being incapable of doing any thing	41.7	50.0	6.3	2.1
getting out temporary	10.6	44.7	23.4	21.3
thinking that sunshine comes after rain	4.2	20.8	43.8	31.3
trying somehow to feel better	6.3	22.9	52.1	18.8
seeking diversion	8.2	36.7	40.8	14.3
worrying about the past	22.9	39.6	18.8	18.8
getting an gry at someone responsible	16.3	49.0	26.5	8.2
avoiding				
avoiding difficult situations	28.6	38.8	16.3	16.3
giving in to avoid difficulties	25.5	40.4	21.3	12.8
asking for help	35.4	50.0	14.6	0
thinking that others have difficult times too	8.2	28.6	30.6	32.7
thinking of things that have not got to do with the problem	10.4	68.8	16.7	4.2
seeking support				
looking for comfort and understanding	25.0	35.4	20.8	18.8
sharing my problems with someone	12.5	50.0	27.1	10.4
showing my feelings	18.8	52.1	14.6	14.6
showing that something is bothering me	22.9	45.8	27.1	4.2
showing my annoyance	12.0	50.0	30.0	8.0

Note. Percentages valid for available N, varying from 47 to 50.

Appendix 5.5: Subscales for coping behavior of prostitutes (N=60) in the 'coping and well-being'-study; range, mean score (SD), mean item score

subscale	range	mean (SD)	mean item score
problem solving	6-24	16.0 (3.7)	2.7
depressed-palliative pattern	7-28	16.2 (0.6)	2.3
avoiding	4-16	9.4 (0.4)	2.4
seeking support	5-20	11.4 (0.4)	2.3

Note. Scores are on a 4-point scale, ranging from 1 (hardly ever) to 4 (very often)

Appendix 5.6: Frequency of used coping reactions in the 'protective behavior'-study; percentage of prostitutes (N=127)

coping reaction	frequencies				
	never	some-times	regu-larly	often	very often
dissociation					
feeling as if I am not in my own body	65.4	15.9	7.5	8.4	2.8
feeling as if I'm not myself	37.4	32.7	9.3	11.2	9.3
feeling as if I'm looking from the outside at myself	50.5	26.2	8.4	11.2	3.7
feeling as if I have lost contact with reality	68.2	16.8	3.7	9.3	1.9
staring without being conscious of the time	42.1	40.2	8.4	4.7	4.7
seeing things somberly	50.5	37.4	5.6	4.7	1.9
seeking distraction	21.7	37.7	21.7	11.3	7.5
being totally taken over by problems	64.5	20.6	5.6	6.5	2.8
problem solving					
going through things	11.2	28.0	24.3	22.4	14.0
purposeful action to solve a problem	10.3	31.8	20.6	23.4	14.0
thinking of different possibilities to solve a problem	5.7	32.1	17.9	26.4	17.9
seeing problems as a challenge	39.6	30.2	13.2	10.4	6.6
putting aside negative feelings	18.7	35.5	13.1	19.6	13.1
thinking that others got difficult times too	18.9	39.6	14.2	18.9	8.5
seeking support					
sharing my worries with someone	15.2	33.3	21.9	19.0	10.5
asking someone for help	38.3	47.7	7.5	4.7	1.9
seeking comfort and understanding	26.4	37.7	10.4	20.8	4.7
showing that something is bothering me	35.2	41.0	13.3	7.6	2.9
denial					
trying to think about problems as little as possible	25.5	38.7	11.3	13.2	11.3
feeling incapable of doing something	53.3	29.9	9.3	5.6	1.9

Note. Percentages valid for available N; minimum N of cases 106

Appendix 5.7: Subscales for coping behavior of prostitutes in the 'protective behavior'-study (N=127); range, mean score (SD), mean item score

subscale	range	mean (SD)	mean item score
dissociation	8-40	15.1 (6.1)	2.5
problem solving	6-30	16.8 (4.7)	2.8
seeking support	4-20	9.0 (3.1)	2.2
denial	2-10	4.2 (1.9)	2.1

Note. Scores are on a 5-point scale, ranging from 1 (hardly ever) to 5 (very often)

Appendix 5.8: Frequency of using drugs in the 'coping and well-being'-study; percentage of prostitutes (N=60)

	frequencies			
drug	hardly or never	some-times	much	very much
alcohol	45.0	25.0	5.0	5.0
soft drugs	51.7	31.7	15.0	1.7
cocaine	70.0	10.0	20.0	0
heroin	83.1	3.4	11.9	1.7
other hard drugs	79.3	8.6	12.1	0
tranquilizers	58.6	19.0	20.7	1.7

Note. Percentages are valid for available N, varying from 58 to 60.

Appendix 5.9: Severity of victimizing experiences in the 'coping and well-being'-study; percentage of prostitutes (N=60)

victimization	severity of victimization			
	absent	mild	moderate	extreme
youth violence				
left home < age 12	72.4	27.5	-	-
bad experiences being institutionalized	70.7	15.5	13.8	-
child physical abuse	59.3	11.1	22.2	7.5
unwanted sex with acquaintance < age 16	57.1	19.6	17.9	5.4
force and violence by a private partner				
held prison	84.7	8.5	6.8	0
threats to family or child	84.5	8.6	3.4	3.4
forced into prostitution	56.7	18.3	15.0	10.0
blackmail	72.4	15.5	8.6	3.4
physical violence by an acquaintance	48.3	10.3	25.9	15.5
forced marriage	94.9	5.1	-	-
sexual violence by an acquaintance	57.1	17.9	19.6	5.4
violence by strangers/at work				
physical violence by a stranger	40.4	40.4	15.8	3.5
unwanted sex by a stranger < age 16	81.8	10.9	3.6	3.6
sexual violence by a stranger	59.6	22.8	14.0	3.5
threatened 31.0	32.8	22.4	13.8	
rest				
sexual advances by helping agents	74.1	19.0	6.9	0
negative social reactions	58.3	18.3	21.7	1.7

Note. Percentages valid for available N, varying from 54 to 60.

Appendix 5.10: Subscales for victimization for prostitutes in the 'coping and well-being'-study (N=60); range, mean score (SD), mean item score

subscale	range	mean (SD)	mean item score
youth violence	4-16	6.2 (2.3)	1.6
force/violence by a partner	7-28	10.5 (4.2)	1.5
violence by strangers/at work	4-16	6.8 (2.5)	1.7

Note. Scores are on a 4-point scale, ranging from 1 (absent) to 4 (severe/extreme)

Appendix 5.11: Severity of experiences with violence in the 'protective behavior'-study; percentage of prostitutes, N

experience	severity of experience with violence				
	absent	mild/ once	more often/ prolonged	severely/ extreme	N
childhood trauma					
unwanted sex with a family member < age 16	84.8	-	9.5	5.7	105
unwanted sex with other < age 16	91.2	-	4.9	3.9	102
violence in the private sphere					
physical violence in the private sphere	71.3	6.1	13.0	9.6	115
forced into prostitution	71.1	4.7	14.8	9.4	127
sexual violence in the private sphere	70.6	13.8	13.8	1.8	109
violence on the job					
sexual violence outside the private sphere	61.3	22.7	13.4	2.5	119
physical violence outside the private sphere	65.9	18.7	13.0	2.4	123

Appendix 5.12: Subscales for victimization of prostitutes in the 'protective behavior'-study; N, range, mean score (SD), mean item score

subscale	range	mean (SD)	mean item score
childhood trauma (101)	2- 8	2.5 (1.3)	1.3
violence private sphere (105)	3-12	4.5 (2.0)	1.5
violence on the job (117)	2- 8	3.1 (1.4)	1.6

Note. Scores are on a 4-point scale, ranging from 1 (absent) to 4 (severely/extreme)

Appendix 5.13: Victimization related to coping behavior in the 'coping and well-being'-study (N=60); Pearson's r

| | victimization subscales | | |
coping subscales	youth violence	violence pr.partner	violence at work
problem solving	-.05	-.05	.15
depressed/palliative pattern	.10	.10	.32
avoiding	.21	.16	.06
seeking support	.09	-.04	-.19
alcohol	.13	.36**	.27
drugs	.00	.10	.19
tranquilizers	.07	.16	.46**

Note. Pairwise deletion of missing values; minimum pairwise N of cases 42.
*:p<.01; **:p<.001

Appendix 5.14: Victimization related to coping behavior in the 'protective behavior'-study (N=127); Pearson's r

| | victimization subscales | | |
coping subscales	childhood trauma	violence pr.sphere	violence on the job
dissociation	.31*	.14	.33**
problem solving	.08	-.03	-.02
seeking support	.11	.02	.10
denial	.35**	.25*	.29*
alcohol	-.14	-.19	-.02
drugs	.20	.32**	.56**

Note. Pairwise deletion of missing values; minimum pairwise N of cases is 86.
*p<.01; **p<.001.